# THE
# SECRET LIFE
## OF
# GENIUS

# THE
# SECRET LIFE
## OF
# GENIUS

How 24 Great
Men and Women
Were Touched by
Spiritual Worlds

## JOHN CHAMBERS

Destiny Books
Rochester, Vermont • Toronto, Canada

Destiny Books
One Park Street
Rochester, Vermont 05767
www.DestinyBooks.com

Destiny Books is a division of Inner Traditions International

**Library of Congress Cataloging-in-Publication Data**

Chambers, John, 1939–
  The secret life of genius : how 24 great men and women were touched by
spiritual worlds / John Chambers.
      p. cm.
  Includes bibliographical references.
  Summary: "A look at the metaphysical experiences that shaped the lives and work
of 24 great men and women from the Renaissance to modern times"—Provided by
publisher.
  ISBN 978-1-59477-272-6
  1. Magic. 2. Occultism. 3. Genius—Biography. 4. Genius—Miscellanea. 5.
Parapsychology. I. Title.
  BF1999.C5136 2009
  130.9—dc22

                                                            2009016854

Printed and bound in the United States by Lake Book Manufacturing

10 9 8 7 6 5 4 3 2 1

Text design and layout by Priscilla Baker
This book was typeset in Garamond Premier Pro with Legacy Sans and Avalon
    used as display typefaces

To send correspondence to the author of this book, mail a first-class letter to the
author c/o Inner Traditions • Bear & Company, One Park Street, Rochester, VT
05767, and we will forward the communication.

*For Gabriel Safdie*

# Contents

# *Introduction*
## Prague's Other Universe

Are there alternate realities?

Does history sometimes bifurcate, asking us to choose between two quite different paths? If there was ever a break in the space-time continuum, it came on the afternoon of November 8, 1620, on the slopes of White Mountain, just outside the gates of Prague, then capital of the Kingdom of Bohemia and today the capital of the Czech Republic.

In just over an hour, the twenty-thousand-man army of the flamboyant Holy Roman Emperor Ferdinand II crushed the twenty-five-thousand-man army of the austere and brilliant Frederick V, King of Bohemia.

The Battle of White Mountain was the opening salvo in Europe's Thirty Years' War, when the Catholic armies of southern Europe flung themselves against the Protestant armies of northern Europe. It ended in 1648 with the signing of the Treaty of Westphalia, which ensured the survival of the Protestant Church.

The Battle of White Mountain also marked a moment in time when a whole other way of looking at reality stood poised to flow across the continent of Europe and on to the New World. This way of looking at the universe, which was opposed to the soon-to-be-born

1

scientific paradigm of Sir Isaac Newton, was a magical, occult system of interpreting and manipulating reality that was being conceptualized and made manifest, in a thousand different ways, by a thousand separate people, in the libraries and laboratories and basements and secluded meeting places of the noisy, cobblestoned, odiferous, but luminous city of Prague.

If Frederick V of Bohemia had prevailed at the Battle of White Mountain, the thought-systems incubating in the city of Prague might have prevailed. If the forces of Ferdinand II, Holy Roman Emperor, had been flung back from the gates of the city, we might be living in a different world today.

Prague in the early seventeenth century was a city seething with strange excitements. Every sort of esoteric, hermetic, cabalistic, alchemical, astral, and envelope-pushing protoscientific art was practiced here. From dark cellars to brightly lit salons, the arcane methodologies honed to perfection in this world capital of the occult were being used to coax into existence complex synergies of magical arts that we cannot now imagine. In ancient clay and timber houses slanting above the maze of narrow streets winding through the Jewish Quarter, rabbis immersed themselves in cabalistic study without fear of persecution. In the bustling main squares, the unadorned white churches of the Hussites rose up in silent tribute to John Hus (1370–1415), the fierce pre-Reformation Czech preacher who denounced the rituals and penances of the Roman Catholic Church and established a reformed church in Europe a century before Martin Luther. (He was burned at the stake for his trouble.)

The melancholic, reclusive, acquisitive Holy Roman Emperor Rudolf II (1576–1612) had claimed Prague as his imperial capital, and in his obsessive pursuit of the philosopher's stone had gathered about him Europe's greatest alchemists. In the emperor's lofty palace perched on a steep hill overlooking the meandering Vltava River, huge "wonder-rooms" whirred and hummed with the magico-mechanical marvels of the age: automata that moved and sang; the intricate "Memnon" statue that whistled in the rising wind of dawn; the "devil in a glass," or *homuncu-*

*lus,* an "artificially created living being" that was actually a glass-blown figure sealed in a giant jar. The Prague of those days would come to be known as the birthplace of the golem—the Jewish Frankenstein's monster. The reputation of the city as a mecca for magical endeavor drew to its shaded gardens the boldest minds of the time: heretical priest/scientists like Giordano Bruno and Tommaso Campanella; magician/mathematicians the likes of John Dee and Edward Kelly; astronomers at the cutting edge of space-time research, such as Johannes Kepler and Tycho Brahe; and many more.

Some of these daring thinkers—it's impossible to know which ones—formed an elusive relationship with a brotherhood so mysterious that its name seemed to blur and change from lip to lip. The Illuminati? The Association of the Rosy Cross? Whatever they called themselves, these author/scholar/scientists, probably based in Prague but nearly always hidden from the public eye, wrote treatises (Thomas More's *Utopia* is the best-known example) describing an ideal city, free of despotism and theocracy, whose citizens enjoyed equal rights and an occult connection with higher realms of being—a city that held forth the promise of a total transformation of humankind.

Frederick V, ruler of Prague and Bohemia at the time of the Battle of White Mountain, was also the ruler of a small principality on the banks of the Neckar in southern Germany called the Palatinate. The capital of this principality was the fabled city of Heidelberg. It was to this city that Frederick brought, in March 1613, his new bride, Elizabeth Stuart, daughter of King James I of Great Britain.

It was because of who Elizabeth Stuart was that the Battle of White Mountain could have gone the other way. James I had given his daughter Elizabeth in marriage to Frederick in a magnificent ceremony in London on Valentine's Day, February 14, 1613. The king intended by this marriage to shore up the alliance between Anglican anti-Catholic Great Britain and the Lutheran anti-Catholic principalities making up most of Germany.

To James I's subjects, this alliance meant the king had taken a radical tilt away from the Hapsburg rulers of Europe's Holy Roman Empire. They saw the coming joint reign of Frederick and Elizabeth over the Palatinate as a beachhead set up in advance of an extension of Protestantism—perhaps a military one—into the Catholic heartland of southern Europe.

Certainly Frederick V believed this when, in late 1619, he was invited by the city fathers of Prague, who had recently expelled the reigning Holy Roman Emperor Ferdinand II from their country, to become the king of Bohemia. Enraptured by the lure of the magico-occult achievements of Prague—Frederick had emulated some of them by placing automata in the gardens of his own Heidelberg Castle—the ruler of the Palatinate traveled from Heidelberg to Prague, with Elizabeth, their children, and a huge train of possessions, to accept the throne of the Kingdom of Bohemia.

But Frederick and James I's subjects—and much of northern Europe—were mistaken about James's intentions. Increasingly bowed under the weight of years and royal responsibilities, James I greatly feared a confrontation with the Hapsburgs. He had sought in secret to counterbalance the marriage of Elizabeth and Frederick with a marriage between his son Charles and a Catholic princess of the Holy Roman Empire. In this he had failed, but his aversion to a showdown with the Hapsburgs had hardened over the years.

This was why, when Ferdinand II's forces marched on Prague in 1620 to challenge the rule of Frederick V, Frederick's father-in-law, James I, sent no supporting army. If he had done this, the balance of power might have shifted. The Protestant rulers of Denmark and Sweden would perhaps have sent their armies to stand beside those of James I of Great Britain, in alliance with Frederick V's Bohemian army, before the gates of Prague.

The great Renaissance scholar Frances Yates writes in *The Rosicrucian Enlightenment*: "The truth probably is that Frederick's chief crime was that he failed. If he had succeeded in establishing himself in Bohemia, all the waverers, including his father-in-law, would probably have wavered over to him."[1]

But Frederick had won few supporters during his year on the throne of Bohemia. Prague fell at the Battle of White Mountain, and a whole other, alternate, magico-occult way of dealing with the universe, which might have begun to sweep westward across Europe if Frederick V had prevailed, was prevented from becoming manifest.

Another factor suggests that on November 8, 1620, Europe stood at a crossroads that might have taken it in a wholly different direction. By one of history's stranger quirks, there fought in the ranks of the Holy Roman Emperor at the Battle of White Mountain a lowly foot soldier who one day would become one of the seminal thinkers of the age. If Bohemia had prevailed, this twenty-four-year-old Frenchman— his name was René Descartes—would probably have died. But he lived. This was the same Descartes who, born in 1596 and died in 1650, introduced the formulation *Cogito, ergo sum*—"I think, therefore I am"—to the world. It was Descartes who paved the way for the transformation of the Western world to the scientific paradigm. His new science decisively rejected the cosmology of the Roman Catholic Church, and also that of the magico-occult world. This latter cosmology affirmed that every particle of matter in the universe is suffused with an equal quantity of spirit. Descartes asserted that the universe is divided into mind and body. The two are radically separate, with body/matter operating according to the laws (however complex) of mechanics only.

In his late teens, Sir Isaac Newton (1642–1727) was profoundly influenced by the thought of René Descartes. Descartes's philosophical/mathematical description of the cosmos split the English scientist off from any allegiance he might have made with magico-occult thinking (though this mode of thinking would always fascinate Newton). Newton would break with the thought of Descartes to create the paradigm of physical reality to which we adhere to the present day (to all intents and purposes)—but the influence of Descartes on Newton in his early years was decisive.

Probably the prodigious Newton would have created his paradigm despite a victory by Frederick V at White Mountain and the early death of René Descartes. It is very likely he would have created his physico-mathematical equations in the face of any flood of magico-occult thinking spreading across Europe.

But if he had not—what sort of a world would we be living in today?

It would be a world without technology as we know it. In the minds of the magico-occultists, spirit (they would have called it "holy spirit," since they regarded it as imbued with a moral/religious dimension) was coextensive with every atom of physical creation. Their magico-science would have evolved a technology that treated every manifestation of matter, leaf to forest to planetoid, with respect and love—as the Beloved. By contrast, our technology—that which evolved from the Newtonian paradigm—is a brute beast, respecting neither nature nor nature's thinking component, man. Near the end of Newton's life, the great scientist and his colleagues made an implicit agreement with the Church that divided the universe into two spheres of influence. Science would be in charge of the physical universe and the Church would be in charge of the spiritual universe; neither could encroach upon the other's territory. In such a way was the magico-occult, with its ethical-religious dimension, drawn away from science, in a series of subtle maneuvers that Newton sensed at the end of his life and profoundly regretted.

Does the ascendancy of the Newtonian way of mastering the universe mean the magico-occult way of dealing with the universe has totally vanished?

The answer is no. There was a certain truth in the way the Prague magico-occultists saw the world. And truth stands alone; it does not need to be believed in to exist. And, in fact, ever since the seventeenth century and earlier, here and there, in the lives of artists and thinkers and very ordinary people, sometimes just for a moment, the magico-occult universe has come bursting through. It has appeared like a waking dream; it has flashed through the exalted nights of visionaries like a comet streaking through the sky; it has unfolded in extended mediumistic séances—"channeling" sessions—that have sometimes given pause to even the most skeptical of experiencers.

By his own account, Benvenuto Cellini was saved from suicide while in a Roman dungeon by the intervention of that other world. Giordano Bruno sought to link what he regarded as the magico-occult thinking of ancient Egypt to a whole new way of construing the modern world. Visions of multiple afterworlds, similar to those of the Prague Illuminati, invaded the consciousness of the Swedish scientist-engineer Emanuel Swedenborg so profoundly that ever afterward he wrote books describing those universes; even the great novelist Leo Tolstoy, while skewering spiritualism in his play *The Fruits of Enlightenment,* could not avoid in his masterpiece *Anna Karenina* bearing witness to the existence of other dimensions. The French novelist Honoré de Balzac wrote seventy-four novels in twenty-nine years by drawing on—or so he intimates—the energy of the "inner self" as elaborated in the treatises of Swedenborg; three of Balzac's novels were seeded by the intuitions of the Swedish seer.

The dreams of visionary poets are glimpses into the realms of the magico-occult. William Blake in eighteenth-century England, Victor Hugo in nineteenth-century France, James Merrill in twentieth-century America—all "channeled," in startlingly similar terms, other, occult universes. (The Irish poet William Butler Yeats pursued through automatic writing a path that, while differing in detail, was the same in essence.) The work of each of these poets depicts a physical universe animated from rock to angel by Spirit. A varied host of other writers, including some we would not expect, have experienced their lives as lit up for a moment—perhaps for a lifetime—by flashes of lightning from the never-to-be-extinguished (and always-yearned-for, since our souls have never ceased to feel its absence) universe of the magico-occult: H. G. Wells, Mary Wollstonecraft Shelley, Carl Jung, Doris Lessing, Harry Houdini, Thomas Mann, Helena Blavatsky, Sri Yashoda Ma—even Sir Winston Churchill and Norman Mailer—all have known for a moment its vibrant presence.

All of their stories—and many more—are told in the following pages.

# One

## Benvenuto Cellini (1500–1571)

### *The Goldsmith and the Guardian Angel*

On a very dark day in mid-May 1539, Benvenuto Cellini, Italy's greatest goldsmith, lay on a dank pallet in the dungeon of the Castle of Sant' Angelo in Rome and decided to kill himself.

He had once escaped from the dungeon, lowering himself down the outside wall on a rope made out of bedsheets. But the bedsheets had torn and he had fallen fifty feet, landing at the bottom of the moat and breaking a leg. He had dragged himself on all fours to the house of a friend, but the friend had betrayed him, and Cellini had been carted back to prison. He'd been thrown into a dungeon far worse than the last. It was deep and clammy and his mattress was soaked through with water seeping in from the walls. From a narrow slot high up on the wall, sunlight filtered down for only an hour and a half a day. Poisonous worms and giant spiders squirmed and scuttled on the floor and in his bed. Because of his broken leg, he had to haul himself by his arms to the side of the cell when he wanted to perform a bodily function.

For a man of Cellini's vitality, a fate like this was worse than death. He wanted to kill himself. But how? His dark cell seemed to be devoid of everything but crawling things and moisture. What could he kill himself with? He looked around carefully. He had an idea.

Cellini writes in his *Autobiography:*

> I took and propped a wooden pole I found there, in position like a trap. I meant to make it topple over on my head, and it would certainly have dashed my brains out; but when I had arranged the whole machine, and was approaching to put it in motion, just at the moment of my setting my hand to it, I was seized by an invisible power and flung four cubits [six feet] from the spot, in such a terror that I lay half dead. Like that I remained from dawn until the nineteenth hour, when they brought my food.[1]

When Cellini awoke, priests were standing over him; they thought he was dead and were administering the last rites. The prison warden—the *castellan*—took pity on Cellini and sent him a new mattress. Cellini writes that, lying on the mattress that night, "[when] I searched my memory to find what could have diverted me from that design of suicide, I came to the conclusion that it must have been power divine and my good guardian angel."[2]

He had a spectacular dream that night that seemed to offer confirmation. He dreamt that he encountered "a marvelous being in the form of a most lovely youth, who cried, as though he wanted to reprove me: 'Knowest thou who lent thee that body, which thou wouldst have spoiled before its time?'" Cellini answered that he "'recognized all things pertaining to me as gifts from the God of nature.'" The beautiful youth responded: "'Hast thou contempt for His handiwork, through this thy will to spoil it? Commit thyself unto His guidance, and lose not hope in His great goodness!'" The angelic form had much more to say that night, according to Cellini, "in words of marvelous efficacy, the thousandth part of which I cannot now remember."[3]

This dream encounter galvanized the imprisoned goldsmith into a frenzy of activity. He mixed crumbled stone with his urine to make ink. He chewed a wooden splinter off the cell door and made it into a pen. He wrote a long poem in the margins of his Bible, a dialogue in which his body scolded his soul for wanting to leave it too early.

While Cellini was writing in his Bible, he began to read it, something he rarely did. He was captivated by what he read. "With profound astonishment," he writes, "I dwelt upon the force of God's Spirit in those men of great simplicity, who believed so fervently that He would bring all their heart's desire to pass." Cellini decided he wanted to imitate these men. No sooner had he thought this when "there flowed into my soul so powerful a delight from these reflections upon God, that I took no further thought for all the anguish I had suffered, but rather spent the day in singing psalms and divers other compositions on the theme of His divinity."[4]

Cellini's imprisonment in the Castle of Sant' Angelo was far from over. There would be desperate new situations for him to overcome. But for each new situation, he would experience another apparently miraculous intervention. Eventually, a frail but free and fiercely joyous Cellini would walk out the prison door to resume his life as a celebrated craftsman, adventurer, brawler, and all-round brilliant rake in the last rambunctious and glorious decades of the Italian Renaissance.

Benvenuto Cellini lived his life in a watershed period in human history, when man, while still passionately believing in God, Devil, angels, demons—all of it—was also embarking on a new and audacious odyssey into the understanding and harnessing of his own powers. Dr. Michael Grosso describes these newly aborning Renaissance men (and, more privately, women) as seeking "through the arts and sciences to push the limits of human achievement toward their godlike potential."[5] Jacob

Burckhardt writes: "When this impulse to the highest individual development was combined with a powerful and varied nature, which had mastered all the elements of the culture of the age, then arose the 'all-sided man'—'*l'uomo universale*'—who belonged to Italy alone."[6]

Leonardo da Vinci and Michelangelo Buonarotti were exemplary of these men. So, in his quarrelsome way, was Benvenuto Cellini, who was born in Florence in 1500 and died there in 1571. From his earliest age, this swashbuckling Florentine genius displayed a remarkable capacity for transcending danger even while he was in the middle of it. One day when he was three, he picked up a scorpion. Not knowing it was poisonous, he refused to put it down. His father had to resort to the stratagem of snipping off the creature's deadly claws and tail while his son was holding it. The danger past, his family "took the occurrence for a good augury," says Cellini. When he was five, his father pointed out to him a salamander "sporting in the intensest coals" of the fireplace. It was thought that salamanders lived in fire; catching sight of one in its natural surroundings was a rare, auspicious event. Once Cellini had seen the salamander, his father boxed his ears so he wouldn't forget what he'd seen. Ever afterward, the goldsmith thought of those boyhood experiences as talismanic of his unique ability to pass through life's disasters unscathed.[7]

Cellini's father made musical instruments and wanted Cellini to become a flautist. Though he had a talent for the flute, the ever-rebellious boy resisted. Cellini's tempestuous nature drew him as strongly to brawling as to music making. His artistic nature drew him even more powerfully to the art of the goldsmith. His father yielded; the mettlesome Cellini, apprenticed to the finest goldsmiths of the day, soon acquired a reputation as a swift, original, supremely talented craftsman.

His reputation as a street fighter kept pace. Cellini was hotheaded and defiant, difficult and self-righteous. He was a fast talker who never stopped arguing, especially with the rich, the high, and the powerful. His attitude problem led to his being regularly banished from urban centers, so that throughout his life he constantly crisscrossed Italy and spent some time in France. He was often on the lam; far more often he was keenly sought after as a fabricator of gold *objets d'art;* of coins, medals, and medallions; and of the occasional piece of sculpture.

The door was always ajar between Cellini and the supernatural world. One pitch-black midnight in 1532, in the deserted Roman Coliseum, with the help of a necromancer and three assistants, he used astral magic to try to summon the spirits of the dead. He only wanted to ask them if he would see his girlfriend, a prostitute named Angelina, again. Cellini says in his *Autobiography* that the spirits appeared and told him he would see her in a month (and this came true). But the blasphemous goldsmith had opened a Pandora's box. Suddenly the Coliseum seemed to burst into flames and fill up with a thousand howling demons. Hallucinating or not, the terrified trespassers on the spirit world ran screaming home—or so Cellini tells us.[8]

In mid-1535, the goldsmith became mortally ill. He hovered between life and death for several weeks. Every night he seemed to wrestle with Charon, the boatman of Greek myth who ferried the souls of the dead across the River Styx to the afterworld. Cellini writes that "the terrible old man used to come to my bedside, and make as though he would drag me by force into a huge boat he had with him." Once, when Cellini was describing this apparition to a friend, "the old man took me by the arm and dragged me violently towards him. This made me cry out for aid, because he was going to fling me under hatches in his hideous boat." The goldsmith finally began to recover. It was only then that "that old man ceased to give so much annoyance, yet sometimes he appeared to me in dreams."[9]

Perhaps it was because he was sure he was under divine protection that Cellini refused to back off from picking a fight with the most powerful man in Italy: Pope Paul III. The goldsmith's long-running quarrel with the pope may have been the chief reason why, in 1537, the stormy Cellini was hauled off to the Castle of Sant' Angelo.

His dramatic rescue by a "guardian angel" from suicide wasn't the only demand he would make on the spirit world during his stay in the castle prison. The castellan, infuriated by the goldsmith's now joyous demeanor, deeply jealous that Cellini was happier than he was, ordered the prisoner to be flung into an even more dreadful dungeon. The guards dragged the goldsmith toward this new place of incarceration with such roughness that he was terrified he would be thrown into the infamous oubliette of Sammabo, down which men plummeted "to the bottom of a deep pit in the foundations of the castle." Arriving at the new cell, which was worse than the last but hardly as bad as Sammabo, Cellini became so joyous that "during the whole of that first day, I kept festival with God, my heart rejoicing ever in the strength of hope and faith."[10]

Reports of Cellini's redoubled joy were the last straw for the castellan. He ordered the prisoner to be taken back to his old cell and issued an order for his execution. He made sure that Cellini heard about this indirectly. Now the goldsmith was truly devastated. His mighty spirit was crushed at last, and, for a second time, he resolved to kill himself.

But this was not to be the end. Cellini later wrote that "at this juncture the invisible being who had diverted me from my first intention of suicide, came to me, being still invisible, but with a clear voice, and shook me, and made me rise, and said to me: 'Ah me! My Benvenuto, quick, quick, betake thyself to God with thy accustomed prayers, and cry out loudly, loudly.'"

"In a sudden consternation," Cellini writes, "I fell upon my knees, and recited several of my prayers in a loud voice. . . . I communed a space with God; and in an instant the same clear and open voice said to me: 'Go to rest, and have no further fear!'"[11]

For reasons that were unclear even to himself, the next day the castellan canceled Cellini's execution order.

The goldsmith rejoiced yet more fervently, working himself into an exalted pitch of altered consciousness. The stage was set for another encounter with the beyond. One night, Cellini vowed to his guardian angel (whom he considered to be always at his side) that he would be content if he could just have one more look at the sun. When he awoke next morning, his cell was darker than ever. Cellini went over the head of his spirit protector, appealing directly to God to give him one last look at the sun.

Instantly, an invisible angel

like a whirlwind, caught me up and bore me away into a large room, where he made himself visible to my eyes in human form, appearing like a young man whose beard is just growing, with a face of indescribable beauty, but austere, not wanton. He bade me look around the room, and said: "The crowd of men thou seest in this place are all those who up to this day have been born and afterwards have died upon the earth." Thereupon I asked him why he brought me hither, and he answered: "Come with me and thou shalt soon behold."[12]

Cellini was taken through a "little low door" onto a narrow street. He noticed sunlight striking a wall. The spirit invited him to climb backward up a huge spiral staircase. Ascending rapidly, the awestruck goldsmith found himself arriving "within the region of the sunlight . . . until I discovered the whole sphere of the sun."[13]

He continues:

The strength of his rays, as is their wont, first made me close my eyes; but becoming aware of my misdoing, I opened them wide, and gazing steadfastly at the sun, exclaimed: "Oh, my sun, for whom I have so passionately yearned! Albeit your rays may blind me, I do not wish to look on anything again but this!"[14]

The rays, now spreading to one side, left an area of whiteness. While Cellini watched, "a Christ upon the cross formed itself out of the same substance as the sun." Then a Madonna appeared, holding a child, escorted by two angels "whose beauty far surpasses man's imagination." Cellini writes: "The marvelous apparition remained before me little more than half a quarter of an hour. Then it dissolved, and I was carried back to my dark lair."[15]

He must have told someone about this "out-of-body" experience. The castellan, angrier than ever at the happiness of his ever-resilient prisoner, decided to have him slowly poisoned to death. But Cellini, no doubt aided by his exalted state of mind, was able to execute a series of wily maneuvers and circumvent this danger.

The courageous goldsmith had brought a permanent souvenir back from his out-of-body journey to the sun: there would ever afterward be, or so he tells us, a halo around his head. Cellini later wrote that this "aureole of glory . . . is visible to every sort of man to whom I have chosen to point it out; but those have been very few." We wouldn't expect Cellini to point out his halo to the castellan. But perhaps he did—or perhaps the castellan saw it anyway. At any rate, for reasons as complex as they are obscure, not long after the goldsmith's visit to the sun, Cellini was finally released from his captivity in the Castle of Sant' Angelo.[16]

It may be that these seemingly divine interventions deep in the dungeons of the Castle of Sant' Angelo were the crucial ones in Cellini's life. But his guardian angel had by no means gone into retirement. The protective forces surrounding the brawling craftsman would never show themselves to more advantage than when, in 1554, they rescued not Cellini, but his greatest work of art, from total destruction.

The goldsmith's supreme artistic achievement is arguably his larger-than-life-sized bronze statue *Perseus Holding the Head of Medusa* (1545–54), which stands to this day in the Loggia dei Lanzi in Florence. Few thought Cellini would be able to cast a bronze statue of such enormous size—eighteen feet in height, including pedestal. Not only did the technology for such a feat scarcely exist in sixteenth-century Italy, but Cellini's many enemies were constantly trying to sabotage his efforts.

Cellini solved the first problem by inventing a new technology. With the aid of ten assistants, in the final weeks of casting the bronze statue he constructed a huge, new, innovative furnace around the baked-clay-and-wax prototype of the *Perseus*.

The final day arrived. At the end of the most strenuous exertions, and even as the bronze was liquefying in the casting furnace, Cellini was overcome by a fever "of the utmost possible intensity."[17] He was sure he would be dead by morning. He dragged himself off to bed, reluctantly leaving in the hands of his ten assistants the difficult, delicate final stages of the casting.

Cellini tells us that he spent the next two hours "battling with the fever, which steadily increased, and calling out continually, 'I feel that I am dying!'"[18] His housekeeper, despairing for her master's life, fought back her tears at his bedside. Suddenly, writes Cellini,

> I beheld the figure of a man enter my chamber, twisted in his body into the form of a capital S. He raised a lamentable, doleful voice, like one who announces their last hour to men condemned to die upon the scaffold, and spoke these words: "O Benvenuto! your statue is spoiled, and there is no hope whatever of saving it."[19]

Howling with rage at these words, Cellini leaped out of bed, pulled on his clothes, and raced through the house back to the workshop. The assistants were standing around helplessly; something was making the molten bronze coagulate in the furnace and they didn't know what to do.

Cellini was certain one of the assistants was sabotaging his masterpiece. With Herculean force he seized control of events. The goldsmith ordered loads of highly combustible oak wood to be rushed from across the street and tossed into the furnace; the furnace blazed up and the bronze began to melt. Icy rain from a storm outside threatened to cool the furnace; Cellini had the assistants block up all the doors, windows, chinks, and crannies in the house, using every rug and curtain he owned. Suddenly, there was an explosion and a tremendous burst of flame; the cap of the furnace had blown off and the molten bronze was bubbling out. All seemed lost—until Cellini, in a furious burst of inspiration, had his assistants throw every one of his two hundred pewter pots, pans, and plates into the furnace. The strategy worked; finally the bronze began to liquefy in the proper manner. Soon the entire statue was cast to perfection. Every ounce of bronze had been used, with nothing left over, and the entire statue had been formed—except for the tip of Perseus's right big toe.

Not only had Cellini not succumbed to the fever, but he'd never felt better. Was the apparition of the S-shaped man one more manifestation of his guardian angel? Or was this Cellini's endlessly powerful creative imagination at work? Or, as his housekeeper laughingly suggested, did the kicks and blows Cellini rained on his staff as he raced back to his workshop frighten away the lethal fever?

Whatever the explanation, Cellini would later write in commemoration of that frenzied hour, "I cannot remember a day in my whole life when I dined with greater gladness or a better appetite."[20]

# Two

# Michel de Nostradamus
# (1503–1566)

## *The Art of Astral Medicine*

In the autumn of 1534, Michel de Nostradamus, the world's most famous prognosticator of the future, dropped out of medical school at the University of Montpellier in France and disappeared.

For a period of three months, he seemed to have vanished. When Nostradamus reappeared at the end of that year, he did not return to the University of Montpellier. He did not resume his medical studies, and he never became a medical doctor in the sense of obtaining a diploma (as Ian Wilson all but proves in his 2007 book *Nostradamus: The Man Behind the Prophecies*). Instead, he spent the next few years touring the countryside as a sort of itinerant apothecary, dispensing remedies of his own concoction such as cypress wood mixed with white roses and acquiring a reputation as one of the few physicians able to deal effectively with the Black Death.

It would not be until 1552 that Nostradamus published the first of his rhymed quatrains called *Centuries,* which sought to foretell the future. And it would be only slowly, over the years, that he built up his practice of drawing up the horoscopes of Europe's rich, famous, and powerful (Rudolf II of Prague was once a client).

But, even though we are still electrified today when we think we have found a correspondence between one of Nostradamus's quatrains and a current event, Ian Wilson makes clear in his book that the vast majority of the horoscopes Nostradamus drew up were radically wrong, and that in almost no cases can we say unequivocally that one of his prophecies came true.

Wilson wonders why it is, given these facts, that the prophecies of Nostradamus have such staying power. How, he asks us, can we account for "the astonishing power of the name 'Nostradamus,' even after more than four centuries, to evoke a deeply superstitious awe amongst the millions throughout the world?"[1]

The answer may lie with those few months of missing time that Nostradamus spent in 1534. When he emerged from them, he may have acquired a power that would carry his name and his works up through the centuries.

We know now that when Nostradamus left the University of Montpellier, he traveled some 170 miles in a southwesterly direction until he came to the little French town of Agen, on the Garonne River. Here he met Jules-César Scaliger. We know this because Nostradamus's secretary and biographer Jean Aimé de Chavigny states unequivocally, "Jules-César Scaliger, an individual of well known and exceptional learning, caused him [Nostradamus] to stay."[2]

Ian Wilson comments that "in all this, why Nostradamus should have gone so far out of his way to seek Jules-César Scaliger, and why at this particular point in time, is by no means easy to determine. That he held Scaliger in high regard there can be little doubt. Later in life he would speak of him as a 'wise and learned man' and (most intriguingly) as one 'to whom I remain more indebted than to anybody else in the world.'"[3] That was all Nostradamus ever said about Scaliger.

But just who was Jules-César Scaliger, anyway?

According to his learned contemporary Jacques-Auguste de Trou, Scaliger was the smartest man who ever lived. De Trou declared that Scaliger was at least as smart as every one of the great thinkers of antiquity, including Pythagoras, Plato, Solomon, and Moses, and that nobody in modern times could hold a candle to him, not even the great Desiderius Erasmus.

The subject of this unrestrained praise was born near Verona, in Italy, in 1484—or so he said. Scaliger shared with Benvenuto Cellini (just sixteen years his junior) two of the frequent characteristics of high achievers of the late Italian Renaissance: he was a brawler and he was a braggart (the word *braggart* had room in it for a certain quantity of less-than-truthfulness). Scaliger claimed to be an artist of genius: he said the painter and printmaker Albrecht Durer had taught him how to draw when he was still in his teens. He claimed to be a warrior of genius, insisting that the emperor Maximilian had bestowed on him the highest military honors for his supreme achievements at the Battle of Ravenna in 1512. He claimed he would become a pope of genius: he had entered the University of Bologna in 1514, he said, with the sole intention—which he communicated to everyone— of taking holy orders, becoming a cardinal, becoming a bishop, then becoming pope.

He didn't become pope. He didn't take holy orders. But he became dedicated to learning. He spent the next eleven years in university study, mastering principally natural science and medicine, but also a huge number of other subjects, including Greek, Latin, Hebrew, music, and all of classical Greek and Roman literature. In 1525 he moved from Piedmont in Italy to Agen in France. Here this lean and commanding man was quick to acquire a reputation as volatile, brilliant, prone to fits of violence, a mesmerizing talker, and a physician of uncanny, almost supernatural, ability. This latter skill included—or so people whispered—a mastery of the arts of astral magic. Of this, Scaliger himself said little, except to a handpicked few whom he swore to deepest secrecy. Certainly he breathed not a word of it to the clergy, who would have assumed he was dancing with the devil and quickly called in the Inquisition.

In 1528, when he was forty-four and she was nineteen,* Scaliger married the petite and voluptuous Andriète de Roques-Lobéjac. Six years later, at about the time that Nostradamus arrived in Agen, there were already five children. Andriète would give birth to fifteen in all, ten daughters and five sons, over the course of twenty-nine years of marriage. Those who knew Scaliger knew that the embraces and other attentions of this young woman had done much to tame the volatility and violent temper of this quarrelsome physician, to the point where he was no longer wary about talking to people he did not know and could reach out to them in his quest to share his knowledge. He seems to have reached out to Nostradamus; once the seer-to-be was in his household, Scaliger must have seen the high intelligence and keen imagination in this young man who had been reared in St-Rémy-de-Provence by a cultivated family and educated in all the arts, including Greek, Latin, and astrology. Nostradamus's silence about this in future years, in addition to some of the soothsayer's achievements, suggests that Jules-César Scaliger may have taught him the art of astral magic.

But what was this astral magic?

In 1460, a monk delivered to the court of Cosimo de' Medici in Florence a Greek manuscript thought to date from before the time of Moses and to be written by the Egyptian god Thoth (the Roman god Hermes). Actually dating from the first or second century AD, this *Corpus Hermeticum* contained knowledge of the qualities of the stars and planets (such as the contemplative faculty, practical intelligence, etc.) that we humans draw into our souls as we are about to take life on earth. The *Corpus Hermeticum* explained how mortals could revivify themselves while alive by reconnecting with these cosmic qualities; it told how we could "draw upon the life of the heavens."[4]

---

*About this the records vary, with some claiming that the marriage took place earlier or that Scaliger was forty and Andriète sixteen.

At the request of Cosimo, the Renaissance philosopher-scholar Marsilio Ficino (1433–1499) translated this work into Latin, calling it the *Pimander*. Ted Anton writes that "the misshapen, pedantic Ficino, his suave, wealthy disciple Pico della Mirandola (1463–1494), and the enigmatic, tormented Giordano Bruno (1548–1600) . . . [studied these techniques of 'astral magic' to enhance] their command of unconscious and erotic, imaginative powers. Magic to them did not mean hocus-pocus, but rather a deep, thoroughly documented world of the imagination connecting conscious and unconscious, individual and cosmos, in a way lost to modern man. However imperfect their 'sciences' were . . . these philosopher-magicians were early masters of cyberspace—the infinite realm of thoughts that the Renaissance called phantasms."[5]

These writings were part of a mysterious tangle of obscure and complex documents, going back to Plato, which asserted that human beings have an inner faculty, the *pneuma,* that translates the language of the divine (i.e., the qualities of the stars and planets, messages from the angels, etc.) into the language of earthly, human thought and feeling. Spirit and matter were so different in essence that they couldn't make contact; the pneuma was the psycho-corporeal organ that made contact possible. Just as a computer is packed with databytes, the pneuma is packed with "phantasms"; these are not unlike the infinitude of individual archetypes making up the Jungian collective unconscious. The phantasms were the symbolic images of every individual thing that could ever exist. Divine thought sought out the corresponding phantasms and, passing through the pneuma, emerged on the other side as a human thought.

The trick of being a successful practitioner of astral magic was to know exactly what each individual phantasm looked like; that done, you could create a replica and display it to the phantasm located in the pneuma. In that way, you might, just *might*—since the symbolic images in the pneuma actually had *more* reality, *more* being, than human thought, and even divine thought—you just might be able to prompt, or trick, or surprise the pneuma into doing something, producing something—*manifesting* something!

But the weird otherness of the thinking of the astral magicians of the late Renaissance baffles our matter-of-fact modern minds. We only know about some of the kinds of images these men experimented with, thinking they might be replicas or near-replicas of the symbolic images that made up the phantasms. The ancient world, lacking books, had invented the *ars memoria,* or art of memory, a collection of concrete images that enabled the ancients to carefully store away pieces of knowledge in their memory. These concrete images were created through human thought and intuition; it was thought they might not be very different in form from the phantasms. That was why, writes expert on Renaissance magic Ioan Coulianu, the art of memory became "a technique for the manipulation of phantasms, which rests on the Aristotelian principle of the absolute precedence of the phantasm over speech and of the phantasmic essence of the intellect."[6]

Ficino, among others, gathered around him every sort of talisman, charm, colored object, intricate occult design, and even bars of music and, endlessly experimenting, tried to discover which assortment of (usually fantastical, odd, and uncommon) *phantasm*-teasers could draw down the powers of heaven in some specific way. Anything to do with ancient Egyptian hieroglyphics and astrological signs (or Decans) might have power; Bruno even designed his own Decans.

You could even, perhaps, feed the pneuma with something that had little or no relationship to reality—and produce something never before seen! Emblems, heraldry, all the vast panoply of late-medieval and Renaissance designs—any of these might trigger an explosion of creative translation in the pneuma. Coulianu writes, "Finally—and here is the origin of the emblems, *impresae* and emblematic legends of the Renaissance—phantasms can, as we have already said, stem directly from the imaginative faculty without an objective support."[7] You could make them up, and the pneuma could make them real.

Such techniques of astral magic did men like Jules-César Scaliger, and very likely Marsilio Ficino, possibly master. Did Scaliger pass this knowledge along to Michel de Nostradamus in Agen in the fall of 1534? To inquire further, let us return to the life of Nostradamus.

The future seer is thought to have returned to Agen, though perhaps he was never far from it. He married Adriète de Roques-Lobéjac. This seems strange; the name is astonishingly close to that of Scaliger's wife, Andriète de Roques-Lobéjac. Nostradamus scholar John Hogue writes that "skeptics have theorized that these biographers [giving that name] mistake Nostradamus's bride for that of Scaliger . . . there is a third possibility—that Nostradamus's "Adriète" was a relation of Scaliger's wife, perhaps a cousin or even a half-sister."[8]

It's believed that Adriète bore the future seer a girl and boy. He practiced medicine in Port-Sainte-Marie, twelve miles from Agen. Then tragedy struck. Nostradamus's wife and two children died in the plague, or such is the legend. The townspeople excoriated Nostradamus; how could a physician so renowned for dealing with the Black Death not save his own wife and children? The Inquisition even wanted to talk to the physician-seer. He fled the area.

We do not know how much of this is true (for example, Ian Wilson gives Scaliger's wife's name as Audriète, not Andriète); we know only that, from shortly after he left the University of Montpellier, a certain aura of the divine—a kind of mega-charisma—began to cling about Nostradamus. From then on, legends of his powers were born and have persisted despite the impossibility of any sort of historical proof. Here is the most famous story of all, in the words of Martin Ebon:

> After the death of his wife and children, Nostradamus traveled widely. He went to Milan, Genoa and Venice. An incident from this period suggests his prophetic powers. Nostradamus is alleged to have knelt before a young and undistinguished village boy, the Franciscan Friar Felix Peretti. When asked why he had humbled himself in such a way, he is said to have replied, "Because I must bow and kneel before His

Holiness." It is a fact that Peretti became Cardinal of Montalto and, under the name of Sixtus the Fifth, was named Pope in 1585.[9]

After some years Nostradamus would reestablish himself in the town of Salon de Crau (now Salon-de-Provence) with his second wife, Anne Ponsarde, who would bear him six children. Nostradamus followed the release of the first batch of his *Centuries* in 1552 with successive volumes appearing in almanac-like form.

Nostradamus's "36,200 weird words of prophecy"[10] eventually included more than eight *Centuries* for a total of perhaps 1,300 quatrains. From the beginning these quatrains were wildly popular. They were made up of a bizarre mix of old French, Latin, and classical rhetorical structures presented in every sort of new and unexpected combination. You could read virtually anything you wanted into these quatrains. As Ian Wilson suggests, we cannot be certain if any of them—except for one, as we shall see—actually ended up foretelling the future.

But were they verses at all?

Are they instead symbolic representations of phantasms, meant to trigger reactions in our souls? Do they have an independent, living reality all their own? Is that why, up through the centuries, they have not lost their power to beguile?

There is one quatrain that indeed does seem to have foretold an event, with striking and disturbing accuracy. The quatrain:

> *The young lion shall overcome the old*
> *On the field of war in a single duel;*
> *He will pierce his eyes in a cage of gold.*
> *This is the first of two stages, followed by cruel death.*[11]

John Hogue tells the story:

By 1556 Nostradamus' *Les Prophecies* was the rage at court. After Queen Catherine de' Medici was shown a quatrain predicting the death of her husband, King Henry II, in a jousting accident, Nostradamus was summoned to Paris. His royal audience was a success and he became an intimate occult friend to the Queen. Nostradamus was safely ensconced in his Salon study when Henry II fulfilled that prophecy in 1559. Following quatrain 35 of Century I to the letter, Henry sustained a wooden splinter from the jousting shaft during the tournament; it rammed through his helmet's golden visor and plunged behind his eye into his brain. On the night of his death, crowds gathered before the Inquisitors, burning Nostradamus in effigy and demanding the priests burn him in earnest. Only Nostradamus's friendship with Queen Catherine saved him.[12]

How did he manage to make this prediction? Martin Ebon paints a picture of the seer at work, using details provided by Nostradamus in his works.

The first edition of *Centuries* had been written, it would appear, in a trance-like state, while Nostradamus was staring into a brass bowl filled with water that acted as a divination device. He was listening to the voices of wisdom, to spirits of the long dead, to his own memory of ancient Egyptian books, to the combination of medical knowledge, mathematics, astrology and astronomy, and to sacred as well as sacrilegious methods of divination available to him, as he put it, because he "had received at birth certain astral aspects which predisposed" him to prophecy, all of which "came from God." Of himself, he prophesized, "After my earthly passing, my writing will do more than during life."[13]

Does this description, taken largely from his own words, constitute proof that Nostradamus practiced the skills of astral magic after the fashion of, say, Marsilio Ficino, constructing through experimentation replicates of phantasms? We can't really tell. For proof—if proof is possible at all—we must look to two other areas in

Nostradamus's life: his career as the author of a series of bestselling self-help, medicinal, pharmaceutical, and culinary arts books, and to his translation into French of a strange, one-thousand-year-old book called the *Horapollo*.

The hieroglyphics of ancient Egypt have never lost their power to fascinate. Deciphered by Jean-François Champollion in 1822 and falling out of use in Egypt at the time of Christ, during the intervening centuries they were thought by mystified commentators to be the words of God. The Deity had delivered the symbols directly to the priests of Egypt; "each image expressed each concept with matchless clarity, because it was a natural [i.e., created by God], not a conventional [i.e., invented by men], sign."[14]

In Alexandria in the fifth century A.D., a Hellenist named Horapollo wrote a manual, *Hieroglyphica* [*Hieroglyphics*], in which he identified, then interpreted, these ancient pictures believed to be things and ideas in their simple, eternal essence. The book was lost from sight for a millennium, showing up in Italy during the Renaissance. Scholars flocked to translate it. For some, the text—now called the *Horapollo*—was a collection of mundane "emblems;" others believed, with the author, that each hieroglyph contained an abstract thought in visual form originally emanating from the mind of God. Among the latter were the astral magicians, who suspected the symbols might be phantasms. In 1545, Nostradamus translated the book with a commentary. His absorption in the text is one indication he was plying the trade of astral magician.

There are also indications in some of Nostradamus's popular medicinal books that he was a practitioner of astral magic.

In 1572, two of the seer's books containing recipes for elixirs were published in German; this translation was published in English in 1995 as *The Elixirs of Nostradamus: Nostradamus' Original Recipes for Elixirs, Scented Water, Beauty Potions and Sweetmeats*. The book contains thirty-nine preparations; here is one of them, Nostradamus's "composition for maintaining the health of the human body, which is very potent and effective":

> Take the ground spice or the crushed powder of sweet musk, of coral and of dissolved pearls, 150 chopped gold leaves, blue lapis lazuli (which has been washed nine times and prepared and likewise ground into fine powder). . . . If you can obtain them [ones used by jewelers and goldsmiths], take as much as four drachms, then a drachm each of offcuts or the residue from the five major gems and excellent pearls, three drachms of fine ivory scrapings, one drachm of fine unicorn [narwhal's horn] scrapings, two lots of lots of bone or gristle . . .[18]

Nostradamus makes extraordinary claims for the curative value of this (to our eyes) outlandish potion:

> Anyone who, each morning an hour-and-a-half before a meal or snack, takes a drachm of this composition with good white wine and malmsey, will be protected against all kinds of sickness . . . if anyone takes it during an epidemic, he will not be infected that day . . . if, mixed with alkanet water, it is taken by someone in his last hour, when he is on the point of death and nature and his sickness are doing battle with each other, it will so invigorate and strengthen the person that the outcome and final judgment on the sickness will be in the patient's favor and nature will obtain the victory. . . . In addition, if a woman would like to have children or heirs, it so arranges the male member and the womb that both seeds unite and remain in the bearing place until it is time for the birth.[19]

Nostradamus's cures must have been very expensive, as the following prescription for "making precious green pomade" suggests:

> If, however, you desire to make your pomade something special, excellent and perfect, better than ever before, then, during the sea-

son when roses are growing and in bloom, take about 300 or 400 white ones, crush them with the pomade in a marble mortar and, when you have done so, leave the mixture to stand for a day or two. At the end of this period take a similar quantity of white roses, crush them once more, as you have been instructed, and when you have done this, put the whole into a pewter vessel, which is perfectly clean and closes properly . . .[20]

Go to any florist's shop today and you will pay $4,000 for eight hundred white roses! That suggests that Nostradamus catered to a very wealthy clientele. It also suggests that Nostradamus didn't mean for his patients to prepare these remedies at all. Rather, he meant for the soul of the patient to be touched by the arcane pictures he was painting of these various ingredients. Take for example the image of eight hundred white roses being squeezed together (and being boiled, as he says later in the recipe, inside a piece of white silk that has never been used before). Is that image really simply a symbol embodied in a hieroglyph, such as the translator of the *Horapollo* might have encountered and which he might have regarded as the eternal form of a concept emanating from God's brain—and even as the replica of a phantasm intended to draw down the healing powers of heaven? Nostradamus often prescribed "unicorn scrapings" in his medicinal concoctions. These were bone scrapings from the horn of a narwhal; this medical ingredient was often used in Nostradamus' time, for example by the physicians who fought to prolong Martin Luther's life as he lay dying in 1546. Might not unicorn scrapings have also been a component, drawn from one or another of the texts the astral magicians scoured, of the replica of a phantasm evoked by the arts of the astral magician to effect a healing?

It would be the subject of another long chapter to discuss—which is more and more being discussed today—the many correspondences, even borrowings, between the hieroglyphic images set forth in Nostradamus's translation of the *Horapollo* and his *Centuries*. If the images described by Nostradamus in the *Horapollo* and in the *Centuries* come to us charged with the vital energy of an astral magic that is able to touch the pneuma of a human being to effect cures or enhance our prophetic powers— if this is so, then we should not be surprised that the prophecies of Nostradamus have retained the power to move us deeply and excite us.

Nostradamus also taught, in his various self-help and medicinal books, the power of positive thinking. In this particular field the seer had many competitors, and we are often not sure which work is his. The dictums below may or may not come from the hand of Nostradamus, but they are contemporary and are exemplary of what he wrote:

- Beware of sleeping blood. That's what makes the organism get old. When your youth begins to fade into the past, get in the habit of going for a good walk as early in the day as you can.
- In winter as in summer, choose a very quiet place, away from the crowd, and seek to get in touch with plants, flowers, and birds.
- Walk slowly without getting upset. Your rhythm doesn't always have to be the same. The body must be flexible. Get your muscles and joints working. But when you begin to get tired, stretch your limbs and relax completely.
- If your head feels heavy, if there's a bitter taste in your mouth, if you're having problems with your digestion, it's not enough just to take medicinal herbs. Every day you should spend twice as much time walking as you do eating.
- Run through the woods alongside a stream. Stop from time to time to breathe in deeply. While you're relaxing, moisten your forehead with fresh water. All this will help you get rid of excess weight.
- It's even recommended that you walk barefoot, as direct contact of the soles of your feet with the ground loosens up the intestines to do their work.[18]
- Drink water (containing fresh sage and mint leaves) whenever you feel the need, but be very careful to swallow just a bit at a time.

- Try to spend the day in a different place from where you usually live.
- Don't think about women when you're fasting. Love helps us live but also burns up too much energy.
- When the fast is over, don't throw yourself on your food. Drink, from a bowl, goat's milk still warm from the milking. The milk will purify your stomach and your intestines. The day after the fast, eat only fruits and honey.[19]
- To digest a copious meal, have joyful people brought to your table. A roar of laughter at the end of a meal is the best digestive.
- Don't envy someone who laughs all the time, and don't complain about someone who never laughs; they're both in bad health.
- Never miss a chance to laugh outright. An instant of good humor will reconstitute your organism.
- Spontaneous laughter serves above all to preserve the mind from pain and fear.
- If you know how to laugh spontaneously, you have the strength to react against illness.
- Laughter acts beneficially on all the organs. If you want to stay healthy, look every day for a good reason to laugh.
- Joyous laughter is better than medication.[20]

# Three

## Ben Jonson
## (1572–1637)

*The Occult as Confidence Game*

Did the Elizabethan playwright Ben Jonson visit China in the first decade of the seventeenth century?

Did the Chinese writer Fêng Mêng-lung visit London around the same time?

To both questions, the answer is certainly no. In the early seventeenth century China was virtually closed to the rest of the world. It maintained trading relations with the West only through trading posts in nearby Portuguese and Dutch colonies. London and Beijing were five thousand miles apart, and travel between England and China was carried out only by protected diplomats and seasoned traders.

How is it then that the plot of Ben Jonson's comedy *The Alchemist* (1610) is exactly the same as the plot of the short story "Khua Miao Shu Tan Kho Thi Chin" by Fêng Mêng-lung, who died in 1646? Dr. Joseph Needham brings this strange coincidence of alchemical plots to light in volume 3 of his magisterial history, *Science and Civilization in Ancient China*. Needham translates the title of Fêng Mêng-lung's story, published in a collection of stories called *Chin Ku Chhi Kuan* (Strange Tales New and Old), with the following couplet:

> *How Spagyrists [Alchemists] with vaunted occult Art*
> *Cozen the Host and with his Gold depart.*[1]

Dr. Needham begins his discussion of the odd similarity of literary plots that are continents apart by summerizing Jonson's comedy:

In Jonson's play a London gentleman, Mr. Love-Wit, leaves his town house on account of the plague, with his servant, Face, in charge, whereupon Face and the alchemist Subtle make use of the premises for cheating a number of characters. These include a wealthy citizen, Sir Epicure Mammon, a clerk and a shopkeeper, also two puritans, Mr. Tribulation-Wholesome and Ananias, together with a quarrelsome young man, Kastril, and his sister Dame Pliant—only Surly, a gamester, disbelieves in the proceedings. In his text Jonson shows considerable knowledge of the technical terms and concepts of alchemy. Then Love-Wit returns unexpectedly, Subtle decamps with his consort Doll Common, and Face arranges a marriage for Love-Wit with Dame Pliant.[2]

What exactly was this alchemy that was practiced in England in the early seventeenth century (and also as it was practiced, it would seem, in China)? Richard Westfall explains in *Never at Rest: A Biography of Isaac Newton* (Sir Isaac was also an alchemist) that "alchemists believed that life rather than mechanism stands at the very heart of nature. All things are generated by the conjunction of male and female; metals differ in no wise from the rest of nature. Like everything else, metals grow in the womb of the earth—rather, metal grows, for if we speak in strict terms, alchemy did not recognize more than one metal. . . . Alchemists were trying to complete what nature had left incomplete. They were growing gold."[3]

Needham also summarizes Fêng Mêng-lung's story, in which a phony alchemist exploits exactly the same theoretical structure described above. He tells us that a learned and wealthy scholar named Phan Fu-Ong becomes infatuated with alchemy. A fraudulent alchemist consents to perform a "projection"—the transmuting into gold of silver supplied by Phan—in Phan's house. The alchemist brings along his beautiful "wife," actually a prostitute. When the alchemical process fails, the alchemist blames it on the fact that in his absence, Phan and the wife had engaged in lovemaking in the laboratory.

At about the same time as this Chinese tale was being written, Jonson's play *The Alchemist* was being performed in London by the King's Men (opening night was probably February 10, 1610). Just who was this English playwright who, if indeed he did not go to China, was so much in the global flow that he produced a work of art whose oddly mixture of crime and the occult was in the air five thousand miles away?

Ben Jonson's great contemporary William Shakespeare (1564–1616) wrote mainly about kings and princes, generals and cardinals, society's movers and shakers—solitary leaders making hard decisions. Jonson didn't. With a few exceptions, such as *Sejanus*, about a Roman emperor, his plays swarm with the low life of society, such as con artists and petty thieves. This is mainly because of Jonson's hardscrabble, urban beginnings. Born in Westminster, a district of London, in 1572, a month after his father died, he was soon saddled with an unsympathetic stepfather and forced to work in his brickyard. Someone of influence noticed the young boy's high intelligence, and Jonson was placed in a first-rate school and educated without charge for three years.

This school taught only Latin. The student learned Latin grammar; he translated prose and poetry into Latin; he wrote compositions in Latin—and if he didn't speak Latin in class he was whipped. Jonson learned Latin perfectly. This enabled him, later on, to adorn his plays with arcane information from hitherto untranslated classical sources.

Withdrawn from school, Jonson was forced to lay bricks again. He rebelled and went off to war in the Netherlands, killing an enemy in single-handed combat as both sides watched and thereby allowing the English to claim the victory without a battle. Back home, he became an actor, then a playwright.

Ben Jonson was always his own worst enemy. He flung himself from one storm center to another, always mixed up in violent relationships, literary polemics, and theatrical feuds. He killed a fellow actor, Gabriel Spencer, in a duel, but got off with only having his thumb branded. He had many friends—but they feared him as much as they respected him.

Jonson made his name among theatergoers with his two comedies *Every Man in His Humour* (1598) and *Every Man Out of His Humour* (1599). These plays displayed Jonson's predilection for thieves, swindlers, blackmailers, con artists, and crooked gamblers. Jonson hated these dregs of society, holding them up to ridicule. But he also loved them; he wasn't far from being one of them. The kind of London this playwright knew—and his own take on it—is best summed up in Jonson's comedy *The Devil Is an Ass* (1616). In this comedy, the Devil sends a junior devil to earth to wreak evil upon Londoners. As the play ends, the minor imp, foiled on every front, is left gasping at the superior wickedness of humankind. "The devil is an ass" by comparison, he concludes. "All my days in hell were holidays."[4]

Jonson's comedy *The Alchemist* brims over with colorful con artists who are astonishingly well-educated. The play is so quintessentially low-life Elizabethan it's hard to imagine how it could have resonated with any Far East culture. Joseph Needham explains in *Science and Civilization in China* that ancient Chinese alchemical practice went hand in hand with the pursuit of certain "elixirs of youth" meant to promote long life and what Chinese Taoists called *hsien*—the state of material immortality, in which the individual becomes a semimaterial spirit, flitting through the world like an astral self. To supplement these elixirs, the Taoists advocated sexual orgies in which unmarried adepts of both sexes got together, sometimes having sex openly. There were hardly public orgies in Elizabethan London, but there was plenty of sexual vitality, spread throughout all classes and including the rapscallion con artists and their marks who make up the cast of Jonson's play.

Given that alchemy was based on the mating of the male and female principles to produce gold, sex was a metaphor, and more, for the alchemical process; it was virtually an adjunct to the alchemist's work. The alleged lovemaking of Phan and the prostitute in Fêng's story seemed to Needham to echo this. Thus he was startled to discover in *The Alchemist* the scenes of Sir Epicure Mammon being maneuvered into sexual love with the prostitute Doll Common, who is masquerading as an alchemist's assistant. The phony alchemist Subtle uses his allegation of lovemaking between the two as an excuse to set off an explosion—caused, he declares, by that lovemaking—that conveniently destroys the alchemical experimentation and frees Subtle from the necessity of actually creating gold, which he has no idea how to do. He remonstrates with Sir Epicure Mammon, the victim of this con artist:

> *Subtle:* [about the lovemaking:] this'll retard
>     The work, a Month at least.
> *Mammon:* Why, if it do,
>     What remedy? but think it not, good Father:
>     Our purposes were honest.
> *Subtle:* As they were,
>     So the reward will prove. How now! Aye me.
>     God, and all Saints be good to us. What's that?
>     [A great crack and noise within.]
> *Face:* O Sir, we are defeated! all the *works*
>     Are flown in *fumo:* every Glass is burst.[5]

Needham is startled to see Jonson seeming to echo in his play the ancient Chinese link between sex and alchemy. He's also impressed by the succinctness with which Jonson makes Subtle—supposedly a fake—

sum up the conventional argument for the validity of alchemy: that an egg with a shell, seemingly so unlike a chicken, can grow inside a chicken, hatch, and eventually become a chicken. In such a way, the alchemists have said throughout time immemorial, do the processes of nature itself demonstrate that something can grow into something wholly different from what it initially was. In analogous fashion, base metals as well can grow, with the help of the philosopher's stone, into gold:

> *Surly:* [But it's impossible] That you should hatch
> Gold in a Furnace, Sir,
> As they do Eggs in *Egypt!*
> *Subtle: Sir, do you*
> *Believe that Eggs are hatch'd so?*
> *Surly:* If I should?
> *Subtle:* Why, I think that the greater Miracle.
> No Egg but differs from a Chicken more
> Than Metals in themselves.
> *Surly:* That cannot be.
> The Egg's ordain'd by Nature to that end,
> And is a Chicken in *potentia.*
> *Subtle:* The same we say of Lead, and other Metals,
> Which would be Gold, if they had time.
> *Mammon:* And that
> Our Art doth further.[6]

It seems to Needham that Jonson has an extraordinarily fine knowledge of the nature of the five-phased steps within the furnace needed for the alchemical process to properly flourish.

> *Face:* These Bleard-eyes
> Have wak'd, to read your several Colours, Sir,
> Of the *pale Citron,* the *green Lyon,* the *Crow,*
> The *Peacocks Tail,* the *plumed Swan.*[7]

Jonson, as was his custom, also plumbed contemporary sources for this play that was meant to expose a whole gamut of confidence tricks based on often fraudulent occult lore. In London in late 1511, three con artists were arraigned at Whitecastle for fraudulently accepting money from a fourth man, whom they promised they would introduce to Mab, the queen of the fairies. Many believed that Mab would allow herself to be introduced to a person with whom she had fallen in love, and that if you met her in this way, she would immediately make you rich. In *The Alchemist,* this scam is inflicted on a "gull" named Dapper.

Jonson had skirted occult themes in his earlier *Volpone* (1607). In this harsh comedy, the rich Venetian merchant Volpone (Italian for "fox") pretends to be dying to dupe people into giving him gifts in hopes he will make them his heirs. Volpone's assistant, Mosca ("fly"), helps facilitate his master's con games throughout the play. Toward the end, he makes himself Volpone's heir without telling his master he has done so. Then he persuades Volpone to play dead to trick one of the suitors—and then Mosca immediately tries, behind Volpone's back, to have his master declared legally dead. That way he expects to get all his money even though Volpone is still alive.

But, in this play that ironically substitutes fraud for alchemy as a way of getting gold, retribution arrives and Mosea and Volphone are found out and punished. A bizarre trio of minor characters in *Volpone* lends a creepy occult edge to the play. These characters are Androgyno, a hermaphrodite; Nano, a dwarf; and Castrone, a eunuch. Volpone calls the three his bastard children and says he has several more like them in the household. Early on in the play, Nano entertains Volpone—and the audience—with a decidedly occult story about the journey of the soul of Pythagoras through several lifetimes.

Pythagoras is the sixth-century-BC Greek philosopher who came up with the Pythagorean theorem while claiming to hear the music of the spheres and to discover the quantitative relationship between music and mathematics. Pythagoras was said to be able to remember twenty to thirty of his past lives.[8] (In his day, the number of past lives you could remember was thought to be a measure of how intelligent you were.)

Jonson drew on every obscure Latin text he knew to have Nano tell us who Pythagoras was after he lived his original life as Pythagoras. In chronological order, the list includes: Aethalides (an Argonaut); Euphorbus (a Trojan killed by Helen of Troy's husband, Menelaus); Hermotimus (an eminent philosopher of classical times); and Pyrrhus (a philosopher-fisherman). Pythagoras then went on to become Aspasia (the prostitute who was the cultured and faithful mistress of the Greek leader Pericles); another prostitute; and Crates (a Cynic philosopher). Then Nano throws in a list of Pythagoras's more recent lives as animals for good measure before bringing to light that in his very first lifetime, the sixth-century-BC Greek philosopher was the son of the god Apollo himself. Jonson lays this catalogue of the many lives of Pythagoras before us quite cynically. He wants to rub in our face the steady deterioration of humanity through the ages—from a god to an animal.

Another member of this weird trio in *Volpone* is the hermaphrodite Androgyno. (The eunuch Castrone is the final member.) The hermaphrodite was a well-known alchemical symbol in Elizabethan times. It stood for the double-headed, single-bodied Hermetic Androgyne thought to unite the two natures of the alchemical Gold-King and Silver-Queen in a single form and essence.[9] The hermaphrodite as alchemical symbol resonated with affinities to the androgynous, "perfect" race that, according to Plato in the *Symposium,* coexisted with humanity at the very beginning of sentient life on earth. A century and a half after *Volpone* was first performed, the Swedish seer Emanuel Swedenborg would embrace the image of the hermaphrodite as the perfect human being, as would Honoré de Balzac in his Swedenborg-inspired novel *Seraphita* (see chapter 9).

Jonson certainly did not go to China. He had, however, subtle, indirect, and enduring ties with occultist Prague and the court of Emperor

Rudolf II. These stemmed from his intimate friendship with Fulke Greville, close friend and enthusiastic assistant to Sir Philip Sydney. Sydney (1554–1586) was a diplomat, scholar, and poet at the court of Elizabeth I who was widely admired as the very model of a chivalrous Renaissance courtier. Sydney was a man interested in, and cognizant of, occult knowledge. He had been Elizabeth I's representative at the coronation of Rudolf II in 1576. Sydney knew well, if clandestinely, the ex-Dominican priest and modern-day Egyptian magus Giordano Bruno.

Sidney and Fulke Greville passed through Prague fairly often. Jonson never knew Sydney, but it's likely he routinely exchanged information with Greville each time the latter returned from a trip to central Europe. They must have spoken often about alchemy. It was not well known at the time that the occultist court at Prague had regular and fairly direct contacts with China and the alchemists of that country. This was because until the fall of the Mongol Empire in 1367, Hungary was a part of the Chinese empire. Culturally, these ties endured. Carefully maintained roads kept the Hungarian capital of Budapest in regular contact with scientific, that is to say alchemical, developments in the Chinese capital. There were Hungarian alchemists at the court of Rudolf II in Prague. It was they who kept the occultist world apprised of the latest developments in alchemy in China—and informed it about the history of Chinese alchemy.

This information would have been available to Fulke Greville; Fulke Greville would have made it available to Ben Jonson.

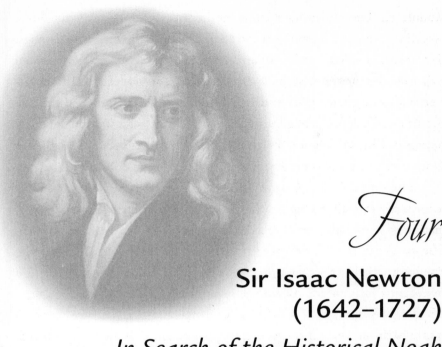

# Sir Isaac Newton
## (1642–1727)

### *In Search of the Historical Noah*

The early-morning sunlight, obliquely striking the snowy heights of Mount Ararat, creates—or such is the impression from a distance—shimmering formations of light so strange they seem to be gateways into another dimension.

Far less often will the passing traveler see along the slopes beneath the snow line, stretched out in a jagged line, a team of toiling climbers scaling the three-mile-high peak in search of Noah's Ark.

These days the Turkish government rarely grants permission to climb Mount Ararat. This is for safety reasons. The legendary mountain rears up out of flat farmlands on the eastern end of Turkey ten miles from Iran and twenty miles from Armenia. This is in the middle of disputed Kurdish territory. The region is awash in rebels, bandits, and conspirators, and adventurers from abroad pass through at the risk of their lives.

Legend says that from the time of the Byzantine Empire (fourth century AD) until 1829, no one tried to climb Mount Ararat. Christians and Muslims alike swore that God had laid down an interdiction against scaling the sacred slopes and thereby profaning the holy Ark hidden somewhere in its snows. The Ark would be revealed only on Judgment Day. A German professor climbed the mountain in 1829 and seemed to escape the interdiction. Or did he? In 1840, Mount Ararat erupted for the last time, gouging a giant hole in the town of Ahora on the northwest side and erasing a monastery—the same one from which the German climber had set out. A second ascent by a German in 1845 was successful and not followed by nature's wrath. A British team scaled the mountain in 1856, failing to find the Ark but convincing its nervous Kurdish guides that British aplomb had finally broken the spell of the divine interdiction placed upon Mount Ararat.

In the second half of the nineteenth century and during the twentieth, perhaps fifty expeditions scaled the peak. None met with disaster, and none found the Ark. Fraud, false reports, and misleading claims muddied the tone of many of these expeditions, and do so to this day.

In the closing decades of the seventeenth century, a man of vast and cool and dispassionate intelligence reflected deeply and at length on the twin riddles of the Flood and Noah's Ark. He considered what happened atop Mount Ararat to be of the greatest importance to humanity.

This was Sir Isaac Newton.

Newton biographer Richard Westfall remarks in *Never at Rest* that Sir Isaac Newton was for him "wholly other . . . a man not finally reducible to the criteria by which we comprehend our fellow beings . . . "[1] Even today, three centuries after, Newton's discoveries form the basis of any high school physics class. He developed the idea that a single force—gravity—was responsible not only for pulling objects to the ground, but also for maintaining in orbit the moon and every other celestial body. Newton formulated the relationship of motion to the forces that affect it, thereby creating the science of dynamics. He invented calculus. He unraveled the secret of light, discovering that it comprises all the colors of the rainbow. He invented the reflecting telescope. He used meticulous experimentation to test hypotheses and then carefully recorded the results, thereby establishing the scientific method that forms the backbone of scientific research today.

Over the past seventy years, we have come into possession of a vast body of completely different, nonscientific deliberations by Sir Isaac Newton. The world has discovered what was only hinted at in the two centuries after his death: that the great scientist had secretly written two and a half million words on biblical interpretation, Christian history, and comparative mythology and one million words on alchemy. These writings surpassed in wordage that of Newton's scientific writings.

Newton's contemporaries had whispered unflatteringly about his secret writings. They thought they were merely the eccentricities of genius and probably amounted to nothing. When he died, these writings were left in the care of his stepniece's husband. They remained there until 1936, when, the estate needing money, they were auctioned off at Sotheby's in London. The entire collection raised the relatively small sum of just over £9,000—substantially less than the $18,000 paid by an unknown buyer for a single sheet from one manuscript at an auction in 2001, when the extraordinary value of these long-hidden writings had finally become known.

British economist John Maynard Keynes went to the 1936 auction and bought some of the manuscripts, reading them in taxis between meetings and calling them "fascinating." Two years later, Albert Einstein was instrumental in having a quantity of the manuscripts sent to the Jewish National and University Library in Jerusalem; he regarded these writings as unique and priceless. Many of the manuscripts ended up at Cambridge University, where scholars examined them with increasing interest, often surprised by the contents. In 1999, a group of scholars launched Cambridge's online Newton Project (www.newtonproject .sussex.ac.uk/prism.php?id=1), which steadily edits and releases the documents online.

Scholars now see that not only did Newton not collapse into nonsensical writings every night, but his nonscientific writings are of great power and importance and were meant to serve as an essential corrective to his scientific writings. Newton scholar Dr. James Force writes that, on account of the Newton Project, the simplistic "two-Newton" interpretation of Newton—one a young brilliant scientist, the other a senile religious nut case—has "gone completely by the boards. We can today see the possibility that one man, a product of many intellectual and religious currents in the seventeenth century, could write great scientific works, great works in church history, in Biblical interpretation, etc., as part of one great enterprise, that of understanding man and his place in the grand scheme of God's creation."[2]

These papers do not reveal that Newton had any sort of encounter with the world beyond. Certainly, he was religious. He was an Anglican who secretly adhered to the sect of Arianism. He believed God existed, but that we could not know His nature. He believed that Christian practice should consist only of worshipping God and loving our neighbors. But he did not believe in the paranormal or in a supernatural realm. He did not believe in reincarnation or in survival after death. He accepted psychopannychism—the belief that the soul remains sunk in sleep after death.[3] (Newton quoted Ecclesiastes 9:5–10 to support this: "The dead know not anything. . . . There is no work nor knowledge nor wisdom in the grave.")

But, as we are beginning to learn from the manuscripts emerging from the Newton Project, Newton, in his nonscientific writings, had arrived at the mountaintop where science and the mystical meet. It was never his intention that the scientific formulae he created be used as tools for the mastery of the physical world. He meant them to be used for harnessing the energy of the spheres. Newton saw humans as potential beings of great power. It was that potential power that he wished to harness. His goal—whose outlines are only now becoming known in the writings released by the Newton Project—was to make of this world a paradise. Newton's immense fear that technology would make of it a wasteland was what drove him on in his nonscientific writings. The key to resolving the contradictions to which he saw his new science giving rise lay in something of inestimable value that Noah had brought with him to Mount Ararat from the pre-Flood world. This was the knowledge of the *prisca sapientia*—the primal knowledge that had seen no separation between spirituality and science.

Sir Isaac Newton was virtually a recluse most of his life. In isolation in his rooms at Cambridge University, he carried out experiments night and day. His post as Lucasian Professor of Mathematics required him to give few lectures in a year, and there were years when he gave none at all.

Along with his genius and the burning curiosity about the universe that drove him on in his work, there were psychological factors that did not make it difficult for Newton to live a solitary existence. He was born in the hamlet of Woolsthorpe, England, on Christmas Day 1642, three months after the death of his father. His mother remarried when he was three, leaving him to be raised by his grandmother. Author Gale Christianson writes that these harsh events "played a significant if not decisive role in the development of his sensitive temperament and always enigmatic character," and that, in later years, "somber and secretive, he moved about his shuttered rooms like some grey disheveled ghost."[4] For the last thirty years of his life, Newton lived in London in the responsible and demanding position of Master of the Mint, and in this role he came into social contact with many men and women. But he always remained essentially an inner-directed, solitary figure.

Through the years, as Newton, with the help of the great astronomer of comets Sir Edmund Halley, gave birth to the reconceptualizing of the laws of the universe that is set forth in the *Principia Mathematica* (1687), his mind was steadily engaged in other, quite different directions. Like most of his contemporaries, he believed in the idea of the prisca sapientia, or "pristine knowledge." This is a notion that runs completely counter to our modern belief in the idea of "progress."

Newton and his contemporaries did not believe it was in the nature of things that the world should get better and better. They believed that the worlds of ancient Greece and Rome were far superior to the one in which they found themselves. The "natural philosophers" of Newton's age—Newton had not invented modern science and the word *scientist* did not yet exist!—believed that the great truths of nature had been known to the more brilliant and morally upright thinkers of the distant past, such as the Greek philosophers Pythagoras, Plato, Archimedes, and Democritus, and to the most gifted figures of the Bible, like Solomon, Isaiah, and Jesus. Newton was convinced that his greatest discoveries, such as the law of gravitation, had been known to these great thinkers of high antiquity, who had expressed them in veiled and allegorical language. Pythagoras, for example, conveyed the concept of universal gravitation through the metaphors of the pipes of Pan and the music of the spheres. The architecture of Solomon's Temple and Stonehenge enfolded in encrypted form ancient formulae describing the true shape of the universe. In the myths espoused by Pythagoras, in the ancient sacred edifices at Jerusalem and Salisbury, could be found the veiled outlines of the primal knowledge—the prisca sapientia.

Noah was a seminal figure in all of this. All that the world would ever know of the most ancient of knowledge had been transported by him on the Ark to the post-Flood world. Through the ages, up to the time in which Newton lived, that knowledge had undergone a steady process of deterioration and corruption at the hands of humankind. Newton dreamed of restoring it to its pristine condition. All of his nonscientific writings that have come to light in the past seventy years reflect his single, vast attempt to mount back up through the centuries and, gradually erasing the ravages of time, arrive at that sacred knowledge, which, he suspected, embodied in its essence the seamless fusion of the spiritual and the scientific.

As strange as it may seem to us today, Newton and his contemporaries believed in the historicity of the Ark. They believed it had tossed for forty days on the floodwaters, come to rest on Mount Ararat, and been left behind as Noah, his progeny, and their wives set out to repopulate the globe. Today we possess few facts about the Flood and the Ark. In 1965, researchers at London's British Museum stumbled on two cuneiform tablets written in Sippar in Babylonia in 1640–1626 BC. These tablets tell how a water god named Enki revealed to a priest-king named Ziusudra God's plan for bringing destruction through floods. There was an actual Ziusudra. He was the historical priest-king of Babylonia's Shuruppak around 2900 BC, and he built a boat and survived. Moreover, there is archaeological evidence of an actual gigantic flood at the site of Shuruppak.

Was Ziusudra Noah? The Shuruppak flood was confined to a small area. Archaeologist Sir Leonard Woolley, excavating the Sumerian city of Ur in the 1920s, found evidence that a flood had indeed occurred in this region between 4000 and 3500 BC. Researcher Paul Johnson writes: "The savior-figure of Ziusudra, presented in the Bible as Noah, thus provides the first independent confirmation of the actual existence of a Biblical personage."[5]

But Newton and his contemporaries had implicit faith in the story of Noah. Newton was determined to unravel the secrets of the patriarch of the Flood. The ascent of Mount Ararat was not the only trail he followed in pursuit of the prisca sapientia. It was necessary that he see through the corruption that had eaten away at the religious practices of more recent times. In fact, Newton had been involved in a massive if clandestine assault on the text of the New Testament since his early twenties.

The long story of the discovery and correction of "corruptions" in the New Testament—corruptions being those changes that have been either deliberately or accidentally made to the original text—began only five hundred years ago.

That story is so complex and rich in detail that we can only touch upon it, and that briefly, in the context of the role that Sir Isaac Newton played.

The great Dutch humanist Desiderius Erasmus (1466–1536) was the first to point out that certain statements in the New Testament declaring that God and Christ were one did not say exactly that in the original texts. Erasmus published his corrections in his new translation of the New Testament from Greek into Latin in 1516. However, these corrections were suppressed by the Roman Catholic Church, with many of its bishops believing that Erasmus should be excommunicated for his heretical statements, and at least one declaring that he should be burned at the stake. Erasmus's disciple, the Spaniard Miguel Servet (Michael Servetus; 1509/1511–1553), was burned at the stake in Geneva in 1553 for singling out, in his books *On the Errors of the Trinity* and *The Restitution of Christianity,* many more corruptions of the New Testament text, most of them having the effect of unambiguously proclaiming the divinity of Christ.

The issue of whether God and Christ were wholly identical remained one fraught with danger for the disbeliever. As late as 1612—thirty years before Isaac Newton was born—two Anglican clergymen, Bartholomew Legate and Edward Wightman, were burned alive in Smithfield and Lichfield, respectively, for refusing to disavow their belief that God and Christ—and the Holy Spirit—were *not* one in the Trinity. Sir Isaac had to tread very carefully when he began to discover, in his early twenties, that there were many corruptions in the New Testament text that changed the words so as to affirm the divinity of Christ. But Newton, vigorously pursuing his researches, came to the conclusion that nowhere in the original manuscripts was it actually stated that Christ was God. (Perhaps no one in history has ever sought to plumb the nature of Christ as exhaustively as did Newton. He pored over biblical manuscripts and the printed editions of all varieties of the New Testament, including Slavonic, Ethiopic, Syriac, Arabic, Armenian, Turkish, French, Latin, and Greek, and examined all the extant commentaries of theologians and early Church Fathers such as Ignatius of Antioch, Justin Martyr, Irenaeus, Tertullian, Origen, Athanasius, Gregory Nazianzen, John Chrysostom, Pope Hilarius, and many more.)

Newton did not dare reveal his findings to the public. (He had never even revealed that he was an Arian, that is, that he believed not that Christ was God but that Christ was God's first creation in the universe.) Instead, on November 14, 1690, he sent two secret letters to a friend, the great English philosopher John Locke, later combining them into a memoir he called "An Historical Account of Two Notable Corruptions of Scripture, in a Letter to a Friend." Newton sent Locke a third letter that same month in which he exposed twenty-five more passages that seemed to declare that God and Christ were one, but which were actually corrupted versions of the original New Testament text.

Newton considered that most of these corruptions were intentional. Richard Westfall writes in *Never at Rest* that Sir Isaac came to be convinced that "a massive fraud, which began in the fourth and fifth centuries, had perverted the legacy of the early church. Central to the fraud were the Scriptures, which Newton began to believe had been corrupted to support trinitarianism [the doctrine that God, Christ, and the Holy Spirit are one]."[6]

In making such a charge, Newton wished to be absolutely sure of his ground. He therefore pursued another line of inquiry in the New Testament, focusing his enormous powers on finding out exactly what had happened at the Council of Nicaea in 325 AD. This was the council at which the Roman emperor Constantine, assembling the bishops of the Church from both East and West, was intent on establishing a single, official version of Christianity; he believed this would help him hold together his newly reunited empire.

At the council, a vote called by Constantine resulted in the triumph of the doctrine, championed by Athanasius, that God and Jesus were one (this doctrine would be fully subsumed into the doctrine of the Trinity before the century was out). The loser was Arius, who spearheaded the movement preaching that Christ was not entirely God, though he was God's first created entity. This latter was Newton's belief, and over the years he put together the most exhaustive examination of Athanasius, Arius, and the Council of Nicaea that has ever been penned: *Questions*

*Concerning the Morals and Actions of Athanasius and His Followers.* This treatise, thirty-five thousand words long, offers overwhelming proof, in Newton's eyes, that Arius was wronged and the Council of Nicaea fixed. It was Athanasius and his followers who had promulgated the doctrine that God and Jesus were one; they would be responsible for many more corruptions in the years to come.

These researches brought Newton to the point where he was satisfied that he had restored the text of the New Testament as it had originally been written. Concurrent with this investigation were his researches into the Old Testament. He scoured this text to discover in what way the Jews had fallen away from the original will of God. It was such a falling away, he believed, that had prompted God to introduce Christ into the world, thus punishing the Jews. Newton believed that Christianity would not have been necessary had the Jews not failed to adhere to Moses's covenant with God. Going farther back, he observed that the Jews had disobeyed Abraham's covenant with God. But this latter covenant had come into being only because the Jews had deviated radically from the first, original covenant, that of Noah with God, made on the day the floodwaters had subsided sufficiently for Noah to beach the Ark on Mount Ararat.

Newton's concern was now to scour the most ancient texts to reconstruct the story of Noah. He wanted to understand exactly which sons of Noah, and which grandsons, had trekked to which parts of the drying post-Flood world to found entire countries and reestablish the emprise of humankind over the globe. He wanted to see how—running parallel to the stages of disobedience of the Jews—the priests of the other new post-Flood religions had presided, whether or not with complicity, over the setting in to their religious practices of the dry rot of corruption. To trace this progression back through time would give Newton a better idea of exactly what primordial wisdom—how much of the prisca sapientia—Noah had brought with him through the Flood. Newton examined in great detail that first day on Mount Ararat. He set forth a precise ordering of the events that surrounded the sealing of Noah's covenant with God. In what follows, we'll combine Newton's account with other accounts and put it all into semidramatic form (which Newton certainly did not do, his prose being starkly denuded of adjectives and adverbs and resembling a string of equations—resembling, in fact, the text of the *Principia Mathematica*).

Let us imagine Noah staggering somewhat as he comes down the gang-way of the Ark. After all, it would have taken him some time to rees-tablish his "land legs" after such a storm-tossed voyage—and wasn't he a drunkard? Few alcoholics have had better reasons for getting drunk than Noah when he brought his colossal Ark, filled with two of every beast in the world, onto this waterlogged mountaintop.

Noah, red-faced or not, but white-bearded, would have been bear-ing before him in his arms a heavy black brazier out of which flames leaped high in the hurrying breeze. This was a brazier he couldn't afford to drop, since it was the only brazier in existence that contained fire from before the Flood. A burnt offering in a temple must be made with a fire that has never gone out, and so this was fire it was essential he have because he must now make a burnt offering to the Lord.

Behind him, moving cautiously, the seven members of his family come down the gangway. There is his wife; his three sons, Shem, Ham, and Japheth; and their wives. One of the sons is carrying a clucking fowl in his arms, while the other two, one pulling, one pushing, are dragging a bleating sheep down the gangway. This is for the burnt offering God has stipulated that Noah make after he has made landfall.

If there is any truth in some of the alternate versions of the Noah story that have come down to us, Shem is probably peering around anx-iously. How far are they from the ground where he'd buried the metal plates? It will be hard for him to identify the place, for now the land is denuded of all familiar vegetation. And he has to be careful; he wasn't supposed to hide for retrieval those metal plates recording all of the sci-ence of his time. Nobody knew he'd done it, not even his father.

Now, in front of the beached Ark, Noah carefully sets the brazier down. His wife and sons and daughters-in-law go about their duties. Perhaps they sense the presence of God looming nearby, for it is with a certain reverence that, bringing out their sharp knives, they thoughtfully slit the throats of the fowl and the sheep they hold between them, draining the blood into the wet earth.

But how can it be that the members of Noah's family are permitted to sacrifice even one fowl and one sheep for the coming burnt offering? Doesn't the Old Testament tell us that Noah transported only two of every species on the earth, a male and a female? Won't this sacrifice mean the end of all sheep and all fowl? No, it won't. Newton quotes Genesis 7:2–3, where we are told that in addition to a male and a female of every species, the Ark carried "seven pairs of all clean animals, the male and female" and "seven pairs of the birds of the air also, male and female." Newton writes, in *The Original of Religions*:

> For so soon as Noah came out of the Ark, he built an altar & offered burnt offerings of every clean Beast & every clean ffowl unto the Lord. . . . And therefore as Noah when he went into the Arck provided for sacrifices by taking in with him a greater number of Clean Beasts & clean ffowls than of unclean ones: so no doubt for the same end he took in with him also the sacred fire with which he was to offer them.[7]

The Ark, huge and brutally weathered, looms above them all. It's as big, according to legend, as one of today's ocean liners. It's also, according to some legends, a computer, or a computer chip, oddly shaped because its dimensions are also meant to encode the divine proportions of the pre-Flood temple of the prisca sapientia. The Ark is not only a boat; it's also a key.

Noah and his family offer up to God the burnt offerings of sheep and fowl. The white smoke billows up along the tar-blackened side of the Ark, rises into the sky, and fades into the azure blue, where the worshippers can see, shimmering in the abating storm clouds, the familiar arc of a rainbow.

Noah and his family don't pray. They don't sing. They move silently, in a solemn circle, around the sacred fire burning in the brazier. Such, Newton assumed (we will see why below), would be the rites of pre-Flood religious worship. Noah sits down suddenly. He is terrified. He's dying for a drink. He knows that God is coming and will speak to him. Again! Him, of all people!

Noah and his family are silent because the animal sacrifice speaks for them.

University of Toronto and Hebrew University Professor of Philosophy and Theology Emil Fackenheim explains in *What Is Judaism?* that animal sacrifice was an early form of prayer, prayer being that which is addressed to God and is always in praise of God—a joyful acceptance of even the worst life has to offer. It is a "holding of oneself open to God,"[8] which ensures for us the "possibility of an incursion of the Divine." When this incursion occurs, Christians call it a "miracle"; for the Jew, it is an event that can take place only if we hold ourselves open, without reservation, to the coming of the Lord. It is an *active process.*

Animal sacrifice was an early holding open of oneself to the Lord. Noah and his family know this state of holding oneself open to God. The animal sacrifice is the prayer that places them in this state of openness as they sit on the drying mountaintop, which is to them a whole new universe. They hold themselves open, and God comes, and Noah makes a covenant with the Lord.

Rabbi Fackenheim writes:

Relying on Gen. 9:1–17, the Talmud formulates seven laws as contained in the "Noachidic covenant." All mankind is bidden to practice justice, as well as to abstain from blasphemy, idolatry, incest, bloodshed, robbery, and the eating of flesh torn from a living animal.[9]

This is one of the closest passes Newton will make at knowledge of the prisca sapientia. He will acquire more knowledge only by tracking back up through the various forms of religious worship that unfolded after Noah's people spread across the world to create new countries. Newton's purpose was to find out when, and in what ways, the religious practices of these newly aborning states deviated from what had been set forth by God in the Noachidic covenant. He began by focusing on ancient Egypt, where, he believed, the clearest historical records survived of the first ceremonies of religious worship in the post-Flood world. Newton calls the first religion of the post-Flood world the religion of the *prytaneum*. Why?

*Prytaneum* is an ancient Greek word referring to a temple built around a central hearth or fire. In ancient Greece, each state, city, or village had its own central hearth and sacred fire, which symbolized the unity and vitality of the community. Newton believed that "the religion most ancient and most generally received by the nations in the first ages was that of the Prytanea or Vestal Temples. This was spread over all nations until the first memory of things."[10] It was in part the remnants of these ancient prytanea, radiating out densely from the countries near the Middle East but also found in other parts of the world, that enabled Newton to deduce the shape of the temple in its first, primordial form. He also used the word *prytaneum* as a generic term. The truest prytaneum of all, he believed, was Solomon's Temple, which most accurately embodied the equations of the primal religion encoded in the shape of Noah's Ark. That was why Newton spent great amounts of time trying to establish the historically true dimensions of Solomon's Temple. He also thought Stonehenge and other so-called druidic structures were likely ancient prytanea. He wrote:

> In England neare Salisbury there is a piece of antiquity called Stonehenge which seems to be an ancient *Prytaneum*. For it is an area compassed circularly with two rows of very great stones with passages on all sides for people to go in and out at. Tis said there are some pieces of antiquity of the same form & structure in Denmark. . . . In Ireland one of these fires was conserved till of late years by the

Moncks of Kildare under the name of Briget's fire & the Caenobium was called the house of fire.[11]

The priests who took part in the religion of the prytaneum were also astronomers. Newton writes: "And thence it was that the Priests anciently were above other men well skilled in the knowledge of the one true frame of nature and accounted it a great part of their Theology."[12] They were also makers of burnt offerings of clean animals to the Lord, for there "burned perpetually in the middle of [this] sacred place . . . a fire for offering sacrifices."[13]

Ideally—going back to the time before the Flood—the religion of the prytaneum was the perfect meeting of spirituality and science. Imagine a planetarium that is also a cathedral, upon whose altar an "eternal" flame burns, that is, a flame that has never gone out, like that of the Olympics, which is supposed, at least metaphorically, to have burned without interruption since the first Olympiad in the eighth century BC.

This planetarium/cathedral doesn't only show all around its vaulted ceiling the starry heavens of a particular night. This place of worship of what Newton sometimes called "astronomical theology" is actually an effigy of the entire cosmos all around us; somehow its soaring proportions precisely reflect the contours of the entire physical universe.

Even to call the religion practiced in this edifice "astronomical theology" is something of a misnomer. Newton reserved that term for a religion that was practiced a little later, by the Egyptians, and which he believed already represented a falling-off from the true religion of the prytaneum. Newton wrote that the primordial religion, with the fire in the center, illuminated by seven lamps representing the moon and the planets, symbolized the "world" (as the universe, in the seventeenth century, was called):

The whole heavens they recconed to be the true & real Temple of God & therefore that a *Prytaneum* [sanctum] might deserve the name of his Temple they framed it so as in the fittest manner to represent the whole systeme of the heavens. A point of religion then which nothing can be more rational. . . . So then twas one designe of the first institution of the true religion to propose to mankind by the frame of the ancient Temples, the study of the frame of the world as the true Temple of the great God they worshipped. . . . So then the first religion was the most rational of all others till the nations corrupted it. For there is no way (without revelation) to come to the knowledge of a Deity but by the frame of nature.[14]

What does Newton mean when he says they "framed" the temple "so as in the fittest manner to represent the whole systeme of the heavens"? Newton scholar Robert Markley writes:

By "frame" Newton does not mean the material existence of celestial objects but the mathematical form that remains a timeless guarantee of a divine intention, a design unaffected by the successive cycles of decay and the corruption of the material world. The *prytane[um]* functions then as a kind of computational code by which true knowledge can be demonstrated and transmitted without interruption, interference or corruption.[15]

But corruption began to set in. The priests forgot that the central fire stood for God, and began to worship the fire for itself alone. Newton writes: "first the frame of the heavens consisting of Sun Moon & Stars being represented in the *Prytanea* as the real temple of the Deity men were led by degrees to pay a veneration to these sensible objects & began at length to worship them as the visible seals of divinity."[16]

Newton elsewhere describes God as "void of external shape, or bounds, a being intangible and invisible whom no eye hath seen or can see, therefore also incorporeal."[17] But it is difficult for mankind to worship something that it cannot see, or feel, or hear, or touch. Newton continues: "And because the sacred fire was a type of the Sun & all the elements are parts of that universe which is the temple of God they soon began to have these also in veneration. For tis agreed that Idolatry began in the worship of the heavenly bodies & elements."[18]

Dr. Markley explains: "[M]en discard an absolute faith in God for a 'veneration' of the secondary effects by which his wisdom can be apprehended, thereby confusing form and content, the ideal and the material, the timeless and the corrupt. Worshipping the mere representations of divine order—the Sun, stars, and planets—turns men and women away from techno-scientific knowledge and true faith and makes them subject to sell-willed delusions."[19]

It was not long before the next step in the process of corruption occurred. Writes Newton,

> Worshipping the sun, the known planets, and the four elements, mankind began to honor the memory of his most illustrious ancestors by naming the planets after them. Finally, mankind, believing that the souls of his ancestors had transmigrated to these planets, began to worship them as gods.[20]

Man has now created a set of gods whom he worships. He has moved farther and farther away from the worship of the one, true, ungraspable-by-the-senses God. The process of corruption has greatly intensified.

Having shown how it was that the pantheon of gods first emerged, Newton is now concerned to show that all of man's pantheons of gods are exactly the same, because they are all based on exactly the same set of original figures, namely, Noah and his family. Newton states in *Theologiae Gentiles Origines Philosophicae* that all ancient peoples worshipped the same twelve gods, if under different names, the originals of those twelve gods being Noah, his children, and his grandchildren. If we compare the pantheons of the twelve gods of the Greeks, the Romans, and the Egyptians, we see that

> the twelve gods were all of a kindred, parents and children, brothers and sisters, husbands and wives to one another, and divers had one

common mother, Cybele. They lived all at the same time, which is called the age of the Gods. . . . And in their age the brothers and sisters for want of further choice became husbands and wives. All which characters agree best to the times next the Flood.[21]

Richard Westfall explains:

Common characteristics distinguished the corresponding gods of all ancient peoples. All peoples worshipped one god whom they took to be the ancestor of the rest. They described him as an old and morose man and associated him with time and with the sea. Clearly, Noah furnished the original model of the god called (among other names) Saturn and Janus. Like Noah, Saturn had three sons. Every people had a god whom they depicted as a mature man, the god they held most in honor. They had translated Ham into Zeus, Jupiter, Hammon, and others. All worshipped a voluptuous woman variously named Aphrodite, Venus, Astarte, *et alia,* originally a daughter of Ham. The histories of the gods of one people frequently became confused with those of another, and peoples invented fables which confounded the origins of the gods by claiming the gods of others for their own.[22]

Other individual characteristics of Noah's family peep through from the pantheons of gods created by the succeeding generations of the family. Newton notes that in many mythologies of high antiquity:

Saturn because of his great age is made the God of time. He was accounted the author of husbandry [cultivation of plants or livestock; farming; agriculture] and in token thereof carries a scythe. Drunkenness was attributed to him and in memory thereof the Saturnalia were instituted. He was painted by the Egyptians with eyes before and behind and reputed the justest of men and the father of truth. And in all these respects he agrees accurately with Noah.[23]

Noah as the god of time and the scythe-carrying god of husbandry was slowly transformed over the millennia into a figure we all know well: Father Time, or the Old Year we toast on New Year's Eve even as he gives way to the incoming, infant New Year. And, since Newton also believed that the god Bacchus was based on a memory of Noah—Noah was, after all, a drunkard, wasn't he?—then it may be true to say that, as we raise our wineglass on New Year's Eve to toast the outgoing Old Year, we are awash in memories of Noah.

The point of all Newton's genealogies—and there are many more—was to demonstrate that our present-day religious practices are hideously skewed versions of the one, true, pre-Flood religion: that of the prisca sapientia. The prisca sapientia, Newton believed, embodied the perfect fusion of spirituality and science. He thought that the tragedy for humanity, of the new science he had created, would be that since spirituality and science were now separate, the way was being paved for a technology shorn of ethics and morality, a technology shorn of all spirituality. In developing his corpus of nonscientific writings, Newton hoped that he might be able to forestall that eventuality. It may be that he hoped he would be able to combine the *Principia Mathematica* with his emerging *Principia Spiritualis,* so to speak, to create a whole new prisca sapientia. But he did not succeed.

Perhaps, though, as Newton's nonscientific writings continue to emerge from the Newton Project, we still have time to take advantage, in a manner Sir Isaac would have wanted, of this, his final contribution to the world.

## *Five*

# Johann Wolfgang von Goethe (1749–1832)
## *The Battle Over Light*

In *Poetry and Truth,* Johann Wolfgang von Goethe tells us that when he was twenty-one, and returning one night on horseback from a visit to his first love, Friederike Brion, "not with the eyes of the body but of the spirit, I saw myself on horseback coming toward me on the same path. I was dressed in a suit I had never worn before, pale grey and with some gold. As soon as I had shaken myself out of this reverie, the vision vanished. It is strange, however, that I found myself, eight years later, once again on the same road, returning from Friederike and wearing, not by design but by chance, just this sort of suit."[1]

Many years later, Goethe told Johann Peter Eckermann that premonitions occur in dreams because we can sometimes "extend the feelers of our soul beyond the limits of our body." He added that such dreams were not simply "presentiments" but constituted an actual "insight into the immediate future."[2]

Goethe had not dismissed the vision he had when he was twenty-one of himself when he was twenty-nine. Increasingly he had come to believe that we are far more than we know, and that even while we live our daily lives, we are not trapped in time and space.

Did this great artist-scientist of Germany believe in the supernatural? No, because he believed that the natural *was* the supernatural. "Mind" organically "grew" the physical world at every point. Goethe believed that the prisca sapientia long meditated on by Sir Isaac Newton was still here; all nature represented the perfect fusion of spirit and science, although we did not have the eyes to see it.

Perhaps, when Goethe was born in Frankfurt, Germany, in 1749, his eyes were already more open than is the case for most of us. Every part of his mind and soul and senses continued to expand through the entire eighty-four years of his life. By the end, his achievements were enormous: his verse drama *Faust* (part I, 1808; part II, 1832) is considered a towering literary achievement, and his collected works comprise 143 volumes and include not only poetry, plays, novels, autobiography, criticism, and correspondence, but also treatises on mineralogy, botany, anatomy, and optics. Goethe was a phenomenon, hardly just a man: "Every new work by Germany's greatest poet and writer was read as soon as it appeared and was totally unpredictable," philosopher Walter Kaufmann writes.[3] Goethe was also *strange*: "His wisdom abides," declares Yale literary scholar Harold Bloom, "but it seems to come from some solar system other than our own."[4]

Born into a wealthy, intelligent, and conscientious upper-middle-class family, Goethe early on displayed a quickness for learning and skill with language. He studied law at the University of Leipzig, graduating in 1770, but ultimately practiced little. He was brilliant, he was insightful, he was vigorous; all this drew men and women to him, women never less than men, for he was as seductive as he was charismatic.

Goethe quickly became a driving force in the twin German literary movements of Sentimentalism and "Storm and Stress." By the age of twenty-two he had published a great many gallant love poems, which were well received, and his five-act drama *Götz von Berlichingen* (1771) had been successfully produced.

Goethe was not molded by the age in which he lived; rather, he was the molder of that age. His works enabled people to discover who they were—almost, to christen themselves with a new name. His novel *The Sorrows of Young Werther* created a sensation when it was published in 1774. Goethe was twenty-four. Werther is a profoundly self-centered young man who falls desperately in love with a woman who is engaged to someone else. The more he finds out he cannot have her, the more desperately he wants her. He goes into exile for a while. Then he returns and goes to see the woman. By this time she is married, to a husband whom she loves. Werther proclaims his love. She rejects his advances. He seizes her husband's revolver and blows his own brains out.

This may sound all too melodramatic to us. But at the time, Goethe was introducing a whole new sensation into society. Goethe liberated males to feel like Werther. Men had not consciously felt this way before. The book struck a pre-Romantic chord, and Werther-type feelings spread like wildfire across Europe. There were twenty-four "Werther" suicides in Germany in 1774 alone. The fad did not die out completely until the end of the century.

In the Catholic-Lutheran Germany of the eighteenth century, suicide was a mortal sin. To portray it in literature was to commit at least a venial sin. Goethe didn't care. In his beliefs and attitudes he was plunging light-years ahead of the society in which he lived. Already at age twenty he had decided that imitating Christ was meaningless. He thought you ought to locate the best in yourself and imitate that. By the time he had entered his thirties, Goethe could speak of Christianity only with derision. He declared in 1782: "I for my part could not be persuaded by an audible voice from heaven that a woman has given birth without a man or that a dead man has risen again; on the contrary I regard these as blasphemies against the great God and His revelation in Nature."[5]

Early on, the poet/novelist/playwright had been a pantheist, believing that God dwelt in a nature made benevolent by His presence. This belief was shattered in June 1777 when his beloved sister Cornelia, only twenty-six, died four weeks after giving birth to her second daughter. Goethe carried with him ever afterward, biographer Nicholas Boyle writes, "a tragic awareness of the possibility that a human being may have to face an ineluctably wretched destiny and that neither earth nor heaven may offer any response to the cry of the heart for love."[6]

God was inscrutable. Perhaps he did not exist at all. But Goethe believed that huge powers resided within the heart of man. In 1775, this wholly autonomous individual took an administrative position in the Duchy of Saxony-Weimar, near Leipzig. For the rest of his life, on and off, Goethe spent a part of every week in the three-hundred-room, twenty-two-staircase, Versailles-look-alike palace of Duke Carl August. His function was to carry out every administrative task that presented itself; these tasks were not trivial, and he was acting prime minister of Weimar for two months. During all this time, Goethe never stopped writing poetry and prose. But he discovered that administrative functions took a toll on his spiritual energies. He turned his attention to the physical sciences, finding that the silent communion with nature these studies afforded him provided a balm to his soul.

Goethe preferred the real world to any secret one. He had nothing but disdain for those secret societies that claimed to harbor the wisdom of the ages. Inducted into the Masons in 1780, Goethe quickly advanced through the customary grades, joining in 1783 the order within the order that made you an "Illuminist." He soon wrote:

> They say you can best get to know a man when he is at play . . . and
> I too have found that in the little world of the brethren all is as it is
> in the great one. . . . I was already saying this in the forecourt, and
> now I have reached the ark of the covenant I have nothing to add.
> To the wise all things are wise, to the fool foolish.[7]

In 1790, he wrote a comedy called *The Grand Kophta*. It satirized the Masons harshly. One of the characters was "Count Cagliostro." Count Cagliostro was a real person, a Rasputin-like Italian who claimed to be several thousand years old. The venerable count was wealthy and said he had mastered the highest occult skills of a Mason. At the time Goethe wrote his play, Cagliostro was touring the courts of Europe, where he conducted séances, made prophecies, bilked noblemen, and in general cut a high-visibility figure as a genius/con man who claimed to be a benefactor of mankind.

In *The Grand Kophta,* Goethe portrayed Cagliostro strictly as a swindler. In 1787, he visited the home of Cagliostro's mother in Palermo, Italy. He discovered that the "Count" was the ne'er-do-well son of a poverty-stricken family. "Cagliostro" had borrowed money from his mother and disappeared with it. When Goethe returned to Weimar, he anonymously repaid the debt to the mother. (The family thought the money came from Cagliostro.) This experience was the last straw, convincing Goethe that those who pretended to possess secret occult knowledge of the world did not deserve respect but only contempt.[8]

Goethe was now well advanced into his scientific studies, which included mineralogy, botany, anatomy, and optics. He conducted his studies with a wholly new point of view, and that is probably why it seemed to some that Goethe was dabbling in the occult; his lines of scientific inquiry were invariably new and strange. Goethe was strikingly original in his researches. He was very soon seeking to discover a kind of primal pattern in rock—an organic template that would account for every kind of manifestation of rock, for every shape. He ended up by concluding that crystallization was the organizing principle underlying all of the mineral world. Goethe was sure that the equivalent of this in human beings was the "intermaxillary bone" in the upper jaw. This bone was the organizing principle establishing a relationship between human and animal. Goethe was sure that through it he would be able to find the underlying unity, visible to the informed eye, behind the multiplicity of animal forms in the natural world. He scoured all vegetation for the "primal plant" (*Urpflanze*); that is, he hoped to find in nature a basic pattern that, reducing all plant form to a repeated sequence of elements—for example, sprout, leaf, and growth point—underlay the complex variety of the vegetable world.

None of what Goethe set forth could be tested using the rigor of the scientific method. He was not seeking the "archetypal" plant or mineral or animal, such as a philosopher might seek in the Platonic archetypes the ideal forms of the world. Goethe did not think there *was* a world of ideal forms. He thought that on earth there was only the here and now, and that such was the whole of existence. At first, the poet/scientist had searched for ideal *Ur-* shapes that might actually exist on earth. Then he had sought out concepts of primal patterns that he thought would encompass every variety of form of plant, animal, and mineral in the world. But now he concluded that existence comprised only that which can be seized in the here and now.

Goethe was thus not a hermeticist or cabalist. He did not believe that the entire physical universe was infused, in every atom, in equal portion, with mind or soul. Nature, it seemed to him, was dumb. Goethe would have agreed with William Blake that "where man is not, Nature is barren." The German poet/scientist came more and more to suspect that when we see soul in nature or in the "beyond," we are merely projecting our hopes and fears into zones likely to be devoid of soul and God.

Goethe therefore vigorously rejected the notion that nature has essence, a soul—something independent of what we can grasp with our five senses. Man being a part of nature, Goethe also rejected the notion that man himself has essence, believing, in the words of Walter Kaufmann: *"Man is his deeds."*[9]

In the *Doctrine of Colors* (1810), which discusses his theory of chromatics, Goethe declared:

> We really try in vain to express the essence of a thing. We become aware of effects, and a complete history of these effects [*Wirkungen*] would seem to comprehend the essence of the thing. We exert ourselves in vain to describe the character of a human being; but

assemble his actions, his deeds, and a picture of his character will confront us.[10]

Goethe was in profound disagreement with Sir Isaac Newton. The German poet/scientist declared that not even light has an essence. Contrary to Newton, he believed that behind or beyond white light as we perceive it there is nothing that can contain the being of colors. "Colors," declared the poet, "are the deeds of light."[11]

Goethe was deeply troubled to see that the clear implication of Newton's theory of light was that we can never accept the reality of what is presented to us through our senses; this was true no matter how purified our vision was. Regarding these conclusions, Walter Kaufmann writes:

> Goethe's immense lucidity [in expressing these ideas] is inseparable from his habit of seeing things instead of relying on pure concepts alone. . . . Goethe always could find words for what he saw and felt. He mistrusted words that were not backed up by any experience. And he had no need of mathematical certainty.[12]

The great attraction of Goethe's assertions about light (utterly unproved from any scientific point of view) lies in the fact they seem to imply that there is a third alternative to accepting the evidence of the senses and accepting the truth of an unseen (if experimentally verifiable) world of equations.

However, there may be another powerful reason why Goethe, to the end of his days, stuck so tenaciously to his theory of "chromatics." Nicholas Boyle explains in *Goethe: The Poet and the Age:*

> A recent exegesis, of great brilliance, has shown that the underlying structure of Goethe's unwearying argument for a new chromatics is that of a defense of Arianism—the heretical belief that Christ was not divine—against the tyrannical sophistries of the established Trinitarian Christology. Light is tortured, indeed crucified, with the

instruments of the scientists, who, like a churchful of theologians parroting inherited dogmas, endeavor to split up the pure simplicity of divinity into seven colors or three persons or some other magical number in which they would rather put their trust than in what their eyes and their reason tell them. It may have been within a couple of months of his moment of conversion [to his new theory of light] that Goethe began to make the comparison of Light suffering at the hands of Newton and his followers with Christ suffering at the hands of the orthodox.[13]

Ironically, Newton was an Arian himself; he did not believe that the crucifixion of Christ had any ultimate significance. It wasn't public knowledge in Newton's time, nor was it in Goethe's, that Newton was an Arian. There is a second reason to suspect that had Goethe known more about Newton's secret and unpublished thought—specifically as it appears in Newton's nonscientific writings—he might have been far more sympathetic to Newton's ultimate thought. L. A. Willoughby writes in *Man, Myth & Magic*:

> The general tenor [of his treatment of the Faust legend] at any rate coincides with Goethe's maxim that "whatever emancipates the mind without giving us control over ourselves is dangerous." Such a warning could, and probably did, have reference to the dangers inherent in the control over the universe that man has acquired through the predictive power of Newtonian science.[14]

Had Goethe known—as no one then did know—how much Newton feared that his own science might be doomed to giving birth to a heartless technology, one without morality, spirituality, or ethics, Goethe might have been more powerfully driven to helping human beings find a way to reassemble the pieces of the shattered prisca sapientia.

# $\mathscr{Six}$

# William Blake
# (1757–1827)
## *The Horse's Mouth*

A block of sculptor's Hopton stone, lowered too hastily through the skylight of a millionaire's mansion, crashes through the bedroom floor and plummets to the floor below. The millionaire and his wife are away on vacation. In the bedroom Alex Guinness, disheveled, unshaven, wearing rags, continues to work with maniacal glee on a huge painting called *The Raising of Lazarus* that takes up the entire wall. On the floor below, a sculptor, gaunt and pale and acting as if possessed, begins to chip away with grim determination at the block of Hopton stone. He doesn't care, any more than the painter upstairs, that this isn't his house and that there's a gaping hole in the ceiling.

This scene is taken from the film version of Anglo-Irish writer Joyce Cary's 1944 novel *The Horse's Mouth*. Painter Gulley Jimson, played by Alex Guinness, worships the poetry of William Blake and quotes it often throughout the novel and the movie.

One of the messages of William Blake's poetry is that we are all terribly shrunken versions of our true selves and that by using our imaginations, which are part of the mind of God, we can expand our beings infinitely and become gods. This is a philosophy Gulley Jimson lives and breathes. Gulley is painting this epic work on the wall of a millionaire's bedroom even though he is penniless, ailing, virtually friendless, an ex-felon, and doesn't have the millionaire's permission. (Gulley was, though, recognized as a genius in an earlier phase of his painting career.) The sculptor on the floor below is like Jimson, though he doesn't quote Blake; this artist, too, acts like a mighty being who can roam the world at will and do anything he wants. Both artists ignore physical reality and create a new reality.

Gulley believes Blake's every word. For him the horse's mouth is Blake's; the poet is filled with the divine.[1] For Blake the horse's mouth is God's. In listening to Blake, and by extension God, we too can be gods.

William Blake was the last great poet to carry forward, though in a unique style, the message of the hermeticists in Marsilio Ficino's translation of the *Pimander:* "Make yourself grow to a greatness beyond measure, by a bound free yourself from your body; raise yourself above all time, become eternity; then you will understand God."[2]

Today the illusory freedoms of technology blind us to the liberating power of this dictum. The English poet of the Romantic era who embodied it was born and bred in a time when technology was turning most of England into a vast factory where children toiled like slaves and sometimes died—a world William Blake, like the novelist Charles Dickens, wanted to see abolished.

Blake produced sprawling epic poems that, until the mid-twentieth century, were thought by most to be the incoherent works of a madman, and some of the most exquisite short lyrical poems in the English language. Who does not know the following lines?

> *Tyger! Tyger! burning bright*
> *In the forests of the night,*
> *What immortal hand or eye,*
> *Could frame thy fearful symmetry?*[3]

Blake claimed to accomplish all he did with the help of angels, who, he said, surrounded him at his birth, and whom as an adult he could see any time he wanted, as clearly as if they were living human beings. When he was four, the face of God appeared to him at the window and made him scream. Another time he watched as the prophet Ezekiel sat placidly on the front lawn beneath a tree. As a child Blake saw a ghost (as opposed to an angel) only once—but it was a "scaly, speckled, very awful" ghost that chased down the staircase after him.[4]

As a child he was untamable. Only with great difficulty could he be made to fit into small corners of society. In *William Blake: The Politics of Vision* (1959), Mark Schorer writes:

> Because as a child he could not brook discipline, and especially the indignity of whippings, William was not sent to school. . . . At an early age, and at his own desire, he was given instruction in drawing, apprenticed to an engraver, and allowed to educate himself as he wished. His attitude toward churches was identical with his attitude toward schools. Except for a brief attachment to a Swedenborgian community, he seems in his youth, as in his age, to have kept himself free from all the claims of all the current dogma: a sectarian without a sect.[5]

Paul Johnson writes that Blake "hovered uneasily between the roles of artist-craftsman and poetic-visionary. He had an excellent training as an apprentice engraver and was extraordinarily innovative in everything he did—watercolors, illustration, color printing, work in tempera, prose and poetry."[6] Johnson shows us how, even as an adult, and an artist whose achievements were increasingly admired by his peers, Blake continued to live in everyday intimacy with the spirit world and the spirits of the dead:

> In this [working-room and bed-] room, Blake would describe his visions, which inspired a growing number of his drawings. While he did so, said [Henry Crabb] Robinson, "it was in the ordinary unemphatic tone in which we speak of trivial matters . . . he said repeatedly, 'The spirit told me.' I took occasion to say, 'You use the same words as Socrates used. What resemblance do you suppose is there between your spirit and the spirit of Socrates?' 'The same as between our countenances.' He paused and added, 'I was Socrates,' and then as if correcting himself, 'A sort of brother. I must have had conversations with him, as I had with Jesus Christ. I have an obscure recollection of having been with both of them. . . .' He spoke with seeming complacency of himself, said he acted by command; the spirit said of him: 'Blake, be an artist and nothing else. . . .'"
>
> Sometimes Blake would draw his portrait heads of visions while visitors were present. "William Wallace," he exclaimed, "I see him now—there, there, how noble he looks—reach me my things!" Having drawn for some time, with the same care of hand and steadiness of eye, as if a living sitter had been before him, Blake stopped suddenly and said: "I cannot finish him—King Edward I has stepped in between him and me." "That's lucky," said my friend, "for I want the portrait of Edward too." Blake took another sheet of paper and sketched the features of Plantagenet [King Edward I]; upon which his majesty politely vanished, and the artist finished the head of Wallace.[7]

Blake did not know how it was that all mankind was not in the same state of visionary awareness as he was. The engraver-poet was preoccupied by the same theme that held in thrall his predecessor, the great English poet John Milton: How had it come to pass that humankind "fell from grace," that we were "banished from the Garden of Eden"—

that it was only through the birth and death of Jesus Christ that we could be put back on the path that led to the Garden of Eden?

Blake felt such affinity for Milton's ideas, poetry, and indeed the whole man himself that he believed he was the reincarnation of Milton, who lived from 1608 to 1674. (Reincarnation may not be the right word; Blake believed that any great artist's work acquires immortality, or, that is, an independent, transcending reality of its own, and that the creative achievement of Milton had been passed along to him, Blake, at his birth. The latter poet felt that his mission was to elaborate on and complete Milton's work as he himself pursued his destiny as an artist.)

But if, like Milton, Blake devoted much of his creative energy to the description and explanation of the fall and redemption of humankind, he did it in a strangely different way than had the more conventionally Christian Milton. Blake lived at a time when technology was supplanting religion, and he was decisively influenced by that group of writers who had fallen through the cracks left by the schism between religion and science. These were the esotericists Boehme, Swedenborg, Paracelsus, Agrippa, and the collective figure of Hermes Trismegistus.

The notion of the fall of man and the banishment from the garden seems quaint and old-fashioned to many of us today, but for nearly two millennia its power was such as to keep Christian men and women bowed low by a sense of their own sinfulness. The idea of the fall implies that people were once perfect but that through the sin the theologians call pride—but that somehow seems to also be bound up with the dawning of self-consciousness—humankind "fell" from God's grace and ever after has been struggling to survive in a world of pain and sorrow. The coming of Christ, who, according to the theologians, died on the cross to "save us from our sins," gave people a second chance, wiped clean the slate that said people had to prove themselves worthy before they could reenter Eden. Still, according to many Christian sects, there were those who would have to work hard to regain Eden.

These are the stories John Milton told in *Paradise Lost* (1667) and *Paradise Regained* (1671), the former work memorable for its description of a fall from grace that included the descent into imperfection of every aspect of the physical world. The angels tilted the earth twenty-three degrees on its axis to make the seasons happen, roses grew thorns, animals grew claws, and so on, until everything was barbed. Man, who was once one with God—as Jesus Christ was—was now formidably cut off from his Maker.

In the later poems, in particular *The Four Zoas* and *Milton,* Blake, influenced by esotericists like Jakob Boehme, driven by his own demanding genius, gave a strange and startling twist to this scenario. He tells us that not only did humankind fall, but that God fell too. In fact, there was not a physical universe at all until God/humanity fell. It was this very fall that gave rise to physical reality as we know it.

Such differences of metaphysical opinion—Milton believing humankind fell away from God in an already created universe, Blake holding that God/humanity fell together, contracting and fragmenting in such a way as to create the physical universe—may look like mere quibbling to those not already hooked on such ethereal debates. But in saying that God and man were one from the beginning, Blake makes us ask some compelling questions that Christianity takes for granted, such as: What was God/humanity like before the fall? What was the state of existence that came before the creation of the physical universe?

Since Blake believed God and humankind were one, he visualized that preexisting "heaven" in the shape of a man, whom he called Albion (a name given to Britain in ancient times). Blake also called this perfect God/humanity, in his prefallen state, Atlantis. The poet believed the myth of Atlantis was a "remembering" of man's first, primordial state in a perfection of godhood that took the form of a single giant man. As Northrop Frye explains in *Fearful Symmetry* (1947):

In the Golden Age before the Fall, humanity or Albion dwelt at peace in its Paradise or Atlantis. The Fall produced a chaotic world and the central symbol of chaos is water. The Platonic story that Atlantis was overwhelmed by a flood gets the meaning of this clearer. The Atlantic Ocean, then, symbolizes the fallen world in Blake; he calls it the "Sea of Time and Space."[8]

For those who believe that Atlantis, however vanished it may be now, was once a hard-and-fast reality, such statements may seem like a letdown. But they are far from that—though grasping Blake's full meaning isn't easy in our world, dominated as it is today by technology-enhanced physical reality. For Blake, the unfallen God/humanity-Albion/Atlantis was far more real than man's puny physical constructions woven from time and space. In our time we are fighting against racism and sexism; Blake might have said we have a long way to go in fighting against "matterism," or "physicalism"—the mistaken notion that physical reality is somehow harder, more real, more nuts-and-bolts, than what we call "spirit."

To understand more fully Blake's meaning, let's continue to follow the progress of God/humanity-Albion as it plummets, figuratively speaking, downward from perfection and the nonphysical universe, through seven successive stages, or "Eyes" (Blake here uses the terminology of Jakob Boehme), until at last it strikes rock bottom. Or, more accurately, becomes its own rock bottom, since it has reached what Blake calls the "Limit of Contraction"—that is, confinement in the time-space universe we know today. Critical to an understanding of this "fall" is Blake's statement, in *The Marriage of Heaven and Hell,* that "Man has no Body distinct from his Soul; for that call'd Body is a portion of Soul discern'd by the five Senses, the chief inlets of Soul in this age."[9] Blake means that as Albion fell, or "contracted," the organs of perception of Albion contracted as well. In other words, Albion's perception of itself progressively devolved; diminishing in acuity and power, Albion made it steadily harder for its components—emerging individual humans—to

> see a World in a Grain of Sand
> And a Heaven in a Wild Flower,
> Hold Infinity in the palm of your hand
> And eternity in an hour.[10]

The world of the artist is one of expanded perceptions, no matter how seemingly hopelessly trapped in space-time reality the artist may be. When Gulley Jimson, the destitute, ailing painter in *The Horse's Mouth,* walks beside the Thames, he doesn't see just a dull old sky: he sees, instead,

> Tide pouring up from London as bright as bottled ale. Full of bub-
> bles and every bubble flashing its own electric torch. Mist breaking
> into round fat shapes, china white on Dresden blue. Dutch angels
> by Rubens della Robbia. Big one on top curled up with her knees to
> her nose like the little marble woman Dobson did for Courtauld. A
> beauty. Made me jump to think of it. You could have turned it round
> in your hand. Smooth and neat as a cricket ball. A Classic Event.[11]

And when he looks at the blank wall in the millionaire's bedroom, he doesn't see just a blank wall; he sees an expanded vision of reality (a painting, *The Raising of Lazarus*), which he immediately begins to fling onto the wall. While doing this Gulley quotes Blake nonstop. Today, we, the shattered debris of Albion, see little more than a few grains of sand and a wildflower—if we're lucky. In the words of Northrop Frye: "When we say that man has fallen, we mean that his soul has collapsed into the form of the body in which he now exists . . . [in accordance with] the interdependence of the universe we see and the bodies which compel us to see it in that way."[12]

But Albion/Atlantis hasn't disappeared. It is all around us—or, more accurately, it is all within us—if we can only perceive it. Such arisen, or expanded, perception has been the goal of seers and mystics through the ages, whether through meditation or drugs or austerities. (The relatively simple psychotherapy of the age in which we live doesn't really do the trick.) Such attainment is not easy; here is Northrop Frye again:

> Now we cannot by taking thought add a cubit to our statures; it is a
> change of worlds that is necessary, the lifting of the whole body to a

fully imaginative plane by getting rid of the natural man. . . . There is no soul within the body evaporating at death, but a living man armed with all the powers of his present body, infinitely expanded. The relation of soul to body is that of an oak to an acorn, not of a genie to a bottle. And there are no natural laws which the risen body must obey and no compulsory categories by which it must perceive. It is impossible to picture this except in terms of what we now see, and providing angels with wings is about as far as we can get. As Blake says, "From a perception of only 3 senses or 3 elements none could deduce a fourth or fifth"; and we have no idea how many imaginative powers we do not possess. . . . Because we perceive on the level of this body, we see an independent nature in a looming and sinister perspective.[13]

Blake will still seem to us to be living in a world of fantasy, to be a lunatic, if we do not try hard to understand that the seemingly ironclad reality in which we live is really just a dream in comparison with the brilliant, bursting, searing, nuts-and-bolts reality in which the unfallen God/humanity-Albion has his being. Let's try an exercise: Imagine, as you read this, that you, now, wherever you are, are nothing but a thought, or that you are merely dreaming—that you and everything surrounding you has no physical reality whatsoever and that everything that is *really* real is for the moment completely hidden from you.

Now, imagine this dream you're dreaming creeping into the realm of nightmare. Do what you always do when you realize your dream is not reality but a nightmare: wrench yourself out of the nightmare. Then, imagine yourself lying in your bed, breathing quickly, relieved it wasn't real . . .

For William Blake, all of time-space reality is, essentially, merely a nightmare, with the occasional brief excursion into something a little better. The poet invites us to wrench ourselves out of the nightmare, to begin the journey up and out into our unfallen self—a journey we cannot begin to imagine, for, as we pursue it, our very organs of perception expand, which is the same as saying that everything expands into something more vast, more strange, more rich than we can possibly imagine. Since the visionary poet is able to catch glimpses of "infinity in a grain of sand" or "eternity in a wildflower," from time to time, Blake is able to describe the journey for us here and there in his poetry, as in the following lines:

> *My eyes more and more*
> *Like a Sea without shore*
> *Continue Expanding,*
> *The Heavens commanding,*
> *Till the Jewels of Light,*
> *Heavenly Men beaming bright,*
> *Appear'd as One Man.*[14]

When the poet's "eyes did expand," he saw not only landscapes and seascapes flooded with sunlight, but also numberless "particles of light," each in the form of a man. As he continues his ever-expanding journey upward and inward, he can expect to attain the ultimate vision: that of the one man, Albion, who is Atlantis, who is the whole universe—who is God and who is himself. Somewhere in his long poem *Jerusalem,* Blake promises us "the end of a golden string"; if we follow it, we will truly find his meaning. The string is still there, for those who dare to grasp it.

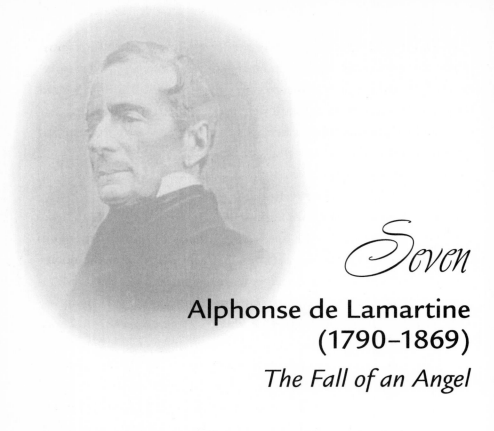

# Seven

# Alphonse de Lamartine
# (1790–1869)

*The Fall of an Angel*

It sometimes occurred to Alphonse de Lamartine, now forty-two and a famous poet embarking on a second career in politics, that he was not an ordinary man at all but, rather, an angel (in terms of beingness, not in terms of character), perhaps even a god, who had fallen in love with a mortal woman (Marianne, his wife) and relinquished his immortality to be with her.

That thought crossed his mind now as, wearing a red frock coat and white riding breeches despite the blistering heat, he stood in the shimmering sunlight of the courtyard outside the monastery at Djoun. He was waiting for an audience with Lady Hester Stanhope, whom a thousand adoring Syrian Arabs called the queen of Palmyra. It was surely the thought of this Englishwoman, who was spoken of as if she were a goddess, that had prompted the return of his obsession about his once having been—perhaps!—an angel.

Of course, he told himself, as he and Dr. Leonardi waited patiently in the blazing sun, he couldn't actually remember if he had ever been an angel, nor was it likely that he ever would, for, having once put on the mantle of mortality, surely a former immortal would not be able to remember what he had been. How could mortal faculties remember what only immortal faculties could embrace?

The voice of Leonardi broke the silence: "The door has been opened. The queen of Palmyra is ready to receive us. Let us proceed."

Lamartine strode forward quickly. The door was ajar; Leonardi, beside him, opened it wide. Lamartine entered. He was in a tiny room that seemed for an instant to be pitch-black by contrast to the noonday sun that filled the sky outside with a single, burning, stupendous expanse of glare. His eyes focused. The room had one small window and was dim with an amber glow. There were two armchairs, a bench, and a thick gold carpet filling up the floor. To one side, against the wall, two Arab boys in white robes—they must have been Druses—gently waved two giant fans.[1]

The queen of Palmyra—he intended to call her Lady Hester Stanhope—was advancing toward him across the opulent carpet. She must have been six feet tall. She wore the white turban and purple headband of an Arab chieftain. Now she was before him; their eyes met at the same level; she stared at him sharply through those dark eyes set above an aquiline nose in a wide florid face.

A hand darted out from the Turkish robe of white silk with flowing sleeves that enveloped every inch of her body in simple folds. Lamartine slipped off his glove and took her hand. "My dear Lady Hester Stanhope," he said. "I am honored to meet the woman who is the niece of one English prime minister and the granddaughter of another."

Lady Hester gazed at him severely. "That, sir, is indeed my family," she said. "But it is *not* me." She smiled warmly. "However, I know *you,* sir. I do not know *who* you are, but I know *what* you are! A moment ago, something—was it the sound of your footsteps on the paving stones outside?—told me that our stars were friendly and that we would be suited to one another. You are one who, like me, loves God, nature, and solitude. Let us talk. We are old friends. We are brother and sister!"[2]

"Indeed, Madame," he replied. But he was very surprised. "Do you really not know who I am?" he asked.

Dr. Leonardi stepped forward from the door and murmured in a soft silky voice: "Madame, you know that I am your servant, Leonardi. Allow me to introduce Count Lamartine. He is a celebrated poet from Mâcon, France. He is a member of the French Academy. No doubt you are familiar with these verses."

And Leonardi carefully recited: *"Eternity, nothingness, past, somber abysses, what do you do with the days you engulf? Speak; will you give back to us these sublime ecstasies that you snatch from us?"*[3]

Lady Hester listened intently. She raised her hands: "My dear Count, you are the celebrated author of 'The Lake'!"

Lamartine bowed distractedly. That poem—and his poem "The Crucifix" (about which he had been asked so many vexing questions)—and all the rest of his poems were not what he wanted to talk about today. He had written those poems a dozen years ago. What he wanted to talk about today—what he had come to Lady Hester expressly to acquire—was knowledge of the divine, knowledge of spiritual worlds beyond, knowledge of the world before the Flood. He had been told that Lady Hester possessed such knowledge. She had obtained it from the Druses, who remembered what the world was like when the cedars of Lebanon sang, when animals talked to men, when men talked to the stars—when all of nature was still suffused with the presence of the divine.

It was to receive such knowledge that Alphonse de Lamartine had come to Djoun in Syria to talk to Lady Hester. He was not to be denied.

It was certainly true that Alphonse de Lamartine had, in 1830, rediscovered, or, as we might put it in the twenty-first century, reinvented, the lake.

He was born in 1790 in Mâcon, France, a town that owed its fame to its nearness to the ruins of Cluny—the towering oak trees that surround this religious site bear witness to its antiquity—considered to be the most grandly beautiful of all the medieval abbeys. The descendant of a sturdy line of minor nobility, Lamartine was, says scholar Charles Lombard, "the center of attention as the only son. His mother and five sisters contributed to the development of his at times almost feminine sensibilities."[4] Lamartine's family favored the views of the Enlightenment, and protected their son from Napoleon I's conscriptions. An effortlessly brilliant student, the young man was free to pass his time somewhat indolently, indulging his two great passions, literature and women.

In 1816, at Aix-les-Bains, he fell desperately in love with Julie Charles, the wife of a celebrated physicist. She returned his feelings. The lovers spent three weeks together on the shores of Lac du Bourget. Fourteen months later—as they were about to meet again at the lake—Julie died. The devastated Lamartine, already on the path to becoming a poet, worked furiously on his craft. "The Lake," written just before the failed rendezvous, was rewritten to commemorate Julie's death. It appeared, along with twenty-three other poems, in *Méditations poétiques,* which Lamartine published anonymously in 1820.

This little volume, writes Dr. Lombard, "created a sensation on the Paris bookmarket."[5] Nature figured vibrantly in every poem. Lombard explains: "Fondness for the natural world, its trees, hills, lakes, and forests, represented nothing surprisingly new. Lamartine, however, made use of this background to insert an intensely personal note into his lyrics in which nature literally seemed to vibrate in sympathy with the poet."[6]

This was, above all, true of "The Lake." But "The Lake" ushered in a newer note as well. Writes Lombard: "Joined to the motif of a return to a place where love knew brighter moments is the concept of the impermanence of time, its fleeting character and instability."[7]

Lamartine hated the experience of the passage of time. "The Lake" mourns Julie, but it also mourns each instant of our lives that, annihilated by the devourer time, can never be retrieved. The lake becomes for the poet, buffeted by the winds of eternity, a metaphor for time itself, which cannot stay. Such was the power of Lamartine's poem, and of this image of the lake, that he changed forever the concept of Frenchmen. Before, a lake was a lake; from 1820 on, it was also an image of time, the moving destroyer.

The enduring popularity of "The Lake" ensured the poet's future success. In 1823 he married the accomplished Englishwoman Marianne Birch. Through the 1820s, he published several more volumes of poetry. In mid-decade Lamartine entered the diplomatic service as secretary to the French embassy in Naples and Florence. In 1830, before departing for the Middle East, he published *Harmonies poétiques et religieuses*.

Throughout the 1820s Lamartine moved increasingly in literary circles. He came to know Victor Hugo, Alfred de Vigny, and Charles Nodier. Lombard lists the new cultural factors that impinged on all these writers at the time, particularly Lamartine:

> . . . Platonism in the 1820's was in the air. Hinduism was also a topic of conversation, and Frederick Creuzer's work on India was widely read. An especially intriguing ideological undercurrent was the persistence of theology, which emphasized man's ability to obtain through natural means a form of direct revelation from the deity. [The Illuminist] Louis-Claude de Saint-Martin was particularly attractive. . . . [He taught that] a select group, the *hommes de désir* (men of desire), possessed extraordinary insights into the divine will and plan. Their duty was to make this revelation known to other men.[8]

Lombard might also have mentioned the mysterious, apocryphal *Book of Enoch,* translated into English for the first time in 1821 by the Irish bishop Richard Lawrence, and rapidly acquiring notoriety.[9] This work greatly influenced Lamartine, as did the writings of Saint-Martin;

the poet wondered if he were not one of those men of desire to whom would be opened up the secrets of the world from the beginning of time. New books flooded into Paris on the Middle East and the Far East. There—to trust the evidence of the religious legends and the philosophies—eternity had a different nature than in the West. It was as if, at the Levant, one passed over almost imperceptibly into a new sort of time. It flowed more slowly; it mattered less. In the lore of the East, one harked back to ancient epochs, when eternity mingled more with time—when the rocks, the trees, the animals—perhaps even humans!— remembered more of when they had been an essential part of the stuff of the universe.

Lamartine decided that he must go at least to the Middle East. He was launching a career in politics; such a trip would help him in this regard as well. In August 1832, he, his wife, Marianne, and their ten-year-old daughter, Julie, slipped anchor at Marseille and set out for Palestine. They docked in Beirut in October. Lamartine immediately set out on a tour of the region, leaving Marianne and Julie behind. Near the top of his itinerary was a visit with Lady Hester Stanhope.

Dr. Leonardi had slipped noiselessly out of the small room in this monastery at Djoun abandoned by the Syrian Christians centuries before and now lived in (for twenty years) by Lady Hester. Lamartine gazed at his sternly smiling hostess. As a young woman she had served tea regularly at the soirées of her bachelor uncle William Pitt the Younger, prime minister of England from 1783 to 1801 and 1804 to 1806 and the mortal enemy of Napoleon. She was the granddaughter of the superb Lord Chatham—William Pitt the Elder—her uncle's father and prime minister of England from 1766 to 1768. Even then she had acquired a reputation for a barely repressed eccentricity and a certain wildness of character. Little wonder, then, that she had suddenly thrown it all up and flung herself with passionate abandon across the Mediterranean to Greece, ending up in this mysterious Syrian monastery deeply beloved of the Druses, who were now also deeply infatuated with her.

Who better to give him knowledge of the occult secrets of the universe?

Lady Hester took Lamartine's hand and led him to an ancient white marble bench festooned with purple cushions. She sat down opposite him, detached and thoughtful, in an ornate white armchair, and crossed her arms. The Arab boys with the swaying fans seemed to have faded into the wall, their presence betrayed only by the currents of cool air that eddied across the room.

Lamartine leaned forward and spoke earnestly. He wished to know about the vanished art of divination. There was not a single nation, not a single people, not a single epoch that did not wonder about that vanished art. A science of divination must then have existed, somewhere far back in time. Was not divination a language the key to which humanity had lost when we descended from a higher state?

She acknowledged his concerns. Yes, knowledge of the science of divination had been lost in Europe, in the West. But it had not been lost in the East. She herself possessed that knowledge. It taught one how to read the stars. That was the key; we had all been born the child of a certain celestial fire—of the star that had presided at our birth.[10]

"But," he asked her, "was there not a time on earth when all of us knew this instinctively? When we knew our star, when we could read our star as if it were a book, when we were in wordless communication with all the species on our planet?" He went on: Did not the Druses remember the first mornings of the world, remember that time before the Flood? Was not the ancient science of divination a secret guarded by that people of rare antiquity, that antediluvian race, the Druses of Lebanon and Syria? Had they not revealed that secret to her?

"They have," she replied.

He implored her: "Madame, reveal to me something of that secret."

She answered, "Sir, destiny has sent you hither, and the astonishing sympathy between our stars permits me to confide to you what I should conceal from the profane world. Know that I have enemies here. It was but lately that I was obliged to defend myself with dagger against the attack of a black slave whom I had brought up. But the Druses are my friends. I will take you to them. They will speak to you."

He rose quickly. "Wait," she said. "Do you believe in the Messiah?"

"The Messiah—?"

"Do you believe that Christ will come a Second Time riding upon a steed as he rode upon the ass at Passover?"

He was ecumenical enough to be able to say—did not all religions come from the same central core?—"Yes."

"Do you believe the legend that that steed will be born fully saddled, already able to receive the Master on its back?"

He stared at her silently.

"That steed has already been born. I have him in my stable. Come."

She led him through dark corridors. Abruptly they emerged into a high, narrow courtyard. All was ablaze with sunlight. The sudden heat seemed to swell, then ebb. Across the courtyard—not twenty feet away—beneath a white-plastered wall glittering in the fiery light, two magnificent Arab steeds, one white, the other brown, stood in a richly decorated stall.

Lady Hester led him across the courtyard. "See," she said. "Examine this bay mare."

He approached the brown mare. She tossed her mane.

Lamartine saw, behind the shoulders of the mare, a long, deep, and sloping cavity, naturally and perfectly a part of the creature's body, resembling exactly a Turkish saddle.[11]

He turned to Lady Hester. "And this—?" he began.

"This mare was born among the Druses," she said. "Many of them are Christians."

He waited.

"And now," she said sternly, "you will meet those who care for this steed. They will give you the knowledge that you seek so ardently."

Behind the stall, in the darkness of the stables, figures stirred. Lamartine could make out two men moving toward him.

"You will be astonished at what they say," said Lady Hester.

With those words, she slipped away.[12]

The next day, he and Leonardi, riding swiftly on horseback, rejoined the rest of the party, which had been sequestered with the horses in a nearby village. They reassembled the expedition and, under the blazing sun, which once more had become relentlessly hot, they moved forward.

Lamartine told Leonardi about the bay mare of the Messiah that had been born already saddled. He told him nothing about the conversations that had taken place late in the afternoon and evening. He had not even written them down. During that day, as they went forward on horseback, he committed every detail of them to memory.

They were inscribing a wide swath through the Levant, one that would take them, in a month, back to Beirut. They passed through the seaport of Jaffa, which the Roman historian Pliny had described as a city from before the Flood, and where, according to tradition, Noah had built the Ark and the Cedars of Mount Lebanon had been landed on the orders of Solomon for the construction of the temple.[13] They came to Baalbek, where Lamartine examined the celebrated Trilithon—three massive, oblong blocks of stone, the largest sixty-five feet by fourteen feet, six inches by twelve feet. It seemed to the poet that only giants could have built the towering monuments of which these massive blocks were only a mute reminder. How long ago must they have lived, he wondered, since nothing was known of these giants?

The next day, on horseback, moving slowly beneath the fiery sun, he reread the lines in Genesis 6:1–4, in the Old Testament, that had first been read to him when he was a boy.

1. When men began to multiply on the face of the ground, and daughters were born to them, 2. the sons of God saw that the

daughters of men were fair; and they took to wife such of them as they chose. 3. Then the Lord said, "My spirit shall not abide in man for ever, for he is flesh, but his days shall be a hundred and twenty years." 4. The Neph'ilim [giants] were on the earth in those days, and also afterward, when the sons of God came in to the daughters of men, and they bore children to them. These were the mighty men that were of old, the men of renown.

There was more. He contemplated the lines of the apocryphal *Book of Enoch,* that text, rejected from the biblical canon, that had been translated from Hebrew and Aramaic into English just nine years before:

VII: 2. And the women became pregnant [from the sons of God], and bore great giants, whose stature was three thousand ells, 3. And who consumed all the acquisitions of men. And when they could no longer sustain them, 4. The giants turned against the men and women and devoured them.[14]

They came to the region once known as Basan, where, according to the Book of Joshua, 12:4, a king named Og had reigned. This king's bed had measured thirteen feet by six feet—not inconsistent with Goliath's height of nine feet. "One of the last of the Rehmaites," Og had ruled a race of giants; it was said that with Noah's permission, he had leapt onto the roof of the Ark, thus ensuring the survival of a remnant of his race after the Flood had passed.

They halted in the ancient city of Réphaïm, called by the Hebrews Argob and by the Greeks Trachonitide. This was the largest of the sixty cities ruled by Og. With Dr. Leonardi and two guides, Lamartine roamed up and down the wide and desolate avenues. Réphaïm still had all its houses—three halls on the ground floor, two rooms on the second floor, massive stone staircases—all of its towers intact, all of its walls, all of its crossroads, paved or with paving stones, and all of the streets. But it had not a single inhabitant. Ordinary humans had never inhabited it. It had been inhabited only by giants. Only the monstrous hands of giants could open and close the doors of these houses, which were made of a single slab of stone six feet high and one foot thick, turning on two pivots sculpted from the stone itself, with one stuck into the top of the doorway and the other stuck into the stone threshold.[15]

The expedition moved forward, almost home now. When Lamartine arrived in Beirut on November 5, he was joyously greeted by his ten-year-old daughter, Julie. She seemed to be in good health. Two weeks later she was gravely ill. She died on December 7.

The Lamartines were crushed by this tragedy. They lingered on in Syria for several months. In early April, the poet received word that he had been awarded the seat of deputy for Bergues. Perhaps this was what kept him and Marianne from total collapse. Their agony was not new: they had lost their first child, Alphonse, a son, in 1822, when he was eighteen months old. But to his projects as poet Lamartine could now add those of a politician. In late April, he and Marianne set sail on a homeward voyage of many stages. They arrived in Mâcon in late October. A politician needed money. If for no other reason, Lamartine set himself to completing the nine-part epic history in poetry of the human soul that he had been planning for years.

Lamartine was not certain that he personally believed in reincarnation. He had always had a feeling, however—sometimes this almost seemed to be borne out by physical evidence—that he had already been a part of the countries he longed to visit, that perhaps he had lived a lifetime in each one. He writes in *A Pilgrimage:*

> I have seldom met with a place or an object the first sight of which did not present itself to my mind rather as a remembrance than as a new idea! Have we lived twice or a thousand times? Is our memory a tarnished glass, which the breath of God can revive? Or, otherwise, has our imagination the faculty of presentiment, and of a sight anterior to the natural eye? The questions are unsolvable.[16]

Robert Mattlé quotes the poet in *Lamartine voyageur:* "I had a presentiment about the Orient practically from my birth. My nature is primitive and sun-directed. The sun draws me to it as it does the sunflower."[17] Lady Hester had revealed to him, during the epochal meeting in Djoun, that his foot was that of an Arab: "Look!" she had exclaimed. "Your instep is very high: there is space between the heel and the toes, when you place your foot on the ground the space is sufficient to let the water flow under it without wetting you. It is an Arabian foot; it is the foot of the East."[18]

So it was no great stretch of belief for the poet to imagine a series of epic poems, which he thought of as a single poem, in which the main protagonist would live a different lifetime in each episode. The poem as a whole would span the lifetime of the human race.

The hero of Lamartine's twelve-thousand-line epic poem, *La chute d'un ange (The Fall of an Angel;* 1838), is a fallen angel, Cédar, who must live through nine successive lifetimes, in this and eight additional epic poems, to reclaim his nature as an immortal. Lamartine completed only two of these epic poems, which he called "Episodes." *The Fall of an Angel* is episode one. A third episode, *Knights,* was stillborn. Henri Guillemin notes that in May 1827 Lamartine "undertook to complete that Episode of *Knights* [*Chevaliers*] that he had begun in May 1827 and which was supposed to show the fallen angel reincarnated in the Middle Ages in the guise of the knight, Tristan. But, after a month of work, the pen dropped from his hand."[19]

Lamartine then launched himself into Episode Nine, which he completed. At the end of this Episode the protagonist finds himself redeemed and reascends to heaven. This epic work, called *Jocelyn,* is set in the contemporary France of Lamartine. Jocelyn is a French priest, who, having dallied with an earthly, carnal amour, ultimately sacrifices himself unselfishly for those he loves, and so is finally—and it is essential to the divine principles at play here that he does not know this will happen, and does not expect it to happen—transported back to heaven as an immortal being. The mortal Jocelyn had retained, without his being fully aware of it, some of the gifts he had as an angel; he could, for example, talk to the animals, declaring at one point:

> *O, my dog! Only God knows the distance between us;*
> *Only He knows what degrees on the ladder of being*
> *Separate your soul's instinct from that of your master;*
> *But only He knows of the secret ties by which we talk.*[20]

Episode One, *The Fall of an Angel,* inspired in part by Lamartine's experiences in the Middle East, takes place in the unknown and forgotten pre-Flood world of Lebanon. Humankind has not yet entirely fallen; we are not wholly in a state of sin. The boundaries between heaven and earth are still blurred. The power of the divine peeks through and people can still talk to the animals and hear the music of the spheres.

The contrast of the intersecting planes of reality can be sharp. Angels hover in the air while primitive peoples roam the still-young hills and the valleys. The angels have descended and copulated with the daughters of men. This has produced a race of giants. Lamartine has no hesitation in presenting these giants as brutal and violent, even evil.

Cédar, one of the angels, is the guardian of a mortal earth-woman, Daïdha. A descendant of Cain, she is barely out of her childhood. Taken by her grace and beauty, Cédar falls in love with Daïdha. He declares his love to her. God cautions him that if he wishes to live out his love with Daïdha on earth, he must become a mortal; he will then experience all the tribulations of the human condition. Cédar doesn't hesitate, and he and Daïdha marry. As they do, the cedars of Lebanon sing praises to the Lord:

> *Holy! Holy! Holy! The Lord whom the hill adores!*
> *Behind his suns, we see it from here*
> *When night's perfumed breath bids us incline*
> *Like humble reeds, beneath his hand we bow!*

*But why do we bend? Because we pray to him,*
*Because an intimate instinct of divine goodness*
*Makes our trunks shiver from tree-top down to root,*
*Like a wrathful wind that reddens our nostrils,*
*And roars in our bellies,*
*Makes the manes of lions' necks ripple.*
*Slip, slip, wandering breezes,*
*Change into murmuring.*[21]

Cédar undergoes many trials. He saves Daïdha when she is trapped in a net by hunters. He rescues her when her parents tie her hair to the bottom of a grotto because she loves Cédar; they had meant to starve her to death if she did not renounce her love. But he can't save her when giants arrive in a flying machine and carry her, along with himself and their two children, off to Babel, the capital city of the giants, ruled over by the evil Asrafiel. (The flying machine is guided by the thoughts of the pilot. It is held aloft in a manner analogous to the operation of a modern-day ramjet: a current of matter that is subtler than ether is introduced into the front end of the craft and expelled out the back, propelling the machine forward.)

The aircraft, its giant crew, and the prisoners arrive in Babel. Asrafiel tells Daïdha that he will kill her two children if she does not give herself to him. She resists. A sorceress assumes the form of Daïdha and tries to seduce Cédar. She fails. Cédar rescues Daïdha and the children one more time, and the four of them flee the city of the evil giants.

To no avail. They lose their way in the desert and while Cédar watches in horror, Daïdha and the two children die of thirst. He builds a funeral pyre, lays their bodies on it, lights it, and then hurls himself on the pyre to join them in death.

He hears the voice of God telling him that he will not be wholly redeemed until he has lived through eight more incarnations on earth; that is the time it will take for him to experience each and every vicissitude of that human condition that he has freely chosen to share. Only when this is achieved—and it happens at the end of *Jocelyn*—will he be able to reclaim his immortality.

Robert Mattlé lists several of the "New Age" influences on Lamartine in *The Fall of an Angel*.

> It was while standing before the isolated blocks and the surfaces of the gigantic walls of Baalbek that he began to believe in the Cyclops-like giants who alone could have been capable of such works; at the same time, he felt horror at this materialistic civilization that had crumbled because God wished to play no part in it. A whiff of Hindustani poetry, wafted to him from India, carried the poet forward on perfumed wings: the idea of expiation—the theory of metempsychoses—used by him as a symbol without his really believing in it, the episode of Nala and Damayanti [in the *Mahabharata*], may well have inspired the adventures of Cédar and Daïdha; and the aerial voyage of the two heroes recalls that of Douchmanta, spouse of Sakuntala [also in the *Mahabharata*].[22]

With Lamartine's descriptions of airships we enter the realm of the *vimanas,* those airships, described with such vigor in the *Mahabharata,* with which the gods of high antiquity in India waged titanic war. (Well over a century after Lamartine wrote, vimanas helped inspire the "ancient astronaut" theories of Erich von Däniken.)

*The Fall of an Angel* was badly received when it was published. Not only was the poem perceived by French society as blasphemous (the French were offended by the huge number of "purple passages"), but it seemed to them that Lamartine reveled in blood and cruelty, and he was accused of sadism. (The word *sadism* did not exist at the time, but in fact his critics were not far wide of the mark; in his youth Lamartine had enthusiastically read the works of the Marquis de Sade.) It was also felt that while there were glorious heights of lyricism in his poem, there were also stunningly long sections of boring repetition. Into the bargain, Lamartine was accused of being sloppy—and in fact there were many purely factual errors in his epic poem.

At the time, Lamartine was not greatly concerned by all this. He was pursuing the political career that would make him the head of a caretaker government in France for several crucial months in 1848. The verdict is mixed on the quality of Lamartine's performance as president of France during that period, but there is no doubt he warded off tyranny and kept alive the hopes of democracy, all the while displaying great personal courage. By the time the poet left politics, he was so hugely in debt that he would spend the remaining twenty years of his life writing hack poetry and, far more often, hack nonfiction.

*The Fall of an Angel* was strikingly original for its time. When we consider all that Lamartine achieved in his seventy-nine years—glory in literature and glory in politics—and how much he suffered, we wonder if he was not striving to live many lifetimes at once, so that he would not have to return from the godhood he would reassume in heaven. It's to Lamartine's credit that, through his poetry, he—one of the first to do so—put such fantastical and compelling ideas into the minds of the French.

# Eight

## Mary Wollstonecraft Shelley (1797–1851)

### The Last Man

The silence is piercing. Between the vacant brownstones, tall grass pokes up from the cracks in the deserted streets. In the shadows cast by the skyscrapers across the avenues, gigantic heaps of rusting cars peer blindly at the sky.

This is New York. A single automobile hurtles down a street. It's driven by actor Will Smith. Beside him on the seat lies an automatic rifle, and alongside that a huge brown dog. The dog is Smith's sole companion. Everybody else in the city—probably in the world—is dead. Plague has swept the planet clean of human life.

Smith's face is numb with despair, his eyes dull with pain. He must get home. Ravenous mutants, once human beings, roam the streets, zombielike, at night. Smith is one of earth's leading scientists, working night and day in an apartment protected by storm shutters to develop a vaccine that will defeat the plague. He's alive because of experiments he conducted when the plague first broke out. But it probably doesn't matter whether he succeeds.

He is the last man.

This is an early scene from *I Am Legend,* the 2007 blockbuster science-fiction film. It was not the first movie to tell this story. In *The Omega Man,* released in 1971, Charlton Heston was the overwhelmed protagonist wandering the deserted streets. In *The Last Man on Earth,* made in Rome in 1964, Vincent Price shouldered the role of the physically and spiritually exhausted sole survivor. All three of these films were inspired by the deeply pessimistic 1954 novel *I Am Legend* by science-fiction writer Richard Matheson.

But the antecedents of this apocalyptic story lately reanimated by Will Smith go back much further than 1954. They can be traced to 1826 and the novel *The Last Man* by Mary Wollstonecraft Shelley, the author of the perennially popular novel (re-created in many films) *Frankenstein, or The Modern Prometheus,* first published in 1818.

In the movie *I Am Legend,* the scientist played by Will Smith discovers other survivors and finds a cure for the plague. But as Mary Shelley's *The Last Man* draws to a close in the year 2100, it seems increasingly certain that Shelley's last man, Lionel Verney, will not be so lucky. The plague in *The Last Man,* never identified, apparently coming from regions near the Nile, has killed everyone in England except Verney. He has become convinced that it has killed everyone in Europe; as he sets out in a one-man boat from the east coast of Italy in hopes of finding survivors in India, he seems to tell us, in the last paragraph of the novel, that he expects to be voyaging for as long as he is alive, seen only by the eye of God:

> I shall witness all the variety of appearance, that the elements can assume—I shall read fair augury in the rainbow—menace in the cloud—some lesson or record dear to my heart in everything. Thus around the shores of deserted earth, while the sun is high, and the moon waxes or wanes, angels, the spirits of the dead, and the ever-

open eye of the Supreme, will behold the tiny bark, freighted with Verney—the LAST MAN.[1]

Mary Shelley often seems remarkably prophetic. In *The Last Man* she writes about a king of England who abdicated and became the Earl of Windsor; something very much like this happened in 1936, when King Edward VIII of England abdicated and became the Duke of Windsor to marry Wallis Simpson, a commoner. Two of Shelley's short stories deal with frozen corpses from ancient times; in 1984, the body of Lindow Man (died in the first century AD) was discovered in a peat bog in England, and in 1991, that of Otzi the Iceman (died about 3300 BC) was found in the Alps. Shelley scholar Mary Devlin tells us: *"Maurice, or the Fisher's Cot,* one of Mary's private manuscripts, was discovered only a few years ago and published in 1998. It deals with issues which are in the news today: missing children and animal rights."[2]

Most of us know that Mary Shelley wrote *Frankenstein* and married Percy Bysshe Shelley, one of the great poets of England's Romantic era. But exactly who was this extraordinary woman who, living in an age when women were hardly allowed to express themselves, wrote with such skill and varied imagination and saw with such chilling insight into the possible apocalyptic future of humankind?

Mary Wollstonecraft Godwin was the daughter of William Godwin (1756–1836), author of the revolutionary social tract *Political Justice,* and Mary Wollstonecraft (1759–1797), virtually the founder of the women's rights movement because of her trailblazing, still popular book *A Vindication of the Rights of Woman.* Both of Mary Shelley's parents had a decisive impact on their times, though often through the influence of William Godwin's devoted disciples; these latter, who often gathered at his house, included Robert Southey, Thomas de Quincey, Samuel Taylor Coleridge, William Wordsworth, and the renowned scientist Sir Humphry Davy, among others.

Ten days after giving birth to her daughter Mary, Mary Wollstonecraft

Godwin died. Her emotionally aloof husband, always preoccupied with his work, was now a single parent. He adored Mary but found it burdensome to raise her on his own. In 1801 he eased the burden by taking a second wife.

But Godwin insisted that Mary be schooled at home. It had quickly become evident that she was precociously brilliant. Her father allowed her to attend the nighttime meetings—sometimes two or three a week—that took place in his living room. Here, his gifted disciples held forth on a wide range of subjects that included Swedenborgianism and occult phenomena. It was quite an education for Mary. She was soon receiving instruction from, and being carefully listened to by, the most original and well-informed literary and scientific minds of the time. Many of Godwin's disciples were atheists and agnostics, venturing into religion only through an interest in pantheism. Nonetheless, from the age of eight to twelve, Mary had a front row seat on mesmerizing stories about ghosts and inexplicable tales of communications from the spirit world narrated with wit and originality by her father's followers. She devoured every book in her father's library—there were thousands—on aspects of the supernatural.

When Mary was seventeen, a dazzling personage entered her life. This was Percy Bysshe Shelley (1792–1822). He was twenty-one and already writing the poetry that would make him great. He began to appear regularly at her father's meetings and became a disciple of Godwin.

Here is how the nineteenth-century critic and poet Matthew Arnold described the ensuing relationship between Mary and Shelley. He writes from Percy Bysshe Shelley's point of view:

> At Godwin's house Shelley met Mary Wollstonecraft Godwin, his future wife, then in her seventeenth year. She was a gifted person, but, as Professor Dowden [early biographer of Percy Shelley] says, she "had breathed during her entire life an atmosphere of free thought." On the 8th of June Hogg [Quentin Hogg, Percy Shelley's best friend] called at Godwin's with Shelley; Godwin was

out, but "a door was partially and softly opened, a thrilling voice called 'Shelley!' a thrilling voice answered 'Mary!'" Shelley's summoner was "a very young female, fair and fair-headed, pale indeed, and with a piercing look, wearing a frock of tartan." Already they were "Shelley" and "Mary" to one another; "before the close of June they knew and felt," says Professor Dowden, "that each was to the other inexpressibly dear." The churchyard of St. Pancras, where her mother was buried, became "a place now doubly sacred to Mary, since on one eventful day Bysshe here poured forth his griefs, his hopes, his love, and she, in sign of everlasting union, placed her hand in his." In July Shelley gave her a copy of *Queen Mab,* printed but not published, [that he had inscribed for Mary] . . . Mary added an inscription on her part: "I love the author beyond all powers of expression . . . by that love we have promised to each other, although I may not be yours I can never be another's"—and a good deal more to the same effect.[3]

In reciprocating Shelley's love, Mary triggered yet greater depths of love in the poet for her. He asked Mary if she would come to Italy with him. Shelley was married, with two children, and the high-minded Mary refused. This only poured fuel on the fire of Shelley's passion. He begged Mary to come away with him. Her upbringing had been so unorthodox—she had heard so many sides of every issue argued brilliantly—that the conventional dictates of society had little hold on Mary. She yielded to Shelley's entreaties. The two set off for Venice with Jane Clairmont, who was the daughter of Godwin's second wife by her first husband and thus Mary's half sister.

The three soon ran out of money. They had to return to London. Society had been scandalized by their departure, and they returned to near-total ostracism. Mary became pregnant. She gave birth prematurely to a daughter, who died after two weeks. She became pregnant again; a son, William, was born in January 1816. The couple fled to Europe once more, again with Jane, who now called herself Claire and was pregnant by

Shelley's close friend the poet George Gordon, Lord Byron (1788–1824).

They had chosen the late spring of 1816 as the time of their second flight. Arriving in Switzerland, they took a cottage on Lake Geneva, near Villa Diodati, where Byron was staying with his friend John Polidori, a physician. The five began to spend most of their time together. They exchanged every sort of idea of the time; they read voraciously; they told ghost stories and made up plots; they played card games; gradually, the subject matter of their conversations veered into the sphere of the supernatural. Martin Ebon writes:

> While Mary herself seems to have undergone few otherworldly experiences, her husband, Percy, recorded many pseudo-psychic phenomena in his hectic and short life. Once, when the Shelleys, Lord Byron, and Claire Clairmont—Mary's half-sister and Byron's mistress—were sitting by the fire telling ghost stories, Shelley suddenly experienced a panic, masquerading as X-ray clairvoyance: He thought he saw right through the young women's bodices, imagined their nipples staring at him, turning slowly into malevolent, jelly-like eyes. He leaped, screaming, from his chair and raced from the room.[4]

In the early summer, nature conspired to keep them cooped up in the house and thereby encouraged a certain morbidity in their conversations. The coldest and rainiest summer ever recorded settled across Europe and much of the Northern Hemisphere. Severe climate anomalies destroyed crops in northern Europe, the American Northeast, and eastern Canada. Scientists now believe these aberrations occurred because of the April 5–15, 1815, volcanic eruptions of Mount Tambora, on the island of Sumbawa in the Dutch East Indies (today's Indonesia), which ejected immense amounts of volcanic dust into the upper atmosphere. In the coming months this dust drifted over many parts of the world, lowering temperatures because less sunlight could pass through the volcanic ash–ridden atmosphere. This eruption in Indonesia had a causative effect on the birth of Frankenstein's monster. The enforced confinement due to the rain and the cold heightened the hothouse atmosphere of Villa Diodati, where five highly imaginative people sought ways to express their anxieties and creative impulses. One night Byron suggested they each try to write a ghost story. Mary seemed lost at first, but was obsessed by the project. They talked heatedly about the latest developments in science: Erasmus Darwin (grandfather of Charles Darwin) had placed a vermicello strand in a glass jar, and after a while it seemed to come alive;* some scientists thought a corpse could be reanimated, perhaps by galvanism, i.e., applying an electric current, known to make muscles contract, to the dead body.

Mary wrote in the introduction to the 1831 edition on the genesis of *Frankenstein*:

> Night waned upon this talk, and even the witching hour had gone by, before we retired. When I placed my head on my pillow, I did not sleep, nor could I be said to think. My imagination, unbidden, possessed and guided me, gifting the successive images that arose in my mind with a vividness far beyond the usual bounds of reverie. I saw, with shut eyes, but acute mental vision,—I saw the pale student of unhallowed arts kneeling beside the thing he had put together. I saw the hideous phantasm of a man stretched out, and then, on the working of some powerful engine, show signs of life, and stir with an uneasy, half vital motion.[5]

Mary began the story of *Frankenstein* during those oppressive but exalting summer days on Lake Geneva, but she did not finish it until the next year, in London. She and Shelley had returned to a London more scandalized than ever by their actions. Tragedy compounded this three months later: Shelley's wife, Harriet, committed suicide. Three

---

*In a note in *The Temple of Nature* entitled "Spontaneous Vitality of Microscopic Animals," Erasmus Darwin refers to a "paste composed of flour and water" in which "the animalcules called eels" are seen in great abundance and gradually become larger, even in a "sealed glass phial."

weeks later, Mary and Percy Shelley were quietly married. *Frankenstein* was brought out in 1818 to immediate acclaim. (It was published anonymously, and for years people thought it had been written by Percy Shelley, or at least heavily edited by him.) Mary was twenty-one when the book appeared; by this time the couple had returned to Italy.

*Frankenstein* has been the theme of so many movies that even illiterates know the story well. A scientist, Victor Frankenstein, creates an eight-foot-tall monster out of bits of flesh acquired from butcher shops. He brings the monster to life with jolts of electricity. Victor is horrified by his creation and abandons it. This makes the monster's life a misery—he is quite unloved and unaccepted—and he visits his misery upon Victor Frankenstein, causing the death of all his dearest friends and even his wife. Finally the monster exiles himself to the Arctic.

The sojourn of the Shelleys in Italy stretched out over many months. Mary wrote and studied. She had three more pregnancies. In all, only the second son, Percy Florence Shelley, would survive to adulthood. On July 8, 1822, the greatest tragedy of all struck: Percy Bysshe Shelley, becoming acclaimed as a poet, drowned when his boat capsized in a storm while he was sailing in the Gulf of Spezio. He was twenty-nine years old.

The devastated Mary showed the strength that had matured in her over the years. She settled all matters in Italy and swiftly returned to London with her son. For the next thirty years, she edited and promoted the works of Percy Shelley while writing five more novels: *Valperga: The Life and Adventures of Castruccio, Prince of Lucca; The Fortunes of Perkin Warbeck; Lodore; Falkner;* and *The Last Man.*

Apart from *The Last Man,* Mary's prophetic and apocalyptic imagination expressed itself more often in her short stories than her novels. In *The Mortal Immortal,* an alchemist—in fact, Paracelsus, about whom Shelley was learned—creates an "Elixir of Immortality." It is consumed by Winzy, a student of Paracelsus who narrates the story at the age of 323 while lamenting: "I have lived on for many a year—alone, and weary of myself—desirous of death, yet never dying—a mortal immortal."[6] The story ends with Winzy wondering, wistfully and hopefully, if he will ever die; he has come to curse the change the medieval "technology" of the Elixir of Immortality has wrought in him. Shelley's future technologies are usually extrapolated from occult sources; her constant aim is to show us that the application of these technologies in no way enhances the real values in life. "Reanimation" and its dire consequences—as in *Frankenstein*—are a frequent theme in Mary's fictional writings; it can be found in her short stories *Roger Dodsworth* and *Valerius*. She also wrote a short story, *Transformation,* about a doppelgänger; this theme was popularized by Robert Louis Stevenson in *The Strange Case of Dr. Jekyll and Mr. Hyde,* about the creation, by a mad scientist, of a second self that is more effective than the first but inevitably less moral. Shelley showed again how a new "technology," meant to enhance the inventor's life, actually brought a curse upon it.

*The Last Man,* arguably Mary's most ambitious novel, was published in 1826 to poor reviews. It was out of print from 1833 until 1965, when the University of Nebraska Press brought out a new edition. In our world of today that seems to be spinning out of control, this novel is particularly pertinent. It opens in 1818, when tourists exploring the cave of the ancient Sibyl near Naples discover a trove of leaves covered with writing in ancient and modern languages. These leaves tell the story of the great plague that decimated the world's population from 2073 to 2100; somehow, they come from the future. In this epoch still almost a century ahead of ours, men and women are deeply caught up in the usual follies of humankind: civil strife, war, greed, infatuation, romance, and hatred.

It is not until the second half of the novel that the plague, almost unnoticed by humans preoccupied with their own selfish needs, begins insidiously to take its toll. By the time its lethal horrors have attracted everyone's attention, it's too late to do much. Good persons and bad, those who try to help and those who exploit the situation—all (except the narrator) fall victim to the plague. Shelley offers no solutions or panaceas and does not assign blame; as Judith Tarr observes in the introduction to the University of Nebraska Press edition:

> There is no apparent order or reason in this progression of trage-dies. Even those who escape the plague cannot [for a while] escape death—all except Lionel. Blind and heedless nature tramples them all alike regardless of nation, rank, or moral quality. All men are indeed equal, and none can escape the inevitable.[7]

Mary Shelley died in 1851 aged fifty-three, deeply mourned by all for the many acts of kindness to others that characterized her later years. A quarter-century before, she had drawn the portrait of a world heedless of the approach of its own destruction and therefore doomed to perish. It seems her masterwork has been resurrected just in time to help our world of today, which also seems to be galloping heedlessly toward disaster.

# Nine

# Honoré de Balzac (1799–1850)

## Triumph and Tragedy of the Inner Self

She was a superhero in whom cross-dressers, transsexuals, and those benefiting from sex change operations might well take an interest, both then and now. She/he was Seraphita/Seraphitus, the hermaphroditic heroine/hero of Honoré de Balzac's *Seraphita,* published in 1835 and the eighteenth of the seventy-four novels produced by the fiery French novelist over a twenty-year period.

In writing *Seraphita,* Balzac meant to describe not a twisted tormented soul but a perfect human being. He delved far back in humanity's mythical past to plumb the story, told in Plato's *Symposium,* of how there was once a third sex, the androgynous, combining the two we know, with four arms and legs, which Zeus cut in half, so that each half forever desires his or her other half. Balzac's fable also looks forward presciently to Jung's concept of every man's having a female inner personality called the *anima* and every woman's having a masculine inner personality called the *animus*.

*Seraphita* wasn't Balzac's only attempt to depict a human being striving for perfection. In *Louis Lambert* (1832), he tells the story of a genius who in his attempt to acquire all the knowledge in the universe goes tragically wrong because he neglects his human side. Both novels utilize Swedish visionary Emanuel Swedenborg's notion that we all have an "inner" and an "outer" self, and that we should strive to cultivate the former, more angelic, spiritual part of ourselves (also akin to the "astral" self). But if we do so at the expense of our outer self, then we smother our humanity. This happens to Louis Lambert: he goes insane at a young age.

The theme of the exploitation of the inner self at the expense of the outer also figures in Balzac's novel *La peau de chagrin* (The Wild Ass's Skin; 1831). The hero, Raphael, gets his hands on an ancient wild ass's skin inscribed with a message supposedly in Sanskrit stating that the person who owns the skin will have any wish granted, but each wish will cause the skin to shrink. When the skin disappears, its owner dies. After many unexpected and alarming vicissitudes, this is the fate of Raphael. The book is a cautionary tale on the destructive influence of society and wealth, but it also warns against the reckless consumption of one's own vital forces.

*La peau de chagrin* uncannily prefigured the fate that Balzac himself would suffer.

*Seraphita, Louis Lambert,* and *La peau de chagrin* are three of twenty novels Balzac included in the "Philosophical Studies" ("Études philosophiques") section of his great cycle of seventy-four novels, *The Human Comedy* (*La comédie humaine*), in which the author sought to depict the physical and emotional fundamentals of men and women in every walk of urban and rural society. A fourth novel, indirectly related to these three, is *The Quest of the Absolute* (*La recherche de l'absolu;* 1834), which tells the story of a Flemish alchemist, Balthazar Claës, who sacrifices friends, family, and home to discover the philosopher's stone. He succeeds, just barely—but at the cost of his own humanity.

⨷

Honoré de Balzac was born in Tours, France, in 1799. He was the second of three sons; his mother had previously given birth to a boy whom she insisted on feeding herself* and who lived only twenty-three days. Terrified that the baby's death was somehow caused by her having nursed him personally, Mme. Balzac refused to nurse her second son at all, and sent little Honoré away to live with the family of his wet nurse. This arrangement lasted for three years. Honoré then lived at home for a little over three years, before being sent to the Collège de Vendôme, a boarding school, where he stayed for six years. His parents rarely visited him during this period. To these twin exiles from home, when he was an infant and then as a boy, Balzac ascribed, probably rightly, many of his later emotional problems. Late in life he cried out in anguish, "I never had a mother."[1]

If the young boy was lacking in parental attention, he did not lack for high intelligence and a vivid imagination. He used his time at the Collège de Vendôme to read prodigiously and to precociously construct a philosophy of the world. André Maurois writes:

> When undergoing confinement in the *culottes de bois* [boxlike cells six feet by six installed in every dormitory for wrongdoers], or under the stairs, the infant philosopher passed his time seeking the *unity of the world* in the concept that Thought and Will were possessed of real substance, fluids analogous to electricity. . . . He pondered, even at that age, on the nature and functioning of the Will. . . . Balzac believed in the almost limitless power of will and in the physical action of thought."[2]

---

*This incident with Balzac's mother doesn't take place in today's world. It takes place in 1799; and, before the publication of Jean-Jacques Rousseau's *Émile* in 1762, middle- and upper-class women in Europe never nursed their children; they always gave them out to wet nurses. Rousseau's book, with its wildly eloquent and brilliant appeals to humankind to return to nature's ways, created a virtual fad for breast-feeding; it became all the rage for women—especially women of the aristocracy—to nurse their babies.

Graduating from Vendôme, Balzac spent a few years at day schools at home. Then he went to Paris to study law. Finding this unsatisfying, he persuaded his parents to support him in Paris for a year while he tried his hand at writing. This they did, although in niggardly fashion. This wasn't enough time for Balzac to start making money, so now he used his theoretical and practical knowledge of the Will to throw himself into several years of grinding out hack novels, often in collaboration, always anonymously. He produced a number of novels that while severely lacking in literary value at least put bread on his table.

In 1829, at the age of thirty, he achieved a breakthrough with his novel *Les Chouans* (the Chouans were a group of royalists who rose up in 1799 against the new government of the French Revolution). Balzac's skills as a novelist had reached critical mass. Critics and readers alike were pleasantly surprised, even thrilled, with this fresh and original book and others of similar quality that soon followed.

The budding novelist began to make money and acquire debts. He became a spendthrift; the more he earned, the more quickly he spent more than he earned. Balzac was corpulent, with untidy hair, bad teeth, and a big mouth. But his vitality, exuberance, and intelligence, along with a certain purity of heart (coupled with his refusal to take no for an answer), made him very attractive to women. He had numerous affairs with upper-class married women older than himself. Not only were these relationships filled with sexual passion, but also the women usually became good and helpful friends to this ardent young writer.

Balzac's connection with spiritual worlds came primarily through his ability to access the energy of his own "inner self"—or, as he often expressed it, his Will. Balzac believed that our thoughts create reality, and he was willing to put out the energy required to make it happen. This is no more evident than in the punishing writing schedule to which he subjected himself for more than twenty years.

Every day, Balzac went to bed at 8:00 in the evening. A servant awakened him at midnight. As the servant placed a lighted candelabra in the center of the writing table, Balzac closed the curtains and put on a writing gown resembling a monk's robe.

While all Paris slept, all through the night Balzac wrote. He lifted pen from paper only when his head reeled with exhaustion. At 6:00 a.m. he stopped and drank several cups of black coffee, thick as gum, which he had prepared himself. He then wrote on, furiously, until 10:00 a.m., when he stopped, took a bath, and ate.

Balzac's day was far from over. Starting at noon, printers' messengers appeared at the door with proofs of pages he had written two days before, a week before—perhaps even for a different novel. He treated these expensive proofs simply as drafts (he shouldered the costs himself), often covering them with more corrections than there had originally been words on the page. He might do this four or five times over a week or two for a single work. The printers' assistants detested setting in type these nearly indecipherable pages. They took turns, refusing to work more than an hour at a time and calling that dreaded time period *l'heure de Balzac*—"Balzac's hour."

The novelist continued this colossal job of correcting until it was time for dinner. (Sometimes, during the day, he visited the printers' offices.) Then he ate, perhaps went out—and by 8:00 p.m. was back in bed.

Balzac adhered to this titanic schedule for over twenty years, departing from it only when he went on the occasional trip outside the city. The majority of the seventy-four novels, numerous short stories, essays, and one three-act drama produced in this way are considered to be great successes, with a dozen or so—in particular, *Le père Goriot* (*Father Goriot*) and *Eugénie Grandet*—considered to be masterpieces.

But—as he somehow always knew he would—Balzac suffered the same fate as Raphael in *The Wild Ass's Skin*. He mined out all his vital fluids, the stuff, perhaps, of his inner self, and died young, at age fifty-one, of numerous ailments including caffeine poisoning.

Despite the wild idiosyncrasies of his personal life, Balzac had, intellectually, an iron grip on the hard realities of everyday existence. His novels teem with all the denizens of ordinary life: aristocrats and maids, businessmen and prostitutes, bank managers and failed writers, magistrates and recreational collectors, soldiers and priests, industrialists and con artists. Frederick Engels, the coauthor with Karl Marx of *The Communist Manifesto,* declared, "I have learnt more from Balzac than from all the professional historians, economists and statisticians put together."[3]

His masterful knowledge of everyday life notwithstanding, Balzac was intensely interested in the paranormal. Biographer Stefan Sweig writes: "He believed in amulets, always wore a lucky ring with mysterious oriental symbols, and before taking any important decision he would creep up five flights of steps to consult a fortuneteller, just as any Parisian seamstress would."[4] His interest could be practical; he was an early proponent of the use of psychometrics (touching an object owned by the victim to clairvoyantly "see" the crime scene) and advocated the use of ESP in crime detection in general. André Maurois summarizes his spiritual/philosophical belief system:

> He was both materialist and, in the broad sense, spiritualist. The spirit pervades all matter. The scale of created things rises from the minerals, whose consciousness is imperceptible, to Man, whose soul is bound to the body, and upward to the angels, which are all soul. Balzac believed, if confusedly, that the evolutionary process, extending from the rock to the saint, would eventually transform men into angels. . . . Though God remains silent, things and living creatures are charged with mysterious messages. There are secret relationships between matter and man, and what is of real importance in the universe is to be found at the level of the infinitesimally small.[5]

Graham Robb adds: "As a rational mystic, Balzac was especially fond of the idea of Leibniz that everything affects everything else. In his *Théorie de la Démarche* [Theory of Human Motion] in 1830 [Balzac wrote] 'A pistol bullet thrown into the water on the shores of the Mediterranean generates a movement that can be detected on the coast of China.' Balzac would have been an ardent popularizer of Chaos Theory."[6]

Balzac's 1832 novel *Louis Lambert,* based on Swedenborg's notion of the inner and outer self, was the author's first foray into literature with elements of the occult. Lambert himself sets forth the Swedish seer's theory:

> There are within us two distinct beings. According to Swedenborg, the angel is the individual in whom the inward being has triumphed over the outward being. If, failing to possess this translucent vision of his destiny, he lets the corporeal tendencies predominate, instead of merely strengthening and supporting the intellectual life, his powers pass into the service of his external senses, and the angel slowly perishes through the materialization of both natures. On the other hand, if he nourishes the inward being with the essences that accord with it, the soul rises above matter and endeavors to get free of it.[7]

However, Lambert allows his inner self to get the better of him. Visiting a forest grove on a class expedition one day, he realizes that he has been there in his dreams; his inner self has visited the grove. This "complete severance of my body and my inner being" leads him to conclude that there is "some inscrutable locomotive faculty in the spirit with effects resembling those of locomotion in the body."[8]

Louis discovers that by thinking fiercely enough about a knife cutting his arm, he can actually feel the pain. His focus on the inner self becomes obsessive. He falls in love with a woman, Claire, whom he has glimpsed only from a distance. He writes her passionate love letters, so much so that he persuades her—by correspondence—to agree to marry him. But as the wedding draws near, he becomes so terrified at his coming encounter with the real world that he decides to castrate himself. His friends only narrowly restrain him. He lives out his days with Claire, though in a semicatatonic state. She, recognizing the potential he once had, protects him lovingly.

Before we move on to Balzac's next occult novel, *Seraphita* (1835), which embraces the Swedenborgian thought-system more completely, let's find out exactly who was this Swedenborg of whom Balzac wrote, in a letter to his Polish fiancée, Madame de Hanska, in 1837: "I am not orthodox, and I do not believe in the Roman church. Swedenborgianism, which is but a repetition, in the Christian sense, of ancient ideas, is my religion, with this addition: that I believe in the incomprehensibility of God."[9]

Emanuel Swedenborg (1688–1772), who spent his life in Stockholm, was initially a scientist and mechanical engineer of some renown. He made discoveries in mathematics and mechanics and came up with a method for transporting boats forty miles overland. He developed a prototype of the submarine and was on his way to inventing the airplane.

At fifty-five, he abruptly found himself prey to intense otherworldly visions. In sudden trance states, or in dreams while sleeping, he talked to the angels, who appeared to him as vividly as did his friends and acquaintances. He recorded these encounters in a series of books, notably *Heaven and Hell* (1758). Swedenborg's revelations became so popular that the French novelist Gustave Flaubert summarized them, albeit disdainfully, in *Bouvard et Pécuchet* (Bouvard and Pécuchet), published posthumously in 1881. Flaubert wrote:

> Swedenborg made long journeys there [to luminous places in outer space peopled by spirits]. In less than a year he explored [through astral traveling] Venus, Mars, Saturn and—twenty-three times— Jupiter. Moreover, he saw Jesus Christ in London, he saw St. Paul, he saw St. John, he saw Moses, and in 1736, he even saw the Last Judgment. He also gave us descriptions of heaven. You find there flowers, palaces, markets and churches, as with us. The angels, who were once men, inscribe their thoughts on tablets, gossip about domestic or spiritual matters, and the office of priest belongs to

those who, in their terrestrial life, have studied Holy Scripture. As for hell, it is filled with a disgusting stench, with hovels, muck heaps, quagmires, persons shabbily dressed.[10]

But it was, and is, hard to dismiss Swedenborg. He came to his visionary experiences from a solid scientific background. His psychic encounters were such as to confound us even to this day: While at a dinner party in Gothenburg with sixteen guests, he observed and reported on a fire in Stockholm 280 miles away (his account included mention of a friend's house that was burning to the ground); every detail of his account proved to be correct. In *Seraphita,* Balzac has Pastor Becker relate the true story of how, in 1758, Swedenborg disclosed to Queen Louisa-Ulrica of Sweden a secret that he said he had learned from her deceased brother, the prince of Prussia, in heaven—a secret that only the queen and her brother knew. Swedenborg was extremely influential; his works impacted a whole generation of nineteenth-century thinkers and writers including Blake, Emerson, Coleridge, Carlyle, Henry James Sr., Tennyson, the Brownings, Thoreau, and Goethe.

*Seraphita* is shot through with Swedenborgianism. Mircea Eliade, in *The Two and the One,* comments on the novel:

> *Seraphita* is undoubtedly the most attractive of Balzac's fantastic novels. Not because of the Swedenborgian theories with which it is imbued but because Balzac here succeeded in presenting with unparalleled force a fundamental theme of archaic anthropology: the androgyne considered as the exemplary image of the perfect man. Let us recall the novel's subject and setting. In a castle on the edge of the village of Jarvis, near the Stromfjord, lived a strange being of moving and melancholy beauty. Like certain other Balzac characters, he seemed to hide a terrible "secret," an "impenetrable mystery.". . . He is a being different in quality from the rest of mankind, and his "mystery" depends not on certain dark episodes in his past

but on the nature of his own being. For the mysterious personage loves and is loved by Minna, who sees him as a man, and is also loved by Wilfred [Wilfrid], in whose eyes he seems to be a woman, Seraphita.

This perfect androgyne was born of parents who had been disciples of Swedenborg. Although he had never left his own fjord, never opened a book, spoken to any learned person or practiced any art, Seraphitus-Seraphita displayed considerable erudition; his mental faculties surpassed those of mortal men. Balzac describes with moving simplicity the nature of this androgyne, his solitary life and ecstasies in contemplation. All this is patently based on Swedenborg's doctrine, for the novel was primarily written to illustrate and comment on the Swedenborgian theories of the perfect man. But Balzac's androgyne hardly belongs to the earth. His spiritual life is entirely directed toward heaven. Seraphitus-Seraphita lives only to purify himself—and to love. Although Balzac does not expressly say so, one realizes that Seraphitus-Seraphita cannot leave the earth before he has known love. This is perhaps the last and most precious virtue: for two people of opposite sex to love *really* and jointly. Seraphic love no doubt, but not an abstract or generalized love all the same. Balzac's androgyne loves two well-individualized beings; he remains therefore in the concrete world of life. He is not an angel come down to earth; he is a perfect man, that is to say a "complete being."[11]

Another of the characters, the pastor Becker, has read all of Swedenborg's works and holds forth on them freely. Seraphita's parents are not only devoted to Swedenborg but also related to him; their sole function on earth seems to have been to rear the pristine, pure, Swedenborgian Seraphita.

There is a great deal of talk in this novel about being a Specialist. This is a Swedenborgian term referring to the top tier of humanity—the great souls, like Napoleon and Jesus Christ, who are capable of singlehandedly changing history. The eponymous hero of *Louis Lambert* has played with the idea that he might be a Specialist. In *Seraphita,* Wilfrid imagines that he himself might be one of this elite few. Seraphita disabuses him of this idea, revealing that it is she who plays the role of Specialist in this earthly lifetime.

Seraphita also reveals to them that Minna and Wilfrid have been readied over several previous incarnations to separate themselves from this world; Seraphita's final task is to initiate them into a state that will prepare them both for Specialisthood, apparently in their next—and final—lifetime. She accomplishes this, bringing about the cessation of all carnal desire in both Wilfrid and Minna. Once in this state, they understand the true nature of Seraphita.

Seraphita/Seraphitus dies, mission apparently accomplished. Standing over the body of the beloved androgyne, Wilfrid and Minna sense themselves leaving their own bodies to embark on an astral journey. They are to tour the lower regions of astral space. The angelic soul of Seraphita/Seraphitus will be their guide.

Balzac's 1834 novel about alchemy and obsession, *The Quest of the Absolute* (*La recherche de l'absolu*), is all the more poignant in that it contains a number of ordinary people who are crushed by the obsessive dream of extraordinary accomplishment of the novel's hero. This is Balthazar Claës, a Flemish alchemist who strives day and night to discover the single, indivisible element in the universe of which all things are made and whose discovery, he believes, will enable him to transmute base metals into gold.

We first meet Claës through the eyes of his loving wife, Josephine, as she endures the dreaded daily routine of hearing the mechanical shuffling of his feet as he tramps slowly downstairs after spending many long hours in his alchemist's laboratory. Balzac describes him standing in the doorway:

> . . . at the present moment the man of fifty or thereabouts might have been sixty years of age. . . . His tall figure was slightly bent;

perhaps he had contracted the habit by stooping over his books, or perhaps the curvature was due to the weight of a head over-heavy for the spine. He was broad-chested and square-shouldered; his lower extremities, though muscular, were thin; you could not help casting about for some explanation of this puzzling singularity in a frame which evidently had once been perfectly proportioned. His thick, fair hair fell carelessly over his shoulders in the German fashion, in a disorder which was quite in keeping with a strange air of slovenliness and general neglect.[12]

As he disappears once more, soon to reascend to his laboratory, Josephine weeps, not only because he has spent the entire family fortune on alchemical supplies (he does this twice over), but also because she knows that occult science has replaced her in his affections. Biographer Graham Robb comments: "There are times when he [Balthazar] seems to be aware of his state of obsessed folly, but he always returns to it, and not even his wife's despair can save him. The house of Claës goes down in ruin. The 'Idea of the Absolute' had ravaged it like a fire."[13]

Ironically, Claës succeeds in the end—although he is not actually present when his apparatus yields up a single diamond, and so can't take notes of the exact circumstances that made this happen, including the random factor of sunlight pouring in through the window. He has lost everything—except for something that Balzac, finally, regards as much greater than a diamond or gold: the undying devotion of a wife.

The wretched Balthazar does not aspire to be a Specialist, nor is there any mention of the term in the book. Balzac himself aspired to be the "Napoleon of literature," and in fact he succeeded. It seems likely this vigorous genius reserved the term for himself.

# *Ten*

## Victor Hugo
## (1802–1885)

### *What the Shadow's Mouth Says*

When Napoleon III seized control of France on December 2, 1851, a number of important intellectuals and politicians who had opposed his rise to power were forced to flee the country.

Not the least of them was Victor Hugo, who, though he wouldn't complete *Les Misérables* for another decade, was already world famous for his poetry, for his novel *The Hunchback of Notre Dame,* and for his tradition-breaking stage plays. Hugo was also a member of parliament whose courageous stand against Napoleon III now made him even more famous. After an eight-month stopover in Brussels, he went on to Jersey, an island in the English Channel, where, arriving before a cheering crowd, he was reunited with his family and began a lengthy stay.

Other famous and not-so-famous political exiles found their way to Jersey island as a place of refuge from Napoleon III. One of the less well known was a small, hunchbacked journalist who had been the editor of the radical newspaper *Revolution* before the coup d'état; this was Hennett de Kesler. He had been arrested during the street fighting of December 4, 1851; been incarcerated aboard the prison ship *Duguesclin* for three months; almost been transported across the Atlantic to life imprisonment at Devil's Island, in French Guinea; and then, abruptly, on the arrival of the *Duguesclin* at Brest, been released and told to get out of France. He had gone to London. Then, after more than two years—in May 1854—he had come to Jersey.[1]

Here he was reunited with Victor Hugo, whom he had not seen since they had defied Napoleon III together on the barricades in December 1851. Kesler, slowly settling into a room near Hugo's house, discovered that something new was occupying a portion of the great man's mind. In mid-1852—seven months after Napoleon III's seizure of power—a craze for communicating with the spirits of the dead through "tapping tables" had swept the country. Most of the intelligentsia and the aristocracy were captivated by this exotic fad and spent several hours a day watching a table leg rap out coded messages from the beyond by banging against a second table.

Kesler had heard a little, not much, about this mania while he was in England. Now he discovered that the great Victor Hugo—who nonetheless still filled his days with literary and political work—was much taken with this new craze. Apparently, the great author communicated with the spirit world, via the tables, two or three times a week.

Now he urged Hennett de Kesler to participate in a séance. Kesler resisted. He was honored and awed by the great man's friendship. He was beholden to Hugo, who gave him money and often had him over to his house for dinner. But Kesler was an atheist. He was most bitterly an atheist, first because of the scorn and ridicule that had been heaped on him since his earliest schooldays on account of the distorted shape of his hunchbacked body, then because of a searing personal loss he had suffered twenty years ago, and now because of the cruelties he had witnessed on the barricades and later in the prison ship.

Hugo persisted in trying to persuade Kesler to attend a séance.

Finally, Kesler could resist no more. On the night of June 2, 1854, he sat down at the tapping tables with Victor Hugo, with Hugo's wife, Adèle, and with Hugo's older son, Charles, who apparently was the medium. Two other political exiles were in attendance.

During that séance, something extraordinary and heart-rending happened—something that had meaning only for him, Hennett de Kesler.

The séance began with his watching tensely, speaking with a courtesy that belied his disdain, as Hugo and his son placed the little three-legged table on the larger four-legged table and then laid one hand each on top of the three-legged table. Hugo explained that you asked the table questions—or, rather, you asked the spirits questions—and then, if you were lucky, the spirits responded by tapping one leg of the three-legged table on the top of the four-legged table. A lengthy series of taps would follow, one tap signifying A, two taps B, and so on, up to twenty-six taps for Z.

That night, for the first twenty minutes, nothing happened.

Then the three-legged table began to shake. There was a long stream of taps. The "spirit"—if it was indeed a spirit—spelled out the word *Marie*. There were more taps; the table-leg, moving swiftly up and down, informed them that Marie had come *to liberate the disbeliever by speaking to him from the grave.* The tapping continued; Hugo, scribbling in a notebook, read them the words as the spirit tapped them out. It seemed that this spirit, when in mortal flesh, had known Kesler—had even been loved by Kesler.

Leaning his twisted body forward, Kesler asked if he was speaking to his grandmother.

The table leg did not move.

Kesler asked impulsively: "Are you the Marquise de Marialva?"

The table leg was still. The participants sensed confusion. Then it shakily tapped out a number of odd phrases; *death's barricade* was one.

Then these two words emerged: *Marie Blanche* (Marie White).

In Spanish *alva* was sometimes spelled "alba," Victor Hugo informed them quickly. "Blanche" was a lesser-known meaning of alba. *Marie Blanche* could be Marialva.

Kesler bent forward, feeling faint. Afterward he would not be able to remember the odd, staccato, often one-word exchanges that took place over the next several minutes.

All he would remember was that suddenly the table had tapped out with firm raps: *Why are you carrying Marie?*

This shocked Kesler. He was carrying around his neck, on a chain hidden beneath his collar, a locket containing a picture of the Marquise de Marialva.

His hand moved involuntarily to protect it.

Kesler looked away, then back at the table. He stammered: "Why have *you* been chosen, *you* of all people, to come to liberate me from my disbelief?"

The table tapped out: *The woman you loved takes precedence over all the other loves in your life. God has chosen her to carry His message to you.*

Kesler fell back slowly in his chair. The spirit did not add to this, but did not depart. They had a brief exchange about Kesler's troubled relationship with his father. Then the little journalist did something he rarely allowed himself to do: he let the memory of Adèle de Marialva's last hours well up in his mind and heart. Then he asked the tapping tables: "Could you say two or three words to describe the thought that is now in my head?"

The table tapped out: *Dagger.*[2]*

Afterward, in his tiny room a mile from Victor Hugo's house, Kesler, sitting back in his single, shabby armchair, surrounded by the meager array of his possessions, lifted the locket from around his neck, opened

---

*The reader is directed to the author's *Victor Hugo's Conversations with the Spirit World: A Literary Genius's Hidden Life* (Inner Traditions/Destiny, 2008), which contains complete translations of the transcripts of the more important of the numerous séances in which Victor Hugo participated on Jersey, along with accounts of the day-to-day activities of Hugo, his family, and his fellow proscrits while in political exile from 1852 to 1855.

it, and gazed at the portrait of the Marquise de Marialva—Adèle de Marialva, whom he had loved twenty years before, whom he had never ceased to love, and who had stabbed herself three times with a dagger and died before his eyes.

The reasons? He hadn't understood them then, and he did not want to think about them now. Sitting in his shabby armchair, he dissolved into tears and wept. Then he tore himself away from the memory and brought himself back to the present. He thought: What just happened with the tapping tables, how could it possibly have happened?

Nobody knew about his love affair with Adèle.

Kesler would repeat this sentence to himself a hundred times over the next several days: Nobody knew. At the time of her death, twenty years before, few had known about the Marquise de Marialva and himself. And now those few were far away, or dead. Victor Hugo did not know about Adèle de Marialva. Nobody on Jersey island knew about Adèle de Marialva.

Then how had the spirits known?

Over the next few weeks, Kesler, affecting a nonchalance he did not feel, plied Victor Hugo with questions about the tapping tables. The great author was forthcoming. He and his family and friends had been communicating with the spirit world since September 1853. Mighty spirits had come: Shakespeare, Molière, Hannibal. Spirits who said they'd never been alive, like the Shadow of the Sepulcher, had come tapping through the tables. The shades of legendary animals, like Balaam's ass, arrived to give them lectures on the nature of the universe. Hugo kept three notebooks in which he recorded the spirits' utterances. He had a thousand ideas about what they were: exactly who they said they were; or a single spirit, pretending to be all the spirits; or his son Charles's intelligence (Charles was the medium), magnified five times through the agency of the tables; or all of the participants put together, somehow unconsciously creating a marvelous network of utterances. And there were other explanations.

Whoever these spirits were, Hugo considered the transcripts of the séances to be the Bible of the Future.

Victor Hugo had so many stories to tell Kesler! One night a spirit came to the exiled Hungarian count Sandor Teleki and tapped out a message in Hungarian for him. Teleki was the only one at the séance who knew Hungarian. Another time, while they were conversing with a spirit calling itself the Grim Gatekeeper, all the dogs in the neighboring streets began to bark. The spirit rapped out sternly, "Shut up, dogs!" Immediately, the dogs were silent.

The "Lady in White" was the shade of a woman who had been executed for infanticide three thousand years ago by the druid priests whose sculpted stone columns, called dolmens, many of them twice as tall as a man, still dotted Jersey island. She spoke through the tables from time to time—and even arranged a rendezvous, a real meeting, in the flesh, on the street outside Hugo's house, for three o'clock one morning. No one had been bold enough to keep the date, but Hugo's doorbell had rung inexplicably at 3:00 a.m.

As he attended the séances more and more often, the phantasms of the tapping tables began to merge subtly with Kesler's awakened yearnings. Did the Lady in White—*La Dame Blanche*—have any connection with *Marie Blanche*—with Adèle de Marialva? Possessed by this thought, he began to flirt inanely with this spirit, even arranging to meet her at a certain hour under a certain tree outside his rooming house. But this was foolishness; he was losing his reason. . . . He didn't attend the rendezvous.

Increasingly Kesler's days were taken up with giving private French lessons to the local residents, with writing articles for radical republican journals, with earning his daily bread in any way he could. He suffered privations; he escaped them by dreaming of Adèle de Marialva. It sometimes seemed to him that he felt, ever so lightly caressing his cheek as he toiled away at his work, something like a light, fresh, subtly perfumed breeze. Was this his imagination? Or was it that the spirit of Adèle having been birthed by the tapping tables into this time and place, was now following him modestly, at a distance—hastening forward at times to touch him lovingly—bringing relief to his starved and desperate soul?

At the beginning of August 1854, Victor Hugo announced an extraordinary event. The great man had written a poem—one that contained the essence of what the tapping table spirits had told him, but one that he had written in homage to the ancient druid priests whose spirits haunted the island. Often at night, visiting in the moonlight the fallen columns of the druid temples scattered across the island, he thought he heard, rustling from the recesses of those columns, from their moss-covered indentations, the whispering of priests, their murmurs of terrified supplication to the gods and goddesses they feared. There was one rough-hewn pillar that, still standing erect and proud under the moon, displayed on its broad and rounded side a deep, jagged indentation that looked to Victor Hugo like a mouth—a mouth filled with shadow, a mouth that spoke to him.

His new poem would be called *What the Shadow's Mouth Says*. He told them all that he would read aloud from the poem beside that same stately column, which the people of Jersey called the Dolmen of Le Couperon, and which was a part of the ruins of a druid temple. It stood like a sentinel on the brow of the hill overlooking Rozel Beach. He would give the reading on the night of the first full moon of August. All who wished could come and hear his poem.

Hennett de Kesler wondered—and knew this must be what madmen wondered—if, through the power of Hugo's words, through the intercession of the gods and the spirit druids assembled there that night, through the power of the full moon, Adèle de Marialva might show herself to him, if only for a moment.

He decided he would attend the reading.

And so it was that at eight o'clock on the evening of August 12, 1854, Hennett de Kesler, his gray terrier Casemate (given to him by Victor Hugo) trotting by his side, began climbing the grassy slope that led up from the beach at Rozel to the druid temple called Le Couperon. He had spent the late afternoon scouring the tide line for local flora and fauna (a hobby dear to him for its lack of expense). At seven o'clock he had eaten his cheese and three biscuits and drunk his water; then, as darkness fell, he had thrust a small bag containing a lantern over his shoulder and begun to hoist his twisted body up the hill, whose grass was still warm from the summer sun.

Victor Hugo, with son Charles, would drive a two-horse carriage to the end of the nearest road. That way they would all be able to get home at the end of the reading.

Kesler had never been able to walk quickly due to his hunchbacked frame. Now he stumbled forward with a slight turning motion, peering ahead, trying to make out the ruined temple whose location Victor Hugo had described so carefully to him.

Tapping table spirits, shades of druid priests—all that notwithstanding, Kesler did not believe that God existed. He believed that evil existed. He could feel it; he could smell it sometimes. Victor Hugo believed that God existed and evil did not. He had asked Kesler: What do you believe in? And Kesler had replied: in friendship, in those women I can respect and admire, in love, in flowers. Victor Hugo had accused him of being a nihilist. But he was not—not quite. He believed in Adéle de Marialva; he believed she might—just *might*—be waiting for him, in some guise more than one of spirit, on this beguiling night.

The clouds that drifted overhead still hid the face of the moon. The sky was now dark. Kesler stopped and taking the lantern out of his bag lit it thoughtfully. What held the universe together, according to these spirits, was an immense chain of reincarnation. All of material existence was imbued with spirit. Soul gravitated from stone to plant to animal to man to angel—passed upward by a process of reincarnation that required great struggle and good actions. But this reincarnation was terrifying in its unforgiving nature. You could labor through a hundred lifetimes to attain the state of human—and then, by virtue of a single heinous act, you could tumble in a single rebirth right back down to the bottom of the ladder of being and reawaken as a stone even though, a reincarnational moment earlier, angelhood had been within your grasp.

This unforgivingness was mainly true of our planet earth. It seemed, especially according to the spirit known as Balaam's ass, that our world was not only a prison planet but also one of the most severe of the prison worlds. Every stone, every plant, every animal, every human on earth had a soul, but in every case it was the reincarnated soul of someone who had committed a frightful crime in a previous lifetime. You could never remember what you had done, but you would always know that you had done something awful, or you would not be here on earth. Remembering or not remembering, you had to strive to do as much good in this one lifetime as you could. That way lay salvation, or elevation to a higher plane—perhaps.

Kesler could believe that our earth was the cruelest of worlds. As he moved forward again, holding the lantern up at shoulder height, he remembered his incarceration on the prison ship *Duguesclin*. He had been thrown into the hold with 140 other political detainees, all foes of Napoleon III, many of them distinguished men. Once a day, scraps of food were thrown into the hold for them as if they were dogs. The hold was infested with fleas. The inside of your coat became infested. But you couldn't throw away your coat; if you did so, you would freeze to death. Once a day, the jailers brought you out on the deck. This was no festive occasion. Once you were out on deck, a net was thrown over the lot of you while on four sides four loaded cannons waited to shoot anyone who tried to escape. You could not mingle with your jailers. Then there were the whippings. Here was the very stench of evil. You wanted to look away, but you were forced to watch.

After three months, when they arrived at the port of Brest, he had been taken to the captain's quarters and told he would be transported to Devil's Island, there to spend the rest of his life. There would be no trial. The sentence would be carried out immediately.

Three days later, when he had hardly slept, when he had hardly eaten—when he had decided to throw away his coat and freeze—they came to him and told him he was free to leave on condition that he get out of France immediately.[3]

Five days later, Kesler had arrived in London.

Now, in the distance, by the light of two lanterns glowing on the roof, Kesler could make out the three columns of the temple. These stood erect, close together, a stone slab lying atop them to make the roof. This was the place from which, millennia ago, the burial grounds of the druids had spread out into the fields.

Kesler moved closer. The clouds had drifted away from the face of the moon, but the night was scarcely any brighter. Much of the moon was an orange-gray. Kesler had heard vaguely there would be an eclipse tonight, though he hardly bothered with such matters these days.

Beside him Casemate, his gray terrier, stopped and bayed strangely at the moon.

Kesler looked down. He had forgotten about the dog. Usually Casemate was silent. But something was bothering him tonight. Kesler peered up at the moon. Tiny specks of black, sparkling at the edges, seemed to streak across its face, plummeting almost straight downward. The evening had been warm and breezy, but now the night was close, oppressive. The wind had dropped; there was no breeze at all.

He was moving forward, while Casement hung back and bayed again at the moon. The druid temple was about fifty feet away. Kesler could make out the figures of Victor Hugo's two sons, Charles and François-Victor. They moved slowly, heavily between the pillars, as if they weighed too much for this planet. He saw the long, angular figure of the always irritated playwright Auguste Vacquerie, slumped against the trunk of a tree; beside him, stretched out on the ground, lay the plump, untidy philosopher Pierre Leroux. Two other political exiles— Kesler was not sure of their names—lounged a little farther back.

He stumbled forward. Victor Hugo emerged from between the figures and, striding out across the grass, came quickly to Kesler and grasped his hand.

"My dear fellow," he exclaimed. "You have come! To what do I owe this honor?"

It was the case that Victor Hugo, whatever he thought of himself, whatever he really was, always behaved among his friends and colleagues as if he were the humblest of the humble, as if he had no right to be here—as if he were honored to be among them at all.

The stars had come out in a part of the sky, but feebly. The air was still close. The interior of the temple, as Kesler approached it, seemed airless. Casemate was baying strangely at the moon again, and Kesler, glancing up at the sky, saw near the constellation Orion what must have been a meteor shower. They were sparks so dim they might have been flecks of gold dust cast across the sky, but he saw them clearly, streaking past the stars and plummeting downward.

Victor Hugo led him to a fallen log just outside the temple and sat him down. Hugo beckoned to the others to sit. They settled into a kind of uneven row on the other side.

The Great Man—he was also their benefactor—had invited them to come, and they could not refuse. But they did not want to be here. They stood, they drooped, they sat, they knelt—they lay stretched out on the ground, huddled in various postures of dejection. It did not surprise Kesler that they should look so pained, so awkward, so uncomfortable: they were, after all, Paris intellectuals; they were spoiled, disdainful, wealthy; they did not like to sit on the damp ground in a wild dark forest with a cliff falling down to the sea on one side and on the other the ghosts of the druid dead crowding in upon them.

They looked haunted and alone and frightened. They looked as if they had fallen from the skies themselves, from a world whose name they had forgotten or never knew, on a trip they never wanted to take, to a world whose name they did not know—as if they themselves had been the very meteors, now taken flesh, that he had seen plummeting down beside the moon.

Victor Hugo stood up and looked around. "*Les enfants,*" he said, "I will begin. Listen. This is what the voice of the Shadow's Mouth has

told me. And I believe," he glanced around, "that all of nature has conspired tonight to help me tell my story. Let me begin."

And, standing in the center of the temple, with two large lanterns
to either side of him, he began, in soft, melodious, measured tones, to
recite his poem:

> *Know that everything has its law, its goal, its way;*
> *That from star to microbe, infinity keeps all parts in*
> *constant touch;*
> *That everything in creation is aware;*
> *The ear hears visions the eye can never see,*
> *Because the created world and being are locked in mighty*
> *discourse;*
> *Everything speaks; the passing air and the seabird that*
> *calms the scudding wave,*
> *Each blade of grass, flower, seed and element*
> *Did you imagine the universe otherwise?*
> *Do you believe that God, who brings forth form from*
> *formula*
> *Would make a forest that never made a sound?*
> *Storm, torrents gushing out from blackest mud,*
> *Rocks rearing out of waves, beasts on the mountain*
> *slopes*
> *The house-fly, bush and blackberry-yielding bramble;*
> *That He would not have given voice to the eternal*
> *murmurings of them all?*
> *Do you think that nature in all its vastness merely*
> *stutters,*
> *That God, in all His greatness, could take pleasure*
> *throughout eternity*
> *In listening only to a deaf-mute's stammer?*
> *No, the abyss is a priest and the shadows are a poet;*
> *No, all is voice and all of it is perfumed;*

*Thought fills up all of this superb tumult.*
*God made no noise without blending it with His Word.*
*Everything moans, like you—or sings, like me, the poet.*
*Everything speaks. And now, mankind, do you not know*
     *why everything speaks?*
*Listen well: it is because the winds, the waves, the flames,*
*Trees, reeds and rocks—everything is alive!*
*Everything is filled with souls.*
*How can this be? This unheard-of mystery!*[4]

Hugo now began to recite eloquently—gorgeously—the story of that great chain of being through which every soul passes, from stone to angelhood, and of that God (it seemed to Kesler this was a God of the Gnostics) who, having left at least an atom of Himself in everything, had long been in retreat from humankind and now dwelt far away, unable (and unwilling, it almost seemed) to intervene in human life. Kesler listened, oddly content as well as anxious, sitting on the grass beyond the inner circle of the temple. He looked around, searching in the woods, among the trees, for . . . What? The glimmer of a sign, telling him that Adèle de Marialva waited for him somewhere nearby—?

His attention was wrenched back to Hugo. The poet had just told them that he was about to jump forward in the poem, to the place where the spirits described the foulness of our earth. Kesler listened reluctantly, mesmerized.

*Prepare you, saddened brow, to sweat yet sadder drops.*
*The wind from heaven tears through me, and what it rips*
     *away*
*I throw to you; take it, and see.*
*And first of all, know*
*That the world you live in is one that terrifies.*
*The gentle dreamer, forced to confront this world*
*Bent beneath infinity's fell weight*

*Raises his arms to the sky and awestruck recoils in*
   *horror.*
*Your sun is gloomy, your earth a den of horrors.*
*You live on the doorstep of a world of punishment.*
*But you are not completely cut off from your God;*
*God—that sun in azure sky, that spark in ashes—*
*Is cut off from nothing; He is that towards which*
   *everything tends.*
*His glance is lightning as much as it is sunbeam*
*And everything, even evil, is His creation*
*Because the mask's interior is still shaped like the face.*[5]

Hugo now moved forward in the poem, leaving out sections, commenting as he did. He was coming now, he said, to what the spirits of the tapping tables—and, for that matter, the ghosts of the druid priests whispering to him from these columns—said about humanity, about our nature. They, the audience, all men and all women, must listen closely, and not upbraid themselves, but understand:

*On your world of prisons filled with rank disease*
*There dwell the wicked of all the universe*
*The condemned who, come from alien skies diverse,*
*Brood in your rocks, bow with your wind-tossed trees.*
*Let me tell the somber tale in all its horror.*
*Your world is a sewage pipe of endless evil.*
*From every point in the sky, spiraling downward*
*With foul and streaming tails, souls plummet*
*To this cosmic end-of-the-line, this latrine-world,*
*This place of punishment—this planet earth!*[6]

Hugo's voice rolled on, and no one in the audience was restless now. Kesler listened, to this great voice, to these mighty words that if they spoke of evil, also returned the coolness to the night and made it, in the mind's eye, seem like day. Kesler looked around him. Perhaps, at least, there were creative geniuses, like Hugo, who could sing of evil in such a way as to render it into beauty. Perhaps, if there was no God, there were at least godlike creators. Perhaps, one day, against the fall of night, against the darkness, Adèle de Marialva would return to him again.

When Victor Hugo moved with his family to the island of Guernsey in the fall of 1855, Hennett de Kesler, along with a number of other exiles, accompanied him. For the last four years of his life, Kesler lodged in Victor Hugo's house. The Hugos did not ask him for room or board.

Kesler died on April 6, 1870. He had stipulated in his last will and testament that his coffin was not to be taken to a church because he "wished no other priest than Victor Hugo." Victor Hugo gave the funeral oration over his grave, in the cemetery of the exiles.

# *Eleven*

## Jules Verne
## (1828–1905)

### *The Prophet as Peter Pan*

Jules Verne is one of the most difficult of all the distinguished authors of the modern era to assess in terms of contact with spiritual worlds. The author of *Twenty Thousand Leagues under the Sea* is an enigma surrounding a riddle. Inside that riddle, the investigator touches upon something so elusive as to be almost an emptiness—a kind of black hole, or a void.

There must have been moments of joy in the life of the man who also wrote *Around the World in Eighty Days, A Descent into the Interior of the Earth,* and seventy-seven other novels, most of which have sold well since the day they were published. UNESCO's Index Translationum for 2008 ranks Jules Verne as the second most translated author in the world, with 4,185 translations of his works on record. (Agatha Christie is first with 6,543 translations and Shakespeare third with 3,603.)[1]

But despite all this fame and fortune, dark clouds hang over most of Jules Verne's life. Sometimes they are quiescent; sometimes there is a steady drizzle; sometimes there are flashes of lightning and the growl of thunder. But the dark clouds never go away.

Here is an example. On March 9, 1886, at about 6:00 p.m., Jules Verne opened the front gate of his house in Amiens, France, and heard two shots ring out. He felt a sharp blow to his left shin and a spasm of excruciating pain.

A voice cried out: "You bastard!" Verne staggered through the front gate. Standing on his front lawn was his nephew Gaston Verne with a gun in his hand. The fifty-eight-year-old author had been walking home behind a neighbor. He shouted to the neighbor for help. A policeman appeared. The three of them subdued Gaston and hustled him into Verne's front parlor. He was soon in custody.

A week later, surgeons operated on Verne's ankle to remove the bullet, but they could not dislodge it. For the rest of his life, Verne walked with a distinct limp and was often in pain. Gaston had been his favorite nephew. The brilliant young man had just become a diplomatic attaché. It was true that he and his uncle quarreled from time to time, but there was nothing to suggest that something like this would happen.

Gaston seemed rational when he tried to kill Jules Verne. He had come up from Paris and had a return train ticket in his pocket. But Verne claimed his nephew had gone insane. The family kept the matter from ever going to trial. They said nothing to anyone about Gaston for the rest of their lives. He was sent to an asylum, and his whereabouts remained a mystery for many years. Only recently have we learned that Gaston spent fifty-two years in an asylum in Belgium, dying there in 1938.[2]

In *Jules Verne: la face cachée* (The Hidden Side of Jules Verne; 2005), Roger Maudhuy offers an explanation for why Gaston might have wanted to kill his uncle. Maudhuy says Jules Verne owned two houses in Amiens; that he was absent from his home for long periods of time; and that he burned all his manuscripts and papers shortly before he died. Maudhuy believes Verne, like former French president François Mitterrand, had a second wife and family and that Gaston Verne was not his nephew, but his son. But Maudhuy offers no evidence at all to support his theory.[3]

Jules Verne was born in Nantes, France, on February 8, 1828. His family was affluent, his father a lawyer. Can we trace the strange grayness of Verne's life to any aspect of his upbringing?

For a long time, people believed yes. Rumor had it that Verne's father beat his young son regularly. The son was said to have run off to sea at age twelve largely to escape the father. It was said that the father had pursued him, brought him back, and continued to beat him. It was further rumored that, in the words of William Butcher in *Jules Verne: The Definitive Biography,*

> Pierre's [the father's] religious fervor led him to self-mortification: to reinforce his wavering faith he would probably fast or even physically punish himself. This masochistic flagellation, recorded by Jules's grandson, was applied with a scourge. . . . Jules perhaps heard muffled groans and moans. Did he possibly wander in one day to find his father in flagrante delicto?[4]

Roger Maudhuy seems to put these rumors to rest. He declares that they were fabricated by Marguerite Allotte de la Fuÿe, a distant relative, who wanted the world to think Jules's climb to fame was even harder than it was.[5] It seems that Jules Verne's upbringing was not unhappy. He left Nantes for Paris in 1848 to study law. He was already thinking of becoming a writer.

There must have been happy times for Verne during his eight-year-long bachelorhood in Paris. His uncle introduced him into literary circles. He hit it off with Alexandre Dumas Jr., the successful author of plays like *The Lady of the Camellias.* Verne began to write plays and operettas himself. Only the one-act play *Les pailles rompues* (Broken Straws), co-written with Dumas, was ever produced; it had two runs in Paris in the summer of 1850. Dumas's father, Alexandre Dumas Sr., the acclaimed author of *The Count of Monte Cristo* and *The Three Musketeers,* also took to Verne and helped him when he could.

Verne completed his law studies. And then the odd, dismal grayness that characterized so much of his life began to reassert itself. In 1856, Verne married Honorine-Anna-Hebée Morel, née de Viane, a twenty-six-year-old widow with two small daughters. He hardly knew her and didn't seem to like her. They set up housekeeping in Paris. Verne bought an interest in the financial agency where he would work as a stock exchange broker until 1863. He got in the habit of staying away from home for longer and longer periods of time. Sometimes his wife knew where he was; sometimes she didn't. His absences became virtual disappearances.

He had never stopped writing. In 1862, he submitted a series of travel stories, *Les voyages extraordinaires,* to the celebrated publisher Pierre-Jules Hetzel. Hetzel published them as the novel *Five Weeks in a Balloon* in 1863. It was an instant success.

Verne began to churn out novel after novel. All were successes. But he had to pay a price—Hetzel insisted that Verne basically write only adventure stories for boys. When Verne didn't comply, Hetzel ruthlessly edited the novels himself, yanking out whatever he didn't like. Verne was not really allowed to mature as a writer, and this must have caused him severe psychological damage.

If Verne's novels were basically adventure stories for boys, how did they come to be so hugely popular? One reason is that they usually contained masterful extrapolations into the future of the scientific developments of Jules Verne's time.

Verne was in the right place at the right time: he loved machines in an era when machines that were getting cheaper suddenly made contact with a middle class that was getting wealthier and now could buy them. Machines were everywhere; they had always delighted Verne, and he had an uncanny knack for guessing how they might evolve. In *From the Earth to the Moon* (1865), a spaceship—or, rather, a cannonball hollowed out to provide living quarters for a crew of three—is blasted out of a cannon and reaches the moon. This 1869 "mission to the moon" of Verne's in some ways prefigured the flight of Apollo 9 a century later. "Our space vehicle," Frank Borman, the astronaut, wrote to Verne's grandson, "was launched from Florida, like [Verne's]; it had the same weight and the same height, and it splashed down in the Pacific a mere two and a half miles from the point mentioned in the novel."[6]

Verne's novels contain numerous glimpses of technological advances that have taken place in our time but were scarcely thought of in his. Journalist Edward J. Altmann writes that in *A Carpathian Castle* (1897) Verne anticipates the hologram: the villain invents a system of projectors that casts a three-dimensional image of the dead heroine onto the ramparts of a castle to trick the hero into thinking she is alive. In *The Chase of the Golden Meteor* (1901), a scientist uses light to change the trajectory of a meteor headed for the earth. (It wasn't until a century later that NASA came up with a plan for using light to deflect the path of a meteor that is on a collision course with Earth.) In *The Ice Sphinx* (1897), scientists discover that the continent of Antarctica is split by a section of unfrozen water hidden under the ice cap. (Only in the 1950s were actual scientists able to use new technologies to discover what appears to be a huge frozen lake hidden under the surface of Antarctica.[7])

One of the few Verne manuscripts Hetzel didn't publish was *Paris in the Twentieth Century* (1863), which was locked in a safe in the Verne family home and forgotten until it was discovered 130 years later by the novelist's grandson. Published in English in 1995, it so impressed "remote viewing" expert Joseph W. McMoneagle that he wonders if Verne did not actually have the power to see into the future. Remote viewing is the ability to telepathically see events that are taking place far away; McMoneagle speculates that Verne may have been practicing temporal remote viewing when he predicted gas-driven cars, fax machines, computers, and streets overrun with electronic advertisements in *Paris in the Twentieth Century*.[8]

Verne evoked the first artificial satellite in *The Begum's Fortune* (1879). In *The Green Ray* (1882), he wrote about the sort of cosmic rays that physicists pursued between the two world wars.[9] Interviewed by

John Lichfield on the hundredth anniversary of Verne's death, Jean-Paul Dekiss, director of France's Jules Verne Centre International, asserted that the novelist was "the first modern mythmaker. He was the first writer to try to tell the story of what happens after God is dethroned, what happens when Man begins to fashion his own world, what happens when Man shrinks the globe and re-creates the terms on which he had existed for thousands of years."[10]

Even as Jules Verne was moving from success to success professionally, troubling personal difficulties continued to cloud his life. Commentators can't really account for the appalling relationship he had with his only son, Michel.

In 1872, Verne hustled Michel, then aged eleven, off to the detention center at Mettray, near Tours. Michel was kept there for eight months, under the care of eminent psychiatrist (the word then was "alienist") Dr. Daniel Blanchard, who diagnosed the boy as having "a small dose of indisputable madness and a frightening perversity."

The boy had been a holy terror almost from the crib. As an adolescent he threatened his cousins and half sisters with assault; they were told to stay away from him. Verne had Michel jailed a second time, in January 1878, then had him forcibly transported to Bordeaux, where he was put aboard a merchant marine vessel bound for the East Indies. Michel turned up back in France fifteen months later. Wholly untamed, he fell in love with Thérèse Tâton, an actress three years his senior. Michel and Thérèse lived together. Eventually, they married, but not before Michel had run off with a seventeen-year-old girl, Jeanne Reboul, by whom he had already had two children. Michel divorced Thérèse in 1885 and married Jeanne. Throughout all this he incurred massive debts, which his father was obliged to pay off. In the year 1880 alone, Verne paid $60,000 to his son's creditors.

The two seemed to have reconciled, in a bizarre fashion, after Jules Verne's death. Verne left a number of unfinished manuscripts. Michel finished a portion of them and had them published without telling anyone he was the coauthor. The novels were not badly written, and they sold well.[11]

In *The Secret Message of Jules Verne: Decoding His Masonic, Rosicrucian, and Occult Writings,* Michael Lamy tells us that as a youth Verne was much given to punning and joking. Lamy writes, "Jules Verne always had a taste for farce and the pun . . . as an adolescent he was a comedian who always made jokes."[12] He was also much taken with puzzle solving and puzzle creating, particularly in the area of cryptograms. These activities spilled over into his adult life: "Similarly, the letters he wrote his parents and his publisher are studded with witty expressions."[13]

Lamy finds that this gift for punning, combined with Verne's skill with cryptograms, served him well in his novels: frequently, there are complex cryptograms and encoded messages at the heart of his books, upon whose correct decipherment the fate of the protagonists hinges. Lamy notes the veiled presence of the initiatory rituals of adult secret societies in Verne's work; this leads him to believe that Hugo was a member of secret societies and that the carrying out of initiatory rituals was often the occult, hidden plot of his novels. He cites *Michael Strogoff* (1876):

It would have been fairly simple for Jules Verne to procure information about the Masonic rituals for the apprentice, journeyman, and master, but not for the high grades, one of which is mentioned in *Michael Strogoff.* There, in fact, we see the hero fighting a bear, and much later, Michael Strogoff is tortured and becomes blind. We can see marked similarities in a passage from Charles Le Forestier's *La franc-maçonnerie templière et occultiste* [Templar and Occult Freemasonry] concerning the grades of Elect or Vengeance: "The candidate presents himself to the Venerable with red-spattered gloves, declaring that the blood that stains his hands was that of the bear, the tiger, and the lion that criminals had raised to guard the entrance to their den. The newly initiated member consents to die in the worst torture, after which his eyes will be ripped from the light with a red-hot iron, if he ever violates his oath of discretion."

This is what happens to Michael Strogoff after he breaks his oath in order to rescue his mother.[14]

Lamy maintains that Verne's late novel *Clovis Dardentor* (1896) displays knowledge of the Priory of Sion (even though it became virtually certain in the early 2000s that the Priory of Sion never existed) and in particular Rennes-le-Château, the French town where a huge treasure was said to have been deposited to ensure the upkeep of the priory. In *The Sion Revelation: The Truth About the Guardians of Christ's Sacred Bloodline,* authors Picknett and Prince write that Verne's novel

> *Clovis Dardentor* (1896), which recounts the adventures of a group of French travelers in Africa, contains not-so-veiled references to people and places connected not just with the Rennes-le-Château mystery but also with the preoccupations with the Priory of Sion.
>
> For example, at the helm of Dardentor's ship as it voyages from southern France to Algeria is Captain Bugarach, and the brooding and distinctive Pic (peak) de Bugarach is a four-thousand-foot-high former volcano, the most prominent feature looking south some 7.5 miles from Rennes-le-Château. This is the only place of that name in France. . . . *Clovis Dardentor* scintillates with significance for the Merovingian story. Clovis was the most famous of the Merovingian kings [said to carry the bloodline of Jesus Christ, which the Priory of Sion was formed to protect]; *ardent* recurs in the Dossiers Secrets [of the Priory] to describe the secret descendants of Dagobert II . . . *or* is gold, suggesting treasure. According to the French researcher Michel Lamy, the name Clovis Dardentor actually means "the gold of the descendants of the Merovingian kings."[15]

Picknett and Prince conclude that *Clovis Dardentor* is "one of the few weirdly true mysteries of the whole Priory business. . . . Yet oddly, according to Gaudart de Soulages and Lamant's *Dictionary of French*

*Freemasons,* Verne's name is even conspicuous by its absence on the register of any Masonic lodge."[16]

Did Jules Verne's terrible relations with his son, Michel, and his nephew Gaston stem from the fact that Jules Verne never grew up himself; that he was always a boy pretending to be a man; and that his son and nephew sensed this and resented his telling them what to do?

A fascination with the encoded, cryptographic language of secret societies combined with a compulsion to insert that language into novels—that is one path Verne's youthful obsession with punning, joking, cryptograms, and games certainly took. But Jules Verne as a man continued to talk like Jules Verne as a boy; it's as if those youthful obsessions not only continued into his manhood, but kept him from really attaining it. Such would explain a curious aspect of his novels: not only do they contain no sex, but they contain no romance and practically no women. John Lichfield comments: "There are no memorable Vernian women. There are almost no Vernian women at all. . . . [Almost all the novels are] 'female-free zones.'"[17]

The great attraction of Jules Verne's novels may lie in his ability, as a perennial youngster, to evoke the vanished world of boyhood and girlhood adventure, one that all adults unconsciously yearn for and even yearn for consciously in times of stress. Verne was a captive of this yearning, which he strove to satisfy all his life. His everyday conversation was the banter of an insecure teenager. He loved sailing and owned expensive, state-of-the-art yachts. Often, he went off on a sail with the guys; these voyages usually lasted quite some time. The trips took place during many of his explained absences and probably during many of his unexplained absences—the trips, and much else that boys love to do.

Verne temporarily satisfied this longing to return to boyhood every time he wrote a book. In his novels, Jules Verne's genius and his yearning come together to re-create the joy of adolescent and pre-adolescent adventures: tree houses and caves as meeting places; secret codes; oaths signed in blood; treasure hunts; and adventure-filled voyages in which routes are determined by the decipherment of clues.

In *Twenty Thousand Leagues Under the Sea* (1866–69), the gang members are Dr. Aronnax, a naturalist; Conseil, his trusty servant; Ned Land, a Canadian harpooner; and the mysterious Captain Nemo, in whose submarine, the *Nautilus,* they all take a trip around the world. Like Jules Verne, these four men are Peter Pans; they are all involved in a treasure hunt that is the equal of any that ever took place in Never-Never-Land. Their great adventure includes a trip to Atlantis, a fight with giant squids, visits to sunken ships, diving suits that allow them to harvest coral from underwater reefs, and a trip to the South Pole. The secret clubhouse par excellence is the *Nautilus:* Nemo's quarters contain a smoking lounge, a bar, and a living room exquisitely paneled in wood from which Old Masters originals hang. There are flowing tapestries, sheets of music in the hand of great composers, a collection of undersea artifacts, a library of ten thousand books (including all the books on naturalism written by Doctor Aronnax)—and an organ.

But the organ has only black keys.

And here the eternal note of sadness in Jules Verne's life returns. The high point of the voyage of the *Nautilus* is a trip to the South Pole, but here the only color is black, or gray. Nemo surfaces at the pole on June 21, the shortest and darkest day of the year in the Southern Hemisphere. He plants a black flag and claims the gloomy continent for himself, crying out, "Adieu, sun! Disappear, thou radiant orb! Rest beneath this open sea, and let a night of six months spread its shadows over my new domains."[18] Earlier, he has told Aronnax, "I am dead, Professor; as dead as those of your friends who are sleeping six feet under the earth!"[19]

Are we talking about the soul of Jules Verne here? Nemo has a secret: a Polish count, he was driven to this life-in-death by the murder of his wife and children by revolutionaries as Verne's *The Mysterious Island* reveals. Was there a strange deadness in Jules Verne for which he found metaphorical expression in the bitter life of Nemo? We may never know. What seems certain is that the adventure novels of Jules Verne, spiced with penetrating glimpses of the future of science, will endure as long as mankind has a future.

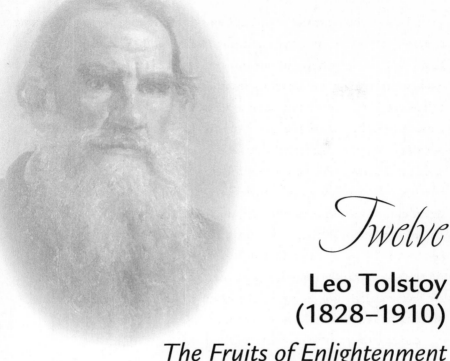

# Twelve

## Leo Tolstoy
## (1828–1910)

### *The Fruits of Enlightenment*

It's dangerous to leap into the middle of one of the great and vast Russian novels of the nineteenth century without knowing the beginning or the end. You risk confusion, or total disorientation, or culture shock. This is no more true than of the works of Count Leo Tolstoy, considered to be as great a literary artist as Shakespeare or Homer, and whose novels, like *War and Peace* (1869), can span decades and draw in characters from every walk of life.

Nevertheless, we'll risk that leap for Tolstoy's 1878 novel *Anna Karenina,* because it will take us directly to the heart of one of the most famous séance scenes in all of literature. The séance takes place in the parlour of a high-society countess in St. Petersburg, Russia. Here we meet Alexei Alexandrovich Karenin, who has come to the séance to ask the spirits if he should grant his wife Anna's request for a divorce; Anna has run off with another man. We also meet Stepan Arkadyich

Oblonsky, Anna's brother, who has come to the séance because he wants to join with his sister in asking Alexei Karenin for a divorce for Anna. (He has also come because he's looking for a job and hopes to get the well-connected countess to pull some strings for him.)

Most important, in this scene we meet the medium, a Frenchman named Jules Landau, who it's very likely Tolstoy modeled after the world-famous Scottish medium Daniel Dunglas Home (1833–1886). Tolstoy had attended one of Home's séances in Paris. The medium was well known to Russian society, having married two Russian wives.

Here's how the scene begins, as seen through the eyes of Stepan Arkadyich Oblonsky, who has just arrived:

> At a round table under a lamp the countess and Alexei Alexandrovich [Karenin] sat talking about something in low voices. A short, lean man with womanish hips and knock-kneed legs, very pale, handsome, with beautiful, shining eyes and long hair falling over the collar of his frock coat, stood at the other end, studying the portraits on the wall. Having greeted the hostess and Alexei Alexandrovich, Stepan Arkadyich involuntarily looked again at the unknown man.
>
> "Monsieur Landau!" The countess addressed the man with a softness and carefulness that struck [Stepan Arkadyich] Oblonsky. And she introduced them.
>
> Landau hastily turned, approached and, smiling, placed his inert, sweaty hand into the extended hand of Stepan Arkadyich and immediately went back and began looking at the portraits. The countess and Alexei Alexandrovich exchanged meaningful looks.[1]

Other guests have already arrived. Seated comfortably in an armchair, Landau slips into a trance. The first words he utters are: *"The person who came last, the one who is asking for something, must get out! Get out!"*[2] Stepan Arkadyich leaps guiltily to the conclusion that this person must be he, since he has come last to the séance and not to talk to the spirits (in fact, he is dismissive of them) but to talk to Karenin and to the countess. Stepan Arkadyich asks the medium if he is the person in question. When told yes, he quickly leaves the seance.

Then Landau answers Alexei Alexandrovich Karenin's question: he tells him he should not give Anna a divorce. Tolstoy writes: "The next day he [Stepan] received from Alexei Alexandrovich a definitive refusal to divorce Anna and understood that this decision was based on what the Frenchman had said in his real or feigned sleep."[3] Stepan sends Anna a telegram telling her Karenin's decision.

Shortly after she receives the news, Anna Karenina commits suicide by jumping under the wheels of a train.

Tolstoy constructed this séance scene with such wiliness that it's difficult to know where his own beliefs lie regarding mediumship. Thomas Berry, in *Spiritualism in Tsarist Society and Literature,* thinks the author didn't believe spirit communication was possible and was trying to belittle Alexei Alexandrovich Karenin in this scene:

> Karenin did not make a move without consulting the mystic (part 7, ch. 20–22). To accentuate the absurdity of Karenin's preoccupation with the medium, Tolstoy arranged for the sophisticated Stiva [Stepan Arkadyich] Oblonsky to visit some of the seances held by Landau. Sensing the skepticism of the visitor, the medium requested that Oblonsky leave. Tolstoy indicated that Karenin was so taken in by the charlatan that he did not realize that Landau was protecting his own interests by having Oblonsky depart.[4]

The Russian-American novelist/critic Vladimir Nabokov, author of *Lolita,* comments more circumspectly on this séance in *Lectures on Russian Literature* (1981):

> It is, curiously enough, owing to the mediumistic visions of a French quack who has found patrons among Petersburg society people, it is owing to him that Karenin decides not to give Anna a divorce—

and a telegram to that effect during a final period of tragic tension between Anna and Vronsky [Anna's lover] helps to build up the mood that leads to her suicide.[5]

By saying "curiously enough" (but not by saying "French quack"!), Nabokov leaves the door open to the notion that Tolstoy is at least implying in this scene the possibility of divine intervention. It's true that Anna does not commit suicide solely because Karenin refuses to give her a divorce, but also because she knows she will probably never see her twelve-year-old son again or be admitted to St. Petersburg society. But it's her husband's decision, precipitated by Landau and relayed by her brother, that's the final straw that drives her to her final act of self-destruction. And hadn't Tolstoy begun *Anna Karenina* with the epigraph: "Vengeance is *mine; I* will repay (saith the Lord)" from Romans 12, verse 19? Was it the Lord Himself who told Landau what to say?

So we can't be entirely sure where Tolstoy's beliefs lie. Even Thomas Berry, apparently so certain that Tolstoy had no belief in Spiritualism, cannot help revealing a touch of ambivalence on the part of the Russian novelist when he writes: "In 1857, in Paris, Tolstoy attended a séance of the famous Mr. Home which the writer recorded in his diary in two short sentences: 'Home neither did nor did not do anything. I ought to try it myself.'"[6] (There's no record that Tolstoy ever did try it himself.)

Even a hint of ambiguity in his portrayal of a medium is a puzzling departure for Count Leo Tolstoy, who almost all his life vehemently denied the existence of a supernatural realm. Count Tolstoy was born in a rambling, forty-two-room manor house on the family's country estate Yasnaya Polyana (Clear Glades) in the rich and rolling farmlands of the Volga valley. His restless spirit carried him through two years of desultory university studies (he took Oriental languages and law at Kazan University, then dropped out) interrupted by bouts of furious dissipation (he squandered huge sums of money on gambling and womanizing). In 1847 Tolstoy returned to his country estate, which he would administer for the rest of his life while mastering such diverse skills as horse breeding, beekeeping, and crop management. He fought in the Crimean War (1853–1856), commanding an exposed bastion at the Battle of Sevastopol and distinguishing himself for bravery. His auto-biographical trilogy, *Childhood, Boyhood and Youth,* published when he was in his twenties, brought him fame by the age of thirty. Between 1857 and 1861 he visited Germany, France, and England twice, learn-ing educational methods he later applied when he opened a school at Yasnaya Polyana for peasant children; eventually he would write and publish a reading primer for the school. In 1862 he married the beau-tiful and intelligent Sonya Behrs, sixteen years his junior; they had thirteen children, seven of whom survived to adulthood. From 1864 to 1878, he wrote *War and Peace* and *Anna Karenina,* the latter consid-ered by many to be the greatest novel ever written. During that period Tolstoy also wrote numerous short stories and novellas.

Beginning in 1878, the now world-famous author underwent a dev-astating spiritual crisis. He denounced his two great novels as egotisti-cal and pointless, mere "aristocratic art." He developed his own brand of Christianity, whose gospel, according to one critic, was "devoid of irrationality, deprived of metaphysical and mystical vision, despoiled of metaphors and symbols, mutilated of its miracles, and sometimes of its parables as well."[7] He told the Russian Orthodox Church (which formally excommunicated him in 1901) that to regard Jesus as a God and pray to him was the height of blasphemy. He declared that the essence of Christ's ministry was to teach men "not to commit stupidities."[8] He became a pac-ifist and vegetarian and, dressed in peasant clothes, worked in the fields with the peasants. Through all this he wrote not only a spiritual autobi-ography (*My Confession*) and numerous essays on religion and philoso-phy, but also additional short stories, one more novel (*Resurrection*), and two short and three long plays. At the time of his death, at eighty-two, this great writer's religious views had influenced numerous radical sects around the world and inspired many distinguished activist-thinkers, such as Mahatma Gandhi, Boris Pasternak, and Martin Luther King Jr.

Despite his amazing accomplishments, Tolstoy was an endlessly tormented man. Looming behind his seeming dismissal of the paranormal was a profound despair at what seemed to him to be the ultimate meaninglessness of life. The critic George Steiner writes in *Tolstoy or Dostoevsky* (1959) that Tolstoy

> suffered from a despair of reason at the thought that men's lives were doomed through illness or violence or the ravenings of time to irremediable extinction. . . . His relentless veracity compelled him to recognize that there is no definitive proof for the immortality of the soul or the survival of any consciousness whatsoever. . . . Tolstoy was harassed to the edge of self-destruction by the apparent absurdity of human existence.[9]

Steiner continues: "Out of this desperate meditation there grew a consoling myth. . . . Tolstoy came to deny the reality of death. He wrote in his *Diary* for December 1895 that man is 'never born and never dies and always is.'"[10] Steiner quotes Tolstoy as later writing that the Kingdom of God "must be established here and now, on this earth and in this, the only real life that is accorded us . . . there is no evidence for the existence of another world and . . . the Kingdom of God must be built by mortal hands."[11] Any communication from an afterworld would weaken an individual's efforts in the here and now, he thought; and, anyway, there was no such communication.

The Russian writer Maxim Gorky (1868–1936) said that the aged Tolstoy and God were like "two bears living in one den."[12] Gorky found Tolstoy's corrosive skepticism terrifying. The author of *War and Peace* was "elemental, nihilistic, malicious, and unfathomable."[13] Gorky felt that it was Tolstoy's violent disappointment at the meaninglessness of life that drove him to unmask every pretension, every civility, in every person. Thomas Mann summarizes in *Reminiscences* Gorky's reflections on Tolstoy's "sly little smile":

There is something not only extra-moral but extra-mental, extra-human, about it; it bespeaks the mystery of the "natural," the elemental, which is not at all kindly disposed, but rather takes pleasure in confusion. According to Gorky, the old man loved to put insidious questions. "What do you think about yourself?" "Do you love your wife?" "How do you like mine?" "Do you like me, Alexei Maximovich?"[14]

But Gorky marveled at Tolstoy's instinctual, primordial connection with life. He watched, mesmerized, as the old man sat motionless and silent at the seashore, head resting thoughtfully on his hands, feet lapped by the water. "He seemed like an ancient stone come alive, that knew and pondered the beginning and end of all things, and what and how would be the end of the stones and grasses of the earth, the waters of the sea, the whole universe from the sun to the grain of sand." Gorky concluded: "In my heart were rejoicing and fear, then all melted together in one single blissful feeling: 'I am not bereft on this earth, so long as this old man is living on it.'"[15]

Tolstoy's elemental connection with nature lay behind the absolute distinction he made between the spiritual healthfulness of rural life and the corrupting influence of urban life. George Steiner writes,

> Tolstoy saw experience morally and aesthetically divided. There is the life of the city with its social injustices, its artificial sexual conventions, its cruel display of wealth, and its power to alienate man from the essential patterns of physical vitality. On the other hand, there is life in the fields and forests with its alliance of mind and body, its acceptance of sexuality as hallowed and creative, and its instinct for the chain of being which relates the phases of the moon to the phases of conception and which associates the coming of the seed-time with the resurrection of the soul.[16]

In an early scene in *Anna Karenina,* Konstantin Levin, a key figure in the book and the one who represents the vibrant and morally healthful spirit of the countryside, argues with Vronsky about spiritualism. The setting is a high-society party in Moscow. Levin rejects tapping-table channeling, which was as popular in the 1870s among the aristocracy of Russia as it was in the 1850s among the aristocracy of France. He declares,

> When electricity was found, it was merely the discovery of a phenomenon, and it was not known where it came from or what it could do, and centuries passed before people thought of using it. The spiritualists, on the other hand, began by saying that tables write to them and spirits come to them, and only afterwards started saying it was an unknown force.[17]

Vronsky, representing an aristocracy cosseted and spoiled by wealth and privilege, replies, "Yes, but the spiritualists say: now we don't know what this force is, but the force exists, and these are the conditions under which it acts. Let the scientists find out what constitutes this force. No, I don't see why it can't be a new force, if it . . ."

Levin interrupts: "Because, with electricity, each time you rub resin against wool, a certain phenomenon manifests itself, while here it's not each time, and therefore it's not a natural phenomenon."[18]

By placing the arguments against spiritualism in the mouth of the virtuous, country-dwelling Levin and those for spiritualism in the mouth of the decadent, city-dwelling Vronsky, Tolstoy seems to show us where his true sentiments lie.

Perhaps Tolstoy's disdain for spiritualism should be placed, however, in the context of his utter contempt, growing worse as he got older, for every sort of human vanity—the kind of searing cynicism that Gorky observed. Certainly, he seemed to express in his later years almost a hatred for spiritualistic table tapping. In 1889–90 he wrote a four-act, antiestablishment, antichanneling comedy-drama called *The Fruits of Enlightenment*. This play was meant first of all for his family and friends, who performed it at his home at Christmas. But it was also intended for the public; soon staged in Moscow, it has been performed fairly regularly ever since, the most recent American production being a Russian-language staging by the seasoned Moscow director Sergei Kokovkin at Middlebury College's Russian School in Middlebury, Vermont, in August 2005.

The action of *The Fruits of Enlightenment* unfolds in the home of the upper-class Zvezdintsev family: mother, father, son, and daughter. Friends and hangers-on circulate through the house, intent mainly on participating in the séances the Zvezdintsevs regularly host. Tolstoy portrays family and guests alike as, in their varying ways, arrogant, idle, ignorant, and frivolous.

The great author has two aims in *The Fruits of Enlightenment:* the first is to show that the shrewd and hardworking servants in the house (and the peasants who live outside it) are morally superior to the condescending and misguided Zvezdintsevs and their friends; the second purpose is to heap ridicule on the beliefs of his time regarding spiritualism. John Gassner writes that *The Fruits of Enlightenment* is

> a devastating, if contrived, satire on the shallowness and credulity of the rich and idle who dabble in spiritualism while squeezing their peasants dry. The intrigue begins when a landowner's muzhiks try to purchase a piece of land on the installment plan. They are refused until a clever chambermaid poses as a spiritualistic medium and by playing that role extorts the master's signature to the bill of sale. This satire is liberally interspersed with amusing details concerning the fatuous behavior of the upper classes and the shrewd earthly ways of the peasantry.[19]

Tolstoy makes it clear in this play that he considers spiritualism to be a form either of self-deception, in which both medium and séance-goers participate, or of outright fraud perpetrated by professionals; in the house of the Zvezdintsevs, the deception is perpetrated by servants who fight for their rights in any way they can.

However, when we reflect on Tolstoy's work, we are led to wonder if it was only Tolstoy the rational man—however powerful and penetrating his powers of analysis might have been—and not entirely Tolstoy the consummate artist, who railed all his life against the possibility that there might be inexplicable phenomena peeking through at us from other levels of reality. We have as evidence not only the puzzlingly ambiguous role of Jules Landau in *Anna Karenina,* but also the disturbingly occult motif—often remarked on by readers and critics—of the shared premonitory nightmare of Anna and Vronsky. Tolstoy biographer Henri Troyat explains:

> A still more awesome menace is Anna's famous dream, in which a little muzhik in rags appears, bending over an iron plate and mumbling incomprehensible words in French, "and she sensed that he was performing some strange ritual over her with this piece of iron, and awoke drenched in cold sweat." She had this nightmare several times; Vronsky himself was affected by it through a kind of telepathy; and the moment Anna throws herself under the wheels of the train, she sees, in a flash, "a little man, muttering to himself and tapping on the iron above her."[20]

Did Tolstoy the seer know more in his heart than Tolstoy the intellect suffered him to accept?

# Thirteen

# Madame Helena Blavatsky (1831–1891)

## *Mistress of Hidden Wisdom*

Some thought she wasn't a real woman at all but the occult re-creation of someone whose dead body had been found on a battlefield in Italy.

Others insisted she had indeed fought on an Italian battlefield (at the Battle of Mentana in 1867 with the revolutionary leader Mazzini) and not only was alive, but had even shown them—while describing how two horses had been killed under her—the scars of five sword and gunshot wounds she had received during the battle.

Most were certain she had been born in Ukraine, spoke nine languages (including Arabic and Hindustani), and had traveled twice around the world alone (an unheard-of achievement for a woman in the mid-nineteenth century).

In the beginning, though, only a select few believed she consorted daily with two "astral" entities, Mahatma Morya, or "M," and Koot Hoomi, whose physical bodies actually resided in Tibet. In the end, however, all had to agree to the undeniable fact that she had authored two enormous tomes, which, each reaching back to the beginnings of life on earth, sought to reveal the earliest expressions of esoteric wisdom on our planet and trace the many transmogrifications of that wisdom up through the ages. Sir Isaac Newton would have been appalled by her methods and beliefs, but he would have acknowledged that she—like he himself in his nonscientific writings—was seeking to resurrect the truths of the prisca sapientia for the modern world.

The woman is Madame Helena Blavatsky, who founded the Theosophical Society with Henry Steel Olcott in New York in 1875, and not long afterward made Adyar, India, a second focus of theosophical activity in the world. Those two centers, the first shifting to Wheaton, Illinois, are active to this day.

The two books Madame Blavatsky wrote, *Isis Unveiled* and *The Secret Doctrine,* were, and have remained, the twin bibles of the theosophical movement. In the words of Richard Smoley, the theme of *Isis Unveiled* is "that there is a 'Secret Doctrine' underlying all religions, that was embodied in precursors of Hinduism and Buddhism. 'Pre-Vedic Brahmanism and Buddhism are the double source from which all religions spring,' Blavatsky tells us. Judaism and Christianity are pale shadows; what truth remains in these degenerate faiths chiefly resides in their esoteric versions—the Kabbalah and Gnosticism."[1]

*The Secret Doctrine* goes even further. But before we discuss it or *Isis Unveiled* in detail, let's find out exactly who Madame Helena Blavatsky was.

Today, Dnepropetrovsk is a flourishing industrial city located thirty miles southeast of Kiev in Ukraine. With a population of 1.1 million, it is the third-largest city in the former Soviet republic.

When Helena von Hahn, the future Madame Blavatsky, was born there on August 12, 1831, it was a town named Ekaterinoslav, with a population of ten thousand. Blavatsky's maternal grandmother, Princess Helena Pavlovna, was a well-known painter and musician who spoke five languages and pursued careers in archaeology and botany. Her mother, née Helena Andreyevna Fadeyeva, was a popular novelist who died suddenly aged twenty-eight; the critic Belinsky called her the "Russian George Sand." Her father, Peter von Hahn, was a colonel and member of the lesser Russian-German nobility whose ancestors were renowned for their bravery in battle.

An omen of impenetrable ambiguity manifested on the day of Madame Blavatsky's birth. She was born so tiny and sickly that her parents had her baptized that very day for fear she would die soon. A candle overturned and set a priest's robe on fire; the church went up in flames; and the newly born Helena narrowly escaped being burned to death.[2]

Her sister Vera wrote of her childhood:

When a child, daring and fearless in everything else, she got often scared into fits through her own hallucinations. She felt certain of being persecuted by what she called "the terrible glaring eyes" invisible to everyone else, and often attributed by her to the most inoffensive inanimate objects. . . . She would shut her eyes tight during such visions, and run away to hide from the ghostly glances thrown on her by pieces of furniture or articles of dress, screaming desperately, and frightening the whole household. At other times she would be seized by fits of laughter, explaining them by the amusing pranks of her invisible companions. . . . For her, all nature seemed animated with a mysterious life of its own.[3]

Helena could be wildly sociable, playing joyfully with her friends, then wildly reclusive, spending entire days in her bedroom reading. She was rebellious and intractable, and generous and frank. When she was eleven, the death of her much beloved mother shattered the family. They moved to the estate of Helena's maternal grandfather, Prince Pavel Dolgorouki, in Saratov, Russia. The prince had died when Helena was seven. He had been a distinguished officer under Catherine II and a prominent Mason who amassed a library of hundreds of rare books on alchemy, magic, and the occult sciences. One of these books was reputed to be an unpublished manuscript by the legendary Count of Saint-Germain (said to be hundreds of years old) accurately foretelling the course of the French Revolution.[4]

Helena took to spending whole days and nights in the library. "I had read . . . [all the books] with the keenest interest before I was 15," she told friends much later.[5] K. Paul Johnson asserts that the Saint-Germain manuscript, authentic or not, "inflamed her imagination with the idea of mysterious adepts manipulating occult undercurrents of European politics."[6]

Four weeks before she turned seventeen, Helena married Nikifor V. Blavatsky, a forty-one-year-old former general and current vice governor of the province. The marriage took place almost by accident. Helena's aunt, Nadyezhda A. Fadeyev, explains:

> She had been simply defied one day by her governess to find any man who would be her husband, in view of her temper and disposition. The governess, to emphasize the taunt, said that even the old man [Nikifor Blavatsky] she had found so ugly, and had laughed at so much, calling him "a plumeless raven"—that even he would decline her for a wife! That was enough: three days after, she made him propose, and then, frightened at what she had done, sought to escape from her joking acceptance of his offer. But it was too late.[7]

The wedding took place on July 7, 1848. The guests included twenty dashing Kurdish horsemen who had once ridden under Nikifor's command. Their presence did not dazzle Helena into allowing her husband to consummate the marriage. Three months of terrible quarrels followed. The unmanageable bride was dispatched to Odessa to rejoin her father. On the way, she disappeared. Several weeks later, Helena showed up in Istanbul, having worked her passage to Turkey disguised as a cabin boy.

From this point until the early 1870s, Madame Blavatsky's life is shrouded in myth, innuendo, half-truths, and a degree of retroactive spin on the part of Blavatsky. In early 1851, the Orientalist Albert Leighton Rawson spotted her in Cairo, where she smoked pot, dressed as a dervish, and studied with the Coptic magician Paolos Metamon.[8] Alfred Percy Sinnett asserts that mid-1851 found her in Paris, where she met "many literary celebrities of the day, and . . . a famous mesmerist."[9] By the end of the year she was in London studying piano.

In London, or so the Swedish countess Constance Wachtmeister tells us, Blavatsky, out walking one day, passed a tall Hindu on the street who—just before he vanished—she recognized with astonishment. Wachtmeister writes: "During her childhood . . . [Blavatsky] had often seen near her an Astral form, that always seemed to come in any moment of danger, and save her just at the crucial point. H. P. B. had learnt to look upon this astral form as a guardian angel, and felt that she was under His care and guidance."[10]

This was the very same entity, Wachtmeister says, that Blavatsky had recognized on the London street. The Hindu reappeared the next day and spoke to Blavatsky, telling her about the Theosophical Society she would found in twenty years, about the difficulties she would have—and that it was essential for her to go to Tibet to study.[11]

It's all too easy to believe that Blavatsky invented some of this. She later claimed that she did indeed go to Tibet, studying for three years with the master whom she had met on the London street—his name was Mahatma Morya, or M—and who had been, and would always be, with her in astral form. (A second "Mahatma," Koot Hoomi, would eventually enter her life and play a similar role.)

The next fifteen years were taken up, Blavatsky tells us, by prodigious world travels that took her to every part of the globe, often for extended stays. She seems to have been scouring everywhere for occult lore and occult experiences; sometimes stories surfaced about her fabled travels. These forays included a brief return to Russia, where she visited with her family and underwent a physical and psychic crisis that, she claimed, precipitated the full maturation of her psychic and mediumistic powers.

Perhaps it was these powers that prevented her from dying in an explosion aboard the passenger ship *Eunomia,* in which she was traveling from Greece to Egypt; only seventeen out of the four hundred passengers survived. She claimed to have blacked out, then found herself swimming in a sea of severed heads and limbs; the disaster robbed her of all her possessions. Finally Blavatsky arrived in Cairo, where (it was now 1872) she set up a spiritistic "closet of miracles"—public séances where passersby could pay to hear the spirits speak. It was here that an English tourist, Emma Coulomb (or that would eventually be her married name), caught Madame Blavatsky red-handed in fraudulent activity—at least, such was Coulomb's claim years later, when her testimony would count for a great deal, as Blavatsky, now head of the Theosophical Society, once again had to answer accusations of fraud.[12]

Helena Blavatsky arrived in New York in 1873. A certain notoriety had preceded her, and curious onlookers gathered at the dock to greet her arrival. At the time a passion for Spiritualism—with special reference to talking to the dead—was sweeping the United States. Blavatsky was in her element; she quickly became a medium with an office in Manhattan.

Henry Steel Olcott entered the picture.

Olcott was a lawyer who fought in the American Civil War as a colonel and was now a reporter for the New York *Daily Graphic.* He was well enough regarded to have been appointed one of a government panel of three investigating Lincoln's assassination. Now he was zealously investigating occult phenomena.

He and Blavatsky liked each other instantly. Olcott was fascinated by the Ukrainian seeress's passion and intelligence; she, by the American colonel's calmness and intelligence. When she asked him to become her manager, Olcott immediately left his wife and three children. He remained Blavatsky's manager for the next decade, even though the two never married and it is unlikely the relationship was ever sexually consummated. (Blavatsky seems to have had an odd streak of chastity, though her enemies accused her of just the opposite.)

In October 1874, Blavatsky and Olcott founded the Miracle Club. In 1875, they changed its name to the Theosophical Society. The word *theosophy* derives from the Greek words *theos* (God) and *sophia* (wisdom); the society's adherents sought knowledge through direct, "divine" illumination rather than through traditional philosophical study and analysis. Theosophy had two goals: to form a bias-free universal Brotherhood of Humanity and to encourage the study of comparative religion, philosophy, and science. The society, heavily promoted, attracted much controversy. Blavatsky decided to write a bible for it. She would rely on her own two special, "astral" advisers, Mahatma Morya and Koot Hoomi. She, in fact, would not write the book; it would be channeled from these discarnate Indians.

If we can believe the testimony of Colonel Olcott, the making of this, Blavatsky's first book, entitled *Isis Unveiled,* was wildly unorthodox. She wrote much of it while Olcott was sitting across the table from her correcting drafts. He wrote in *Old Diary Leaves:*

> Her pen would be flying over the page, when she would suddenly stop, look out into space with the vacant eye of a clairvoyant seer, shorten her vision as though to look at something held invisible in the air before her, and begin copying on her paper what she saw. . . . I remember well two instances when I, also, was able to see and even handle books from whose astral duplicates she copied quotations into her manuscript, and which she was obliged to "materialize" for me, to refer to when reading the proofs, as I refused to pass the pages for the "strike-off" unless my doubts as to the accuracy of her copy were satisfactory.[13]

On one occasion when Olcott refused to okay the pages, Madame Blavatsky replied,

> "Well, keep still a minute and I'll try to get it." The far-away look came into her eyes, and presently she pointed to a far corner of the

room, to an *étagère* on which were kept some curios, and in a hollow voice said: "There!" and then came to herself again. "There;
there; go look for it over there!" I went, and found the two volumes
wanted, which, to my knowledge, had not been in the house until
that very moment.

Olcott located the quotations, made the corrections, and then, at
Blavatsky's request, returned the two volumes to the place on the *étagère*
where he had found them. "I resumed my seat and work, and when, after
awhile, I looked again in that direction, the books had disappeared!"[14]

The works of Blavatsky produced by these methods—first *Isis
Unveiled* and then, more than ten years later, *The Secret Doctrine*—
were huge accretions of learning, unruly mountains of knowledge shot
through with weird, incredible, splendid insights. They were colossally
derivative, but that did not stop the 1,500-page *Isis Unveiled* from selling one thousand copies in the first ten days—a sensational figure for
the time—and the *New York Herald Tribune* from calling it one of the
"remarkable productions of the century."[15]

Blavatsky scholar/researcher David Caldwell writes that "*Isis
Unveiled* outlines the history, scope and development of the Occult
Sciences, the nature and origin of Magic, the roots of Christianity, the
errors of Christian Theology and the fallacies of established orthodox
Science, against the backdrop of the secret teachings which run as a
golden thread through bygone centuries, coming up to the surface every
now and then in the various mystical movements of the last two thousand years or so."[16]

Blavatsky begins the book with a discussion of the *Book of Dzyan*.
This is a sort of protobook, or Ur-book, that she has seen in the library
of the mahatmas in Tibet, and which she now sees, in astral form, before
her inner eye. It is "An Archaic Manuscript—a collection of palm leaves
made impermeable to water, fire, and air, by some specific unknown
process. . . . On the first page is an immaculate white disk within a dull
black ground. On the following page, the same disk, but with a central

point . . . "[17] It is written in a language called Sinzar, and, while quite real in itself, the *Book of Dzyan* is also the Platonic form or archetype of every holy book that was to follow.

What does the *Book of Dzyan* say?

"A conviction," writes Blavatsky (and/or the Mahatmas Morya and Koot Hoomi),

> founded upon seventy thousand years of experience, as they allege, has been entertained by Hermetic philosophers of all periods that matter has in time become, through sin, more gross and dense than it was at man's first formation; that, at the beginning, the human body was of a half-ethereal nature; and that, before the fall, mankind communed freely with the now unseen universes. But since that time matter has become the formidable barrier between us and the world of spirits. The oldest esoteric traditions also teach that, before the mystic Adam, many races of human beings lived and died out, each giving place in its turn to another.[18]

The universe is permeated by a kind of psychic "ether," called Akasha (which means "space" or "sky" in Hindu philosophy). In the nineteenth century, this all-pervading, subtle principle is called the "universal ether." In high antiquity it had many names, being variously known as the Chaos of the ancients; the Zoroastrian sacred fire; the Atas-Behram of the Parsis; the Hermes-fire; the St. Elmo's fire of the ancient Germans; the lightning of Cybele; the burning torch of Apollo; the flame on the altar of Pan; the inextinguishable fire in the temple on the Acropolis and in that of Vestra; and the fire-flame of Pluto's realm.[19] According to Colin Wilson, "This psychic ether explains, for example, the operations of telepathy and clairvoyance, which are 'waves' in the ether. It also *records* everything that has ever happened, and these 'Akashic' records are available to clairvoyants and mystics. . . . She [Blavatsky] adds that anyone who can read the records of the past can also read the future, since it is already present in embryo."[20]

Madame Blavatsky believed that, in ages past, practical knowledge of the ether made magical practices possible. In making *Isis Unveiled* into a survey of the literature of magic, witchcraft, alchemy, Eastern thought, and Western science, her aim was to redeem magic from the disfavor into which it had fallen since the rise of science in the seventeenth century. The secret science of the Astral Light, of the vital ether—of Akasha—had been transmitted down through the centuries by a secret brotherhood of adepts and was available to all who were ready to receive it. One such brotherhood was that of the Tibetans with whom Blavatsky had studied.

The sheer weight of all the far-out facts Madame Blavatsky crammed into *Isis Unveiled* precipitated a critical storm. For the most part the public loved the book, though some took issue with its anticlerical tilt. On the whole, the savants of the day, while acknowledging the breadth and depth of Blavatsky's learning, could not avoid savaging her for the uncritical way she had thrown everything together.

In 1888, Helena Blavatsky—now in England after having spent close to a decade in India—published her second major volume, *The Secret Doctrine*. At 1,500 pages, it was as prodigious as its predecessor. Here she provides the text of the seven stanzas (or "slocas") of the *Book of Dzyan,* with commentary. It gradually becomes clear to the reader that this protoprimordial poem is cast in the same mold as, for example, Plato's mystical dialogue the *Parmenides;* it is a description of how the Many emanated from the One—how God, being perfect, paradoxically brought imperfection into being with the creation of the physical universe. But the *Book of Dzyan* is not a philosophical argument; rather, it is a lushly concrete epic poem in the same genre as William Blake's *The Four Zoas*. (See chapter 6.)

Blavatsky chronicles in *The Secret Doctrine* the transformations of the etheric substance as, released from the undifferentiated Godhead, it unfolds through time and space, acquiring a physicalness that increasingly excludes the spiritual and takes on sinfulness. This brings her to the doctrine of the root races. (The *Book of Enoch,* which influenced Alphonse de Lamartine, was one of Blavatsky's sources.) Colin Wilson describes the ascendance of the root races:

> According to her later doctrine—sketched only briefly in *Isis Unveiled*—man is not the first intelligent dweller on earth. The first "root race" consisted of invisible beings made of fire mist. The second race was slightly more solid and lived on an island continent called Lemuria—or Mu—in the Indian Ocean, and consisted of ape-like giants who communicated telepathically and lacked the power of reason. The fourth race lived in Atlantis, and achieved a very high degree of civilization. They were destroyed by natural cataclysms; the last part of Atlantis, an island called Poseidonus, went down after a battle between selfish magicians and the people of an island called Shamballah. Our present race is the fifth root race, and—where matter is concerned—we are the most "solid" so far. This means that we find it far more difficult to express the power of the spirit; yet matter also enables us to be far more potentially creative than earlier root races. The root races—the sixth and seventh—that will follow ours will again be more ethereal.[21]

Why do we know nothing about these earlier civilizations? Because of the cosmic catastrophes that have periodically wiped the slate clean on our earth. Blavatsky expounds on the Sideral, or Great Year, of the ancients, particularly of India; this is the cyclical movement of our planet among the stars that takes place over a period of more than twenty-five thousand years and was thought by the sages of antiquity to trigger, when it came full circle, geological catastrophe.

The controversy surrounding the publication of *Isis Unveiled* in 1877 had exhausted and distracted Madame Blavatsky. She decided a clearer connection to the mahatmas was needed and that this could only be had by her moving closer to her guides; the Theosophical Society must relocate to India. Blavatsky had little trouble persuading Olcott. The two set sail from New York in late 1878, and in February 1879 disembarked at Bombay.

There they founded the influential *Theosophical Journal*. The two traveled extensively through India. In May 1882, they acquired an estate at Adyar, near Madras, and the headquarters of the Theosophical Society was moved there by the end of the year.

For some time now, Helena's physical appearance had been hardly prepossessing. She weighed 230 pounds and some called her "the old hippopotamus." She wore the same bright red flannel blouse for months on end. She chain-smoked and calmed her nerves with marijuana. She had a volcanic temper. But Blavataky could mesmerize with her charm; she spoke with forcefulness and utter originality—she was charismatic— and by virtue of much writing and numerous visits and alliances with Hindu religious and secular leaders, she was able to attract considerable attention to the society and make its influence felt both in India and in the United Kingdom.

In 1884, however, she ran up against huge difficulties. K. Paul Johnson summarizes in *The Masters Revealed:*

> . . . charges of fraud against Madame Blavatsky were made that year by two disgruntled employees, Alexis and Emma Coulomb, who claimed to have participated in fakery of psychic phenomena aimed at proving the Mahatmas' existence. Among the Coulombs' charges were that the Shrine [in the Adyar Theosophical Temple] was designed to allow letters [ostensibly from the Mahatmas] to be inserted through a sliding panel in the back, making it seem that they materialized inside it paranormally. Their accusations led to an investigation by Richard Hodgson, sent to India by the Society for Psychical Research. He concluded that the Masters were nonexistent and all their alleged phenomena fraudulent, but Theosophists rejected his report as based on lies by the Coulombs. For the past century, opinion on the Hodgson report has been polarized between

those who regard it as definitive proof of fraud and those who reject it as totally unjust.[22]

Helena Blavatsky refused to be downcast. But she left India, spent some time on the continent of Europe, and then settled in London. There, she continued to be influential, and there she wrote *The Secret Doctrine*. She died on May 8, 1891, worn out at fifty-nine and finally succumbing to a host of illnesses including heart disease, rheumatism, Bright's disease, and complications from influenza.

A century later, in 1986, vindication seemed to be in the works for Helena Blavatsky. It had become clear that the report of the Society for Psychical Research (SPR) regarding allegations of fraud against Blavatsky had been hastily put together and hastily approved, with great prejudice against the founder of the Theosophical Society. Sylvia Cranston writes in *H.P.B.* that the SPR "issued a press release stating that 'the exposure' of the Russian-born Occultist, Madame H.P. Blavatsky by the SPR in 1885, is in serious doubt, with the publication in the *SPR Journal* (vol. 53 April 1986) of 'a forceful critique of the 1885 report,' by Dr. Vernon Harrison, a 'long-standing member of the SPR.'"[23] Central to the report was the unanticipated conclusion that the letters put forward as fraudulent communications from the mahatmas fabricated by Blavatsky had really been concocted by her accusers, who were employees fired by Blavatsky and looking for revenge.

Richard Smoley concludes, "Blavatsky is the seminal figure of the New Age. Nearly all of alternative spirituality owes her a great debt, and many seekers today accept her ideas and premises without knowing where they came from."[24] Perhaps today, with our world seemingly teetering on the brink of catastrophe, her writings are worth a second look.

# Fourteen

# William Butler Yeats (1865–1939)

## *Metaphors for Poetry*

It was on the coast of Normandy, in France, in the late summer of 1917; one hundred miles away, the guns of World War I still sounded. The Irish poet William Butler Yeats, aged fifty-two, strolling along the beach, asked the tall slender woman beside him, Iseult Gonne, aged twenty-three, if she would marry him.

With her large brown eyes, small, well-shaped nose, and full, slightly parted lips, Iseult was stunningly pretty. Willowy, six feet tall—almost as tall as Yeats—she was also touchingly awkward. Now she stopped and looked shyly and thoughtfully at the poet.

When she was fifteen years old and Yeats had been her friend and mentor for as long as she could remember, *she* had asked *him* to marry *her!* The poet had turned her down with exquisite flustered tact. At the time he had been in love with her mother, Maud, for some sixteen years. In the beginning of the relationship he had asked Maud to marry him; she had turned him down.

Since then, Yeats had gotten heavier, with streaks of gray running through his curly hair. But his dark glittering eyes and fine straight nose ensured that he would be handsome into old age. She knew that two weeks ago he had again asked her mother to marry him, and Maud had again said no.

Now, here on the beach in Normandy, awkwardly, feeling much love for this great man who had always been her friend, Iseult Gonne turned down the marriage proposal of William Butler Yeats.

Ten days later, heading back to England on the Channel ferry, Yeats felt more than the usual mix of wild emotions. He was sure he would always be in love with the brilliant and ineffably vulnerable Iseult with her alert beauty as taut as a tightened bow. But he wondered if some *frisson* of incestuous desire for her might not also lurk in his heart. Certainly the whole world thought so. Did not everyone know that he had been in love with Maud Gonne, Iseult's mother, for many, many years? Did not many of them believe (although it was not true) that he himself was the father of the inimitable and illegitimate Iseult?

But it was time for him to marry even if he could have neither Maud nor Iseult. He was sick of his wild and wandering shuttlecock ways, spending a month here on the estate of a friend near London, a month there with Lady Gregory at Coole Park near Galway in Ireland. His poetry, the management of his theater, his many appearances in public—for now he was a world-famous poet—all these duties pressed in upon him. He needed a permanent place from which to face the world. He yearned for a home, a hearth—for children. His astrologer had told him that November 19, 1917, was an auspicious date for him to marry: then, or a date just before. So well aspected a time to marry might never come again, he had been told. He had to hurry.

Disembarking at Dover, Yeats felt a pang of grief as he resolutely turned his thoughts away from Iseult. He must focus on the women— and their daughters—from whom he might be able to choose a wife.

It wouldn't be easy. Iseult—and Maud, though his passion for her had begun to recede—still sang their siren songs.

Yeats could not know that in rejecting him on the beach in Normandy, Iseult had placed the poet on an enchanted path that would lead him, in two months, to a wife of the rarest gifts and an encounter with spiritual worlds the likes of which he could never have dreamt, even when, as a boy, he yearned to vanish into a fairyland of spirit beings and never again return to the mortal world.

Just who was this Yeats who was about to make a marriage and meet the beyond? William Butler Yeats was born and educated in Dublin, Ireland, and spent most of his childhood in Sligo. His father, John Butler Yeats, was a distinguished if improvident painter who didn't always finish his commissions. Yeats attended art school for two years, but poetry was his passion. He had been fascinated from his youth by Irish legend and occult lore. In his twenties he fashioned, adding a *soupçon* of French Symbolism, a new language of poetry—one lyrical, and yearning, and magical. He had *élan* and industry. By thirty he had become a famous poet, beloved for such verses as *The Lake Isle of Innisfree*.

Yeats was always deeply attracted to magic and worlds beyond our own. Very young, he dreamed that a boat carrying his grandfather William Pollexfen had collided with another boat and sunk. The next morning his grandfather arrived home on a horse not his own to tell them his boat had indeed sunk and eight passengers had drowned. Other psychic experiences followed. In his twenties, inspired by visits to Madame Blavatsky's London Theosophical Society, he conducted experiments in magic. He tried to make the soul of a flower visible but failed. He had more success working with his uncle George Pollexfen. The two attempted telepathy: at Rosses Point, in Sligo, Yeats walked by the shore while his uncle walked on a cliff or sand hill above. Without speaking, Yeats imagined a symbol, and Pollexfen "would practically never fail of the appropriate vision." The experiments intruded into the dreams of Pollexfen's servant lady, Mary Battle, who had "second sight."

Yeats wrote: "We never began our work until George's old servant was in her bed; and yet, when we went upstairs to our beds, we constantly heard her crying out with nightmare, and in the morning we would find out that her dream echoed our vision."[1]

Yeats never left off experimenting with magic. He never left off climbing social ladders, either. He was a brilliant and sociable talker, charming and witty and original. He was a man of many friends and quickly become a pillar of Irish and English literary establishments. The poet was a driving force behind Ireland's Literary Revival and helped found the Abbey Theatre, in Dublin, which was dedicated to the development of Irish playwrights. Yeats wrote plays for this theater and early on was its director. He was passionately concerned with politics and, while increasingly an Irish nationalist, he was sensitive to the needs of the English. Thus the figure who seemed to wander forlornly through the streets of London and Dublin in late 1917 looking for a wife was no sort of an eccentric loser. He was a poet of genius, coming into his own on the world stage, and he would soon find a wife who would offer him more than he could ever have imagined.

In September 1917, Yeats traveled to Ireland, then traveled back to London. He visited poets and playwriting friends; he visited his family; he especially visited lady friends, including those with daughters. He sought support; he sought advice; he listened; he observed; and he considered whom to woo.

And then—was it merely an accident? Had he unconsciously, or almost consciously, arranged it?—he bumped into Iseult Gonne on a street corner in London. In a rush of unbridled passion, he proposed to her again. She turned him down again. He became violently unhappy.

Then, the unexpected intervened.

In 1911, when she was just eighteen, he had caught a glimpse of a young woman named Georgie Hyde-Lees. She later told him that if he actually noticed her then, it was simply as "a girl perched in some window of her mother's house."[2] They had met again in 1914 and discovered they shared an interest in the occult. He encouraged her to join the Hermetic

Order of the Golden Dawn, dedicated to the practice of magical rituals and spiritual development, and sponsored her initiation into the order's Temple of the Stella Matutina branch in London. Her temple "motto" or "secret name," he remembered, was Soror Nemo Sciat—Sister No One Must Know. His was Frater D. E. D. I.—Brother D. E. D. I.

Now, in September 1917, he visited Georgie's mother, Nelly Tucker, whom he had known for years. Georgie happened to be there. They talked. She was a wartime nurse in a London hospital. In the past three years, she had read voraciously in occult literature—Paracelsus, John Dee, Jakob Boehme, Emanuel Swedenborg—and in philosophy—Pico della Mirandola, Plato, Plotinus, Spinoza. As she talked, there was the glint of high intelligence in her eyes and a lovely gleam in her red-brown hair.

He asked her mother's permission, then asked Georgie to marry him.

She accepted immediately.

He felt joy and consternation. He was shaken by the swiftness of events. The astrological deadline was approaching. Georgie's mother was suddenly unsure: Yeats was fifty-two and Georgie was twenty-five; he was twice as old as her daughter. But Georgie was steadfast in her acceptance. Yeats thought of Iseult, wavered—then became exultant and rushed ahead with the marriage arrangements.

In subtle stops and starts, with turnings, hesitations, and intimations of great happiness, the engagement period flashed by. Flustered, fearful, bashful, Yeats notified only a few friends. The banns were posted the day before the wedding, which took place on October 20, 1917, at Harrow Road Register Office in North London. Ezra Pound was best man. The other witnesses were Pound's wife, Dorothy (who was Georgie's best friend), and Georgie's mother, Nelly Tucker.

When she met her two months later, Yeats's sister Lily would describe Georgie as "not good-looking, but . . . comely; her nose is too big for good looks; her color ruddy and her hair reddish brown; her eyes are very good and a fine blue, with very dark, strongly marked eyebrows." There was a "look she often had, as of a light shining out from her. . . . It is most attractive."[3]

No one could mistake her strength of character and her luminous intelligence.

Yeats and Georgie dallied in London. After two days, the couple slipped away for their honeymoon to Ashdown Forest Hotel, at Forest Row, in Sussex, not far from London. Their courtship had been so brief that they did not really know each other. For all his years and fame, Yeats had had few sexual encounters; it is possible that Georgie had had none. For two days they sat bashfully apart from one another in their hotel rooms or bustled about busily to avoid an encounter.

The day before the wedding, Yeats, overwhelmed by ambivalence and fright, had become convinced he was still hopelessly in love with Iseult. He had written her a letter, confessing his doubts and giving her the name of the hotel in Sussex. Iseult wrote back, consoling the poet and professing, not love for him, but great affection. The letter arrived at the hotel. Yeats read it, then told Georgie all about it. He confessed his tormented feelings.

The young bride was devastated. Nelly Tucker had known Yeats for a long time and knew about Iseult; she had warned her daughter that Yeats was marrying her on the rebound and might leave her. Georgie now thought her mother was right. She considered packing and leaving her poet-husband immediately. They had been man and wife for just four days.

Something happened to change the mood completely. While talking, Georgie picked up a pencil and let her hand wander across a piece of paper. Words trooped unbidden into her mind. The pencil wrote them down. There were no spaces between the words, which trailed off the edge of the paper. Georgie felt that something had been written through her. The two of them looked at the piece of paper. It read, "With the bird all is well at heart."[4]

Yeats thought excitedly that "the bird" must be Iseult. But Georgie's hand was still gliding across the paper. The pencil wrote: "Your action was right for both but in London you mistook its meaning." A moment before, Yeats had felt relief; now he did not know what to think. Then Georgie wrote—it seemed to him as if someone, somewhere, was reading his thoughts—"You will neither regret nor repine."[5]

Yeats did not think the author of these lines was Georgie. Long steeped in the lore of the occult, open to the notion that angels come among us, he saw this as an intervention by a higher power to ease his way through the first days of his marriage, and perhaps much longer. He wrote in his journal that night, and would reproduce the entry in his book *A Vision,* published eight years later:

> On the afternoon of October 24th 1917, four days after my marriage, my wife surprised me by attempting automatic writing. What came in disjointed sentences, in almost illegible writing, was so exciting, sometimes so profound, that I persuaded her to give an hour or two day after day to the unknown writer, and, after some half-dozen such hours, offered to spend what remained of life explaining and piecing together those scattered sentences. "No," was the answer, "we have come to give you metaphors for poetry."[6]

What did Georgie think?

Many years later, in 1946, seven years after the death of Yeats, she told literary critic and Yeats scholar Richard Ellman that on the first day of the automatic writing her idea had been to "fake a sentence or two that would allay his anxieties over Iseult." As she recalled it, that was what she had done, and "Yeats was at once captured, and relieved."[7]

But then she went on to say, as Richard Ellman reports:

> Then a strange thing happened. Her own emotional involvement—her love for this extraordinary husband; and her fears for her marriage—must have made for unusual receptivity . . . for she suddenly felt her hand grasped and driven irresistibly. The pencil began to write sentences which she had never intended or thought, which

seemed to come as from another world. As images and ideas took penciled form, Yeats went beyond his initial relief about his marriage. Here were more potent revelations: he had married into a Delphi [the place where the oracle of the Greeks dwelt].[8]

As husband and wife worked awkwardly, but with the dawning of love, through the early stages of their marriage, this automatic writing became almost a daily habit. In the first week and some, Georgie produced ninety-three pages of writing. Initially the presiding "spirit" called itself the "unknown Communicator." Seizing upon the distinction—which Yeats had expressed in his newly published *Per Amica Silentia Lunae*—between man's combat with himself and his combat with circumstances, the hurrying pencil set forth an "elaborate classification of men according to their more or less complete expression of one type or the other."[9]

This was only the beginning. The communications continued for three years. The spirits came 450 times, roughly three times a week. Close to four thousand pages of transcript came into being. The Yeatses maintained their running conversation with the spirit world nonstop through the next year, which saw them first visit Ireland, then stay in Oxford, England, while Yeats worked vigorously on his poetry. The spirit communicators accompanied the pair the next year as they crossed America by rail on a lecture tour; they even addressed Yeats directly with words spoken by Georgie as she emerged from sleep in a Pullman sleeping car. In the third year, it became clear that the spirits could make their presence known not only through written and spoken words, but they manifested in other phenomena as well. Yeats tells us in *A Vision:*

Sweet smells were the most constant phenomena, now that of incense, now that of violets or roses or some other flower, and as perceptible to some half-dozen of our friends as to ourselves, though upon one occasion when my wife smelt hyacinth a friend smelt eau-de-cologne. A smell of roses filled the whole house when my son was born and was perceived there by the doctor and my wife and myself, and I have no doubt, though I did not question them, by the nurse and servants. Such smells came most often to my wife and myself when we passed through a door or were in some small enclosed place, but sometimes would form themselves in my pocket or even in the palms of my hands.

. . . Sometimes they commented on my thoughts by the ringing of a little bell heard by my wife alone, and once my wife and I heard at the same hour in the afternoon, she at Ballylee and I at Coole, the sound of a little pipe, three or four notes, and once I heard a burst of music in the middle of the night; and when regular communications through script and sleep had come to an end, the communicators occasionally spoke—sometimes a word, sometimes a whole sentence.

. . . Sometimes my wife saw apparitions: before the birth of our son a great black bird, persons in clothes of the late sixteenth century and of the late seventeenth. There were still stranger phenomena that I prefer to remain silent about for the present because they seemed so incredible that they need a long story and much discussion.[10]

During this time, Yeats had many theories about what the spirits were. He had always believed in the existence of a spirit world, and that the boundaries of our being extend much farther than we imagine. He wrote in *Essays and Introduction* in 1901:

I believe in the practice and philosophy of what we have agreed to call magic, in what I must call the evocation of spirits . . . in the visions of truth in the depths of the mind when the eyes are closed, and I believe in three doctrines. . . .

1. That the borders of our mind are ever shifting, and that many minds can flow into one another . . . and create or reveal a single mind, a single energy.

2. That the borders of our memories are shifting and that our memories are part of one great memory, the memory of nature herself.

3. That this great mind and great memory can be evoked by symbols.[11]

Yeats's understanding of spiritualism and spirit visits was challenged by the weird complexity of these spirits who came to him. They were of two kinds: the "Communicators," who seemed to wish to truly impart wisdom to Yeats, and the "Frustrators," who seemed to elbow the Communicators out of the way from time to time to deliberately mislead Yeats and Georgie. The poet would be told that he was talking to a Frustrator only if he asked if this were so when he was actually talking to a Frustrator; even the Communicators seemed unable to tell Yeats if he had just been talking to a Frustrator. The baffled poet received this enigmatic warning: "Remember, we will deceive you if we can." But was this a Communicator speaking? Or a Frustrator?[12]

The spirits also called themselves, as Brenda Maddox reports in *Yeats's Ghosts,* Guides and Controls: "'Fish' was what George considered a Guide. In her explanations to Yeats about the messages coming to her from the spirit world, she differentiated between Controls, spirits who once were human and who offered wisdom, and Guides. Guides bore the names of natural objects and gave advice on spiritual matters, as 'Fish' demonstrated by briskly ordering the couple not to make their Irish trip until after a long period of rest."[13]

Yeats set down in *A Vision* his final, bewildered thoughts about where the spirits came from.

I have heard my wife in the broken speech of some quite ordinary dream use tricks of speech characteristic of the philosophic voices. Sometimes the philosophic voices themselves have become vague and trivial or have in some other way reminded me of dreams. Furthermore their doctrine supports the resemblance, for one said in the first month of communication, "We are often but created forms," and another, that spirits do not tell a man what is true but create such conditions, such a crisis of fate, that the man is compelled to listen to his Daimon [guardian angel or guide; familiar spirit]. And again and again they have insisted that the whole system is the creation of my wife's Daimon and of mine, and that it is as startling to them as to us. Mere "spirits," my teachers say, are the "objective," a reflection and distortion; reality itself is found by the Daimon in what they call, in commemoration of the Third Person of the Trinity, the Ghostly Self. The blessed spirits must be sought within the self which is common to all.

Much that has happened, much that has been said, suggests that the communicators are the personalities of a dream shared by my wife, by myself, occasionally by others—they have, as I must some day prove, spoken through others without change of knowledge or loss of power—a dream that can take objective form in sounds, in hallucinations, in scents, in flashes of light, in movements of external objects.[14]

The spirits set forth a cosmology. It had much in common with ideas Yeats had been entertaining for years. It turned on three principal concepts: that the range of human personality can be represented by the twenty-eight phases of the moon; that the individual soul passes through each of these phases, which run from total objectivity through total subjectivity in a series of reincarnations; and that civilization moves in cycles of two thousand years, each cycle, or "Great Wheel," being heralded by a sort of divine rape followed by acts of violence.

The gamut human personality runs is composed of two types of persons: those who gain power through their struggle with the external world and those who gain it through their struggle with themselves. The first type is generally men and women of action, obliged to do battle with circumstances; the second is the artist and the visionary, compelled to live, to some extent, and at the expense of daily life, in the world of the imagination. Often, in their next incarnations, men and women become the opposite of what they have just been.

Yeats and the spirits broadened this scheme to include entire civilizations. Each two-thousand-year cycle, or Great Wheel, was heralded by the descent of a divine, birdlike entity into our everyday world. Acts of violence accompanied this descent. The first two-thousand-year period to which the spirits drew attention began four thousand years ago when Zeus, father of the Greek gods, descended from Mount Olympus as a swan and raped the mortal woman Leda. Leda gave birth to Helen, who was abducted to Troy by Paris. Agamemnon, Helen's husband, mobilized a coalition of armies, sailed to Troy, and at the end of ten years defeated the Trojans and seized Helen back.

The fall of Troy marked the end of the previous Great Wheel cycle and opened the way for the ascendancy of the Greeks in the next cycle and the eventual dominance of Rome. The Trojan prince Aeneas, fleeing the burning city with a remnant of his people, would eventually found Rome.

Yeats evokes the inception of this age in the poem *Leda and the Swan*. Zeus comes to earth, rapes Leda, and immediately sets in motion the chain of events leading inexorably to the destruction of Troy:

> *A shudder in the loins engenders there*
> *The broken wall, the burning roof and tower*
> *And Agamemnon dead.*[15]

The two-thousand-year cycle of Greek and Roman dominance comes to an end when God, or the Holy Spirit, descends to earth in the form of a dove and impregnates Mary. Jesus is born; this will bring about, after several centuries, the end of the Roman Empire and the dominance of Christianity. The act of violence accompanying the divine rape of Mary is Christ's crucifixion.

Yeats and the spirits believed that man in the twentieth century is at the end of another historical cycle. What form will the new Great

Wheel take? A sense of foreboding pervades Yeats's poem *The Second Coming,* as the narrator declares "things fall apart, the center cannot hold." The poet frets:

> *And what strange beast, its hour come round at last*
> *Slouches toward Bethlehem to be born?*[16]

The spirits had told Yeats at the beginning, "We have come to give you metaphors for poetry."[17] This proved to be true; until the sessions ended in 1921, gemlike phrases issued periodically from the Communicators to adorn and deepen Yeats's poems.

In 1922, William Butler Yeats was named one of the first senators of the Irish Free State. By that time he and Georgie had two children, Anne and Michael. In 1923, Yeats won the Nobel Prize for Literature. He would be as effective a senator as he was a manager of the Abbey Theatre. He never ceased to write great poetry (whether he was helped in this by the love affairs he had in the last decade of his life is a matter about which literary historians are inconclusive). Yeats died in 1939, mourned by his family and the Irish nation.

When *A Vision* was first published in 1925—a revised edition of the work appeared in 1937—nobody knew that this volume represented only a tiny part of the almost four thousand pages of transcripts. Georgie maintained close control over the transcripts until her death in 1968. She stipulated in her will that the complete text was not to be released to the public until fifteen years after her death. The task of editing and publishing the full text eventually fell to Yeats scholar George Mills Harper of the University of Florida, in Gainesville, who headed a committee of six scholars. In 1987, Professor Harper's explanatory volume *The Making of Yeats's "A Vision"* appeared. It was followed by the publication in three volumes, completed in 1992, of the entire transcript of what Harper and his committee labeled the *Vision Papers.*

Journalist Brenda Maddox read through the three volumes. In *Yeats's*

*Ghosts: The Secret Life of W. B. Yeats,* published in 1999, she declared that with this comprehensive publication, "the Automatic Script was revealed for what it was: a circuitous method of communication between a shy husband and wife who hardly knew each other, whose sexual life had got off to a troubled start, and for whom the occult and the sexual were virtually indistinguishable."[18]

Maddox asserts: "Three-quarters of what was delivered [during the sessions] was devoted to matters so personal as to be unusable in the book of philosophy, *A Vision,* that he [Yeats] was to make out of it. The 'scattered sentences' [in the original transcripts] were strangely preoccupied with Yeats's sexual life; indeed the messengers seemed at times to have been reading Marie Stopes's *Married Love,* a highly popular book that stressed the husband's duty to give his wife sexual satisfaction."[19]

Maddox concludes (it is the whole thrust of her book):

> That the Script had another purpose [than communicating metaphysical truths] is transparently obvious now that Yeats's *Vision Papers* can be read in detail. It handed Georgie the levers of control over the marriage. The couple had married so precipitately that the basic decisions about their future remained to be taken: where they would live, how they would organize their finances, and even whether they were to have a family. By falling into her stenographic trances, Georgie was doing more than hold her marriage together. She was preparing Yeats to father a child. Whether from her own wish for a baby, from her awareness of his determination to placate his ancestors, or from her eagerness to cement the marriage (probably from all three), her pages give procreation a high priority—as if she sensed that it was going to be difficult. Yeats's "incredible experience," whatever else it was, was a preliminary to conception. . . . From the time of the move to Oxford, the Automatic Script may be read as an exercise in family planning.[20]

Maddox attributes a massive feat of mental sleight-of-hand to Georgie, not to say a certain degree of dishonesty. R. F. Foster, Yeats's official biographer, is basically in agreement with Brenda Maddox: "Effectively the 'automatic script' represents her [Georgie's] own creative work; it also hints at her decisive intervention on various issues where she may have felt he needed guidance."[21] Foster does suggest that, from time to time, Georgie did not necessarily have complete conscious control over what she was "automatically" writing. Was Georgie involved at best in a curious emotional/psychological/creative dynamic that virtually took on a life of its own?

There may be more to it than that. In a metaphysical digression toward the end of *A Vision*, Yeats comes close to suggesting that people's encounters with the spirit world may be for quite different reasons than we think: they may represent an effort by the dead, having slipped back into some unknown and undifferentiated realm outside of time and space, to recover the memories of who and what they were. This is discussed in chapter 19 of this book, where Yeats's thoughts on the subject are placed in the context of C. G. Jung's descriptions of his own encounters with the spirit world. A simple dismissal may be doing a great injustice to these automatic writing communications, which Yeats, a poet of high intelligence as well as splendid imagination, took with the utmost seriousness from the day they began until the last day of his life.

# *Fifteen*

# H. G. Wells
# (1866–1946)

## *Did the Father of Science Fiction Have a Near-Death Experience?*

She was not clear whether it was night or day nor where she was; she made a second effort, wincing and groaning, and turned over and got in a sitting position and looked about her. . . . She seemed to be in a strange world, a soundless, ruinous world, a world of heaped broken things. And it was lit—and somehow this was more familiar to her mind than any other fact about her—by a flickering, purplish-crimson light.[1]

It sounds like a description by one of the survivors of the A-bomb exploding over Hiroshima, Japan, in August 1945. But it isn't; rather, it's a description by a French soldier of a German atomic bomb exploding over the Eiffel Tower in the latter part of the twentieth century.

The above scene is from *The Last War: A World Set Free,* a novel by science-fiction writer H. G. Wells published in 1913. In the novel, Wells also provides a detailed description of an artificially induced chain reaction, stoked by an artificial element called Carolinum, whose "degeneration passed only slowly into the substance of the bomb."[2] Not until the early 1930s did any scientist think such a thing might be possible.

In *The War in the Air,* a novel published in 1908, the English novelist/social prophet was every bit as prescient. The novel describes a surprise air attack on Manhattan, and in doing so sets forth the disposition of power as it actually would be during the Second World War: the Japanese rule the Pacific, while the Germans conquer Europe under the leadership of a charismatic fanatic who is half Napoleon, half "Nietzsche's Overman revealed."[3]

The further away in time we get from H. G. Wells, the more uncannily prophetic he seems. Certainly, not all his imaginings have come true. There has been no invasion from Mars (*The War of the Worlds,* 1898), nor have there been any feats of time travel (*The Time Machine,* 1894–95). But scattered here and there through Wells's many novels, short stories, and essays are not only astonishingly apt descriptions of things that would come to pass, but also speculative ideas that would not emerge until close to one hundred years in the future.

The short story *The Man Who Could Work Miracles,* published in 1898, dramatizes the notion, first popularized by medium Jane Roberts in her 1970s Seth books, that our thoughts create reality, and also the concept, vividly fleshed out in the *Back to the Future* movie trilogy of the 1980s, that if we were to travel back to the past, we would change the present and also the future. The hero described in the title of the short story *The Man Who Could Work Miracles* discovers that he can make anything happen and create any object, simply by wishing it so. He begins with minor feats, like materializing a rose. Then he gets into righting social injustices. Eventually he gets so carried away with what he's doing that he wishes the day wouldn't end. In effect he is wishing the earth would stop rotating on its axis, and this is what happens—and the force of momentum tears everything movable loose from our planet's surface and carries it crashing forward in a cataclysm of destruction. The narrator hastily wishes himself back to the time before he acquired these powers, also wishing that he will never acquire them and that he will forget he ever did. This happens, and the story ends with the earth rotating calmly on its axis and the narrator oblivious to the earth-destroying alternate universe he created, and then made vanish.

How was Wells able to be so startlingly accurate in so many of his predictions of the future? Was he actually able to see the future?

Herbert George Wells was born into a working-class family in Bromley, Kent, that was so poor it seemed unlikely the boy would ever even qualify for college. At age fourteen, Wells was apprenticed to a draper; despising this trade, he broke away, attended night school, and briefly became a teacher's assistant at the Holt Academy in Wrexham, Wales. Eventually, Wells would receive a scholarship to study biology, attend lectures in London, and in 1888 acquire a college degree in science, thereby paving the way for his brilliant career as a writer. But it was while he was at Holt, in 1886, just before his twenty-first birthday, that an event may have taken place that would change, more radically than any sojourn at a college, the entire future course of H. G. Wells's life.

The author writes in his *Experiment in Autobiography* (1934) that in his first term at Holt he was playing football with some students when one of them threw him roughly to the ground. Wells managed to get to his feet but felt very ill. He had a throbbing pain in his side. Staggering off the field, he somehow made it back to his rooms. He writes: "In the house I was violently sick. I went to lie down. Then I was moved to urinate and found myself staring at a chamberpot half full of scarlet blood. That was the most dismaying moment in my life. I did not know what to do. I lay down again and waited for someone to come."[4]

He seems to have lost consciousness for the next few hours. Then, "Nothing very much was done about me that evening, but in the night I was crawling along the bedroom on all fours, delirious, seeking water to drink. The next day a doctor was brought from Wrexham. He discovered that my left kidney had been touched."[5]

The doctor didn't expect H. G. Wells to live. But the future author, after languishing in bed for many days, slowly began to recover. He went back to work but started coughing blood again. Tuberculosis was diagnosed. This disease and its complications would dog Wells all his life.

In 1896, ten years after his accident at Wrexham, Wells wrote a short story, *Under the Knife,* in which the narrator slips out of his body during surgery and undergoes a sort of "near-death experience" (NDE). In 1906, Wells wrote a short story, *The Door in the Wall,* that seems to present in startling detail all the elements of a near-death experience as they would come to be known to medical science almost a century later.

In *The Truth in the Light: An Investigation of Over 300 Near-Death Experiences* (1997), authors Peter and Elizabeth Fenwick conducted a poll of near-death experiencers (NDErs) in which they sought to find out what had happened to them after they had gotten beyond the customary white light and glowing tunnel experiences of a "typical" NDE. A quarter of the respondees said they had been "left standing at the entrance [to the afterworld], but prevented from going in by some kind of barrier, a point of no return, beyond which they know they cannot go."[6] Sometimes the barrier was psychological; other times it was physical, such as the "low green trellis fence"[7] reported in one case, or the "wrought-iron gate—a tall church-window shaped gate"[8] reported in another.

The otherworldly entities beyond the barrier often presented themselves in groups of three. One respondee found herself standing before three "young Indian men . . . young Indian princes, or rajas";[9] another found himself in the presence of "three old Chinese men who all had long white beards, and who also wore white robes."[10] Often only the being in the middle faced the experiencer directly.

The authors found that the well-known NDE "life review" often contained tantalizing glimpses of the experiencer's future. One interviewee, arriving at a church, observed "two large trestles, each with a book resting on them." A spirit guide, flicking through the pages, which were blank, stated: "This will be your life if you go back." Suddenly the empty pages filled up.[11] The respondee, though conflicted, decided he had no choice but to return to life.

At the beginning of Wells's "The Door in the Wall," the narrator, Wallace, then age five or six, finds himself standing in front of a mysterious green door. He wants to go in, but feels "either it was unwise or it was wrong of him."[12] Yielding to temptation, he enters, and finds himself in a gorgeous garden with "something in the very air of it that exhilarated . . . something in the sight of it that made all its color clean and perfect and subtly luminous."[13]

The boy proceeds down a wide path and meets three beings: two panthers who escort him and a "tall, fair girl"[14] at the end of the path who picks him up and kisses him. The girl leads him to a "spacious, cool palace,"[15] where he experiences a timeless interlude of events and game-playing whose details he will forget. A second triad of beings appears: "two dear playfellows who were most with me"[16] and "a somber dark woman, with a grave, pale face and dreamy eyes . . . who carried a book, and [led me] into a gallery above a hall."[17] The woman opens the book and, the narrator tells us, "in the living pages of that book I saw myself. . . . In it were all the things that had happened to me since ever I was born."[18]

This apparent classic NDE life review turns into something bigger: "Then, I turned the pages over, skipping this and that, to see more of this book and more, and so at last I came to myself hovering and hesitating outside the green door in the long white wall, and felt again the conflict and the fear."[19] The boy begins to turn this final page and is stopped by the woman. They struggle; the woman yields; the narrator just glimpses the page, then finds himself no longer in the enchanted garden but in "a long gray street in West Kensington, . . . weeping aloud . . . because I could not return to my dear playfellows who had called after me, 'Come back to us! Come back to us soon!'"[20]

The boy has returned to grim reality; all through his life he will long to return to the enchanted garden. He happens upon the green door three more times. Each time he doesn't go in, feeling that entry is somehow forbidden. Each of these occasions has caught him in the midst of hurrying to a rendezvous crucial to his worldly success; to linger in the garden would be to jeopardize that success.

At the end of his life, set to become a cabinet minister, the narrator—perhaps; we will never know—yields to that vision that seems to issue from the innermost depths of his soul. He disappears. His body is found in an excavation shaft; apparently, he has fallen through a construction doorway.

Was there a door like the one in *The Door in the Wall* in the deepest regions of H. G. Wells's soul? Did the future author of *The Time Machine* suffer a near-death experience on the night he almost died from a football accident, one that flung him into a place beyond time and opened a channel between that place and his imagination? If not, how did Wells know—as he seems to have—the fine details of near-death experiences that have only become known in the late twentieth century, when medical science has advanced to the point where victims can be resuscitated from the very brink of death? In some of the classic NDEs of our time, the NDEr is shown large-scale future events. In *Saved by the Light* (1994), for example, author/experiencer Dannion Brinkley, struck by lightning and "dead" for twenty-eight minutes, finds himself standing in a crystalline "cathedral of knowledge," where Beings of Light give him one hundred and seventeen glimpses of future events—ninety-five of which had come to pass (by Brinkley's count) by 1993, eighteen years after his experience.[21]

During his night of agony at his digs in the Holt Academy, was H. G. Wells granted such visions, and more?

If he was, why didn't he tell us?

One reason may be that Wells was not only a skeptic (at least for public consumption) but also a Victorian, and Victorians tended not to talk much about their private lives. Wells had more need than most to be close-mouthed; twice-married, the father of two sons, he was a notorious philanderer who had at least two illegitimate children, a dozen extended love affairs, and hundreds of brief sexual encounters. He kept an ongoing secret diary of his liaisons that, according to a stipulation in his will, was to be published only after all the women named in the diary had died. This came about in 1983 with the death of author Rebecca West, mother of Wells's illegitimate son Anthony West; the diary, entitled *H. G. Wells in Love: Postscript to an Experiment in Autobiography,* was published in 1984. It may be that Wells's necessary habit of great reticence spilled over into other areas of his life as well, including that of his personal psychic experiences.

Whatever the causes, Wells's ability to anticipate not only future scientific developments but also "New Age" themes of the late twentieth century is truly amazing. He wrote a short story about an encounter with an angel: In *The Wonderful Visit* (1895), an angel is accidentally shot down by a game-hunting vicar. Fallen from a "fourth dimension" of ideal beauty, the angel goes back home because he is disgusted by humanity's degraded nature. Astral travel is a theme: In *The Plattner Story* (1896), the protagonist astral-voyages to a shadowy realm parallel to our own that resembles the "waiting rooms of the dead" described by astral traveler Robert A. Monroe in *Far Journeys* and *Ultimate Journey.* In a twilight zone illuminated by the flickering light of a dim green sun the traveler comes upon spectral counterparts of the living—disembodied heads called "Watchers of the Living"—who crowd around the dying to monitor the departure of their souls to heaven. *The Mysterious Case of Davidson's Eyes* (1894) is about seeing from a distance—"remote viewing." A lab explosion causes scientist Davidson's seeing to leap to a deserted South Pacific island while the rest of him remains in London. Blind for a time to his actual surroundings, Davidson eventually experiences his eyesight receding from the island and returning to him in London.

In our time there has been interest in "past-life regression therapy"—hypnotizing patients and helping them access memories of previous lives to see if those lives are affecting their health in this one. There has also been interest in "future-life progression—hypnotizing clients and helping them move into the future to view a possible future life. Wells's "A Dream of Armageddon" (1901) reads remarkably like a story about future-life progression." Every four or five days, the protagonist dreams of living in an apparent future lifetime. So vivid are these dreams that he appears to awaken and live in that future reality as he dreams it. Each dream brings him into greater possession of the details of that future life. He learns that his future self is Hedon, a dynamic national leader living in a country "away there in the north."[22] Hedon abandons his position for love and goes to live with his beloved in a futurized Capri. His absence provokes the enemies of his country to attack; in the ensuing battle, he and his companion are killed. Then the dreamer finds himself in an even worse predicament: a lifetime far in the prehistoric past, where he exclaims at the end of the story—will these be his last words?—"My God! Great birds that fought and tore."[23]

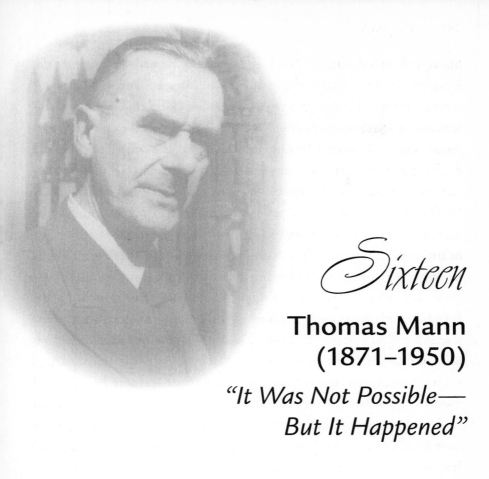

# Sixteen

# Thomas Mann (1871–1950)

## *"It Was Not Possible— But It Happened"*

In June 1912, the thirty-seven-year-old German writer who was destined to win the Nobel Prize for Literature in 1929 sat in the front car of a train that wound its way up an Alpine mountainside in Switzerland. Thomas Mann was headed for the town of Davos. As the train rattled over narrow defiles, he reflected that there were often one or two passengers on this train for whom this trip up the Alps was a journey of no return.

Davos lies in a mile-high Alpine valley that often seems to be floating in the clouds. Today it is celebrated for the World Economic Forum, which takes place there every year. A century ago it was famous for the tuberculosis sanatoriums whose stern facades, rising up stolidly from the snow-covered hills surrounding the town, served to remind the visitor of the brevity of life. Mann was on his way to the Waldsanatorium to see his wife, Katia. She had come down with a lung ailment six months before that no one could identify. She had come to Davos in hopes of finding a cure. Mann prayed that this breathtaking ride up the mountains, with towering peaks reaching to the clouds on the one hand and rugged cliffs plunging down to the valleys on the other, was one his wife would enjoy again, on her way back to Germany.

Katia met him at the station. She seemed hearty and healthy. Very soon, Mann wasn't sure he could say this for the Waldsanatorium. Over the three weeks of his stay he became increasingly oppressed by his surroundings. The air was fresh but oddly odorless; it lacked humidity, it was without content. In the sanatorium, the funereal silence of the corridors was broken only by the abrupt giggle of a patient or by a coughing fit so horrific, so eerily without gusto or any connection with life, that this feeble welling-up of toxic fluid[1] from rotting lungs seemed to issue from somebody who was already dead.

It was as if the sanatorium restaurant was frequented by ghosts—ghosts that ate silently, made silly jokes, engaged in vicious gossip. Mann couldn't help feeling that sanatoriums like these, isolated as they were from real life, with their endless catering to the patients' whims and their exclusive focus on the minutiae of disease, were dangerous to young people—and tuberculosis was almost always a disease of the young.

The writer had been at the sanatorium for ten days when, probably because he sat out on the balcony in the cold damp weather, he came down with a bronchial ailment. He went with Katia to her regular examination. The physician thumped Mann's chest and told him he had a moist spot on his lung and should stay at the sanatorium for six months.

Mann refused. He would later write: "If I had followed his advice, I might still be there! I wrote *The Magic Mountain* instead. In *it* I made use of the impressions gathered during my three weeks' stay."[2]

Arrived back home in Munich (Katia would follow later with a clean bill of health), Mann completed his novel *Death in Venice* and began *The Magic Mountain*. The story rapidly assumed proportions he hadn't dreamt of. Then the turmoil of real life intervened—as it had in 1910, when Carola, his beloved second sister, had committed suicide, or in 1912, when Katia had gone off to the sanatorium and left him in charge of their four children. This time, the intervention was catastrophic and universal. In August 1914, World War I broke out. It would rage across Europe for the next four years, leaving Germany defeated and in ruins.

The first fifteen years of Thomas Mann, who was born in Lübeck in 1875 and died in Switzerland in 1955, were relatively serene, marred mainly by fights with his father over his hatred of school. He didn't respond well to formal education and once at university only audited courses. Mann decided early on to devote himself to writing, soon achieving success with his novel *Buddenbrooks,* published when he was twenty-seven. Fame, marriage, and children (eventually there would be six) followed in rapid succession. Once World War I broke out, he stopped writing fiction entirely. Exempted from military service, Mann defended his country's policies while devoting much time to a long essay on the writer's independence from politics, *Reflections of a Non-Political Man.*

In 1918, amid the wreckage of a humiliated Germany, Mann began to write fiction again. He resumed work on *The Magic Mountain* while completing a host of other novels and short stories. Then, in Christmas week of 1923, as he was beginning the final section of *The Magic Mountain,* he had an encounter with the paranormal.

Munich under Germany's Weimar Republic was as crowded with bizarre and extravagant lifestyles as a hothouse is with tropical plants of exotic shapes and sizes. This was fertile ground for the exploration of paranormal phenomena. The city was a mecca for mediums and "occultists"—investigators of the occult to whom flocked a public hungry for novelty and escape. Dr. Albert Freiherr von Schrenck-Notzing was a German baron, medical doctor, and occultist to whose séances, conducted at his home, prominent members of Munich society came by special invitation. Von Schrenck-Notzing had discovered a new medium, the nineteen-year-old Willy Schneider, who not only channeled messages but also manifested physical phenomena. In the last week of December 1923, Mann received an invitation through a friend.

Thomas Mann was an agnostic in the matter of occult phenomena. He felt what he called a certain "theoretical sympathy" for the subject. But thinking about the supernatural made him edgy. Thus it was that—as he tells us in his essay "An Experience in the Occult"—Mann and his friend made their way to Dr. von Schrenck-Notzing's Munich mansion "in high spirits, exhilarated, curious, in a mood between bluster and funk, something like the feelings of a young man going for the first time to a girl."[3]

Twenty people milled about von Schrenck-Notzing's sitting room. There was a handful of artists, but the guests were predominantly scientists and doctors. The host introduced the medium, Willy Schneider, a slightly built, young, and bashful dentist from Schwabing. Initially, the atmosphere of the room seemed ordinary, even humdrum, to Mann. That would change.

Von Schrenck-Notzing helped Willy put on a one-piece black garment that stretched from his neck to his ankles and was meant to show the audience there was nothing concealed on his person. The physician/occultist then wrapped the medium in a dressing gown on which luminescent ribbons had been sewn so the guests could follow Willy's movements in the dark.

The medium sat down in a chair against a curtained backdrop, while the guests seated themselves in a semicircle some ten feet away. Mann was chosen to be the "first control." He sat down facing the medium, with "his two knees between mine"[4] and holding Willy's hands. The medium's landlady, Frau P., was the second control. She bent over Willy and held his wrists.

Mann looked around, taking in the physical trappings of the room. Five feet from Willy, there was a small table on which von Schrenck-Notzing had placed

a lamp in a red shade, the table-bell, a plate of flour, a little slate and a piece of chalk. A sizable waste-paper-basket stood upside-down by the table, with a music box on it . . . [a] typewriter the Baron set somewhere on the carpet near himself; then he strewed felt rings about the floor within the circle. They were luminous . . .[5]

The séance began. Mann writes: "After two or three minutes, he [Willy] shivered. A shudder ran through him, and his arms, taking mine along, began to perform pumping and thrusting motions. His breath came short and quick."[6] The guests had been told to expect two personalities, "Erwin" and "Minna," to manifest; they leaned forward eagerly. Von Schrenck-Notzing explained that it was Erwin who was responsible for Willy's violent movements. Minna would appear in good time. She would behave more subtly.

The guests listened intently. Willy gasped out that they should form a chain—hold hands—and talk. The baron explained that this was to keep the guests from watching too eagerly for phenomena; they should, rather, maintain a "hovering attitude." Time passed. Willy was speaking in "quick groans and pants."[7] His heavy breathing and perspiring struggles reminded Mann of a woman's labor while giving birth.

Three-quarters of an hour went by. Willy thrashed and turned while Mann held his hands and knees. The medium slipped periodically into deep sleep, from which he awakened suddenly and violently, writhing and shaking in his chair. The guests held hands and chattered loudly. A zoology professor played the accordion. The music box was set going. This was all meant to help bring on the phenomena. The setting, Mann observes, was "fantastic."[8]

It was time for a breather. Willy emerged from his trance and chatted amiably with the guests.

The séance resumed. A Polish painter, Von K., who had attended an earlier séance at which Minna manifested, took over from Mann as first control. Mann took over from Willy's landlady as second control. Close to another hour went by. Willy pumped and twisted to and fro, tossed and trembled. He whispered; he foamed at the mouth. The guests talked. The music box played.

A subtle change descended upon the room. Willy paused and asked for a handkerchief. Von Schrenck-Notzing took one out of his pocket and tossed it on the floor.

One of the guests muttered huskily, "It's coming," as the handkerchief

> rose from the floor . . . with a swift, assured, almost beautiful, movement. . . . It was not that it was wafted up, empty and fluttering. Rather, it was taken and lifted, there was an active agency in it, like a hand, you could see the outline of the knuckles, from which it hung down in folds; it was manipulated from the inside, by some living thing, compressed, shaken, made to change its shape, in the two or three seconds during which it was held up in the lamplight. It was not possible—but it happened. May lightning strike me if I lie.[9]

The handkerchief fell to the floor. It rose again, faster than before. You could see "something clutching it from within, the members of something that held it—it looked to be narrower than a human hand, more like a claw."[10] The handkerchief dropped to the floor, then rose for a third time. It flung itself toward the table, missed, and fell to the floor, where it lay still. Mann writes that "never before had I seen the impossible happening despite its own impossibility."[11]

Now an invisible hand lifted up the bell and rang it. The presence rang a doorbell the baron had placed on the upside-down wastepaper basket. The basket tipped over, levitated, dropped to the floor. The music box had been turned off; now it was playing. The typewriter keys clicked loudly and at length. This clattering, states Mann, was "in the highest degree startling, bewildering, ridiculous."[12]

A form began to materialize,

> a longish something, vague, and whitely shimmering; in size and general shape like a human forearm, with closed fist—but certainly not recognizable as such. It comes and goes . . . lighted by a sort

of flash of white lightning that issues from its own right side and wholly obscures whatever shape it has—then it is gone.[13]

During all this time Willy, held tightly by the controls, ceaselessly tossed and turned. Whispered sounds escaped him intermittently. At one point he laid his forehead on Von K.'s hand, resting quietly as the manifestations went on. Then the séance was over. Willy emerged from the trance, his face and hands bathed in sweat.

How did Thomas Mann feel about this séance?

He writes that from time to time he experienced a "slight seasickness. Profound wonderment, with a tinge, not of horror, but of disgust."[14] The phantom—whatever moved the objects—did not seem to him to be evil but, rather, "shy, sly, stealthy . . . equivocal . . . quite well-meaning but weak-minded and embarrassed."[15]

In the concluding pages of "An Experience in the Occult," Mann discusses the mechanics of what happened and wonders if Minna was "the partly exteriorized medium himself."[16] He reflects on the theory of "ectoplasm," the half-spiritual/half-physical substance exuded from mediums and thought to constitute the material of the manifestations. He puts forward his own theory: the "telekinetic phenomena" are "the medium's magically objectivated ideas."[17]

Mann has saved the best for the last. At the end of his essay, he describes an earlier séance with Willy, one he did not attend. The ectoplasmic body of Minna, if that was what it was, had, in full view of everyone, laid its hand six times on a piece of soft wax on the table.

After the séance, "at the bottom of the index finger and on the wrist, wax had been found on Willy's hand."[18]

Mann's encounter with the paranormal had a powerful effect on him, as we will see when we look at his greatest novel, *The Magic Mountain*, published in 1924.

In *The Magic Mountain*, a young engineer, Hans Castorp, makes the same breathtaking trip up the mountain as did Thomas Mann. A correct and ultrarepressed German, Castorp comes to Davos for three weeks to visit his cousin Joachim Ziemssen, who is being treated for tuberculosis at the International Sanatorium Hofberg. Castorp is very soon diagnosed with a bronchial ailment. Like Mann, he is advised to stay for six months. Unlike Mann, he stays—for seven years.

Mann uses Castorp's stay at the clinic as a vehicle for exploring issues of European bourgeois society, including the destructiveness of that society as a whole, which was to lead to World War I. Castorp conceives a mixture of lust and love for a fellow patient, a Russian woman, Clavdia Chauchat. He engages in endless debates with an Italian, Settembrini, who is a liberal, a humanist, and a supporter of democratic ideals and morality, and a German, Naphta, who defends the forces of decay: radicalism and extremism, fascism, anarchism, and communism. (Does this sound academic, dull, boring? The Thomas Mann who hated school had a genius for making ideas come alive, for making them seem like actual living beings in his novels. The reader will discover this on reading *The Magic Mountain*.) Driven this way and that through the years by the powerful play of these personalities and ideas, Castorp takes refuge in a third way of perceiving reality: occultism.

Mann means to make it difficult for us to dismiss out-of-hand the paranormal events he introduces near the end of this novel. Elly Brand, a plain-looking, sweet-natured, nineteen-year-old Danish girl, arrives at the sanatorium. She has mediumistic powers: she can find hidden or lost objects. Her guardian spirit, Holger, whispers the locations in her ear. Elly's achievements persuade the patients to conduct two séances in the room of one of them. Hans Castorp will be present at both these séances.

At the first séance is "a medium-sized round table without a cloth, placed in the center of the room, with a wineglass upside-down upon it, the foot in the air. Round the edge of the table, at regular incidents, were placed twenty-six little bone counters, each with a letter of the alphabet written on it in pen and ink."[19] The ten guests each place a finger on the wineglass; after a wait it abruptly races to the letters and, skittering from one to the other, spells out "Holger." Holger was a poet, it spells out, and then writes out a great deal of poetry. Castorp asks how long he will be at the sanatorium. The wineglass seems confused and spells out something nonsensical. There is the sudden loud pounding of a fist on the door. There is a second crashing knock on the center of the table. The lights go out; a presence pulls a guest's hair; and an object materializes on Hans's lap: an X-ray of the lungs of Clavdia Chauchat, his beloved.

The second séance takes place a week or two later. In between, the physician-in-chief has conducted experiments with Elly Brand and witnessed the same phenomena—handkerchief-lifting, wastepaper-basket turning—that Mann witnessed at Dr. von Schrenck-Notzing's séance. Castorp is first control at this séance, holding Elly's knees between his own while tightly gripping her wrists. Mann replicates the elements of the earlier séance, except that this time Holger is asked not to answer questions or make handkerchiefs hover in the air but to raise from the dead the spirit of Castorp's cousin Joachim Ziemssen, who died at the sanatorium some months before.

Elly writhes, struggles, moans, is violent, falls asleep for two hours as the guests chatter and hold hands so as not to focus their thoughts on the manifestation they hope will happen. Hans finally suggests they play a record his cousin loved, a song from Gounod's opera *Faust*. They do so—and the ultimate happens: out of the agony and confusion of Elly's seeming birth pangs, an apparition is born. Halfway across the room, Joachim sits as he did in his "last days, with hollow, shadowy cheeks, warrior's beard and full, curling lips."[20] He wears an unfamiliar military uniform with an odd, upside-down, cook-pot-like helmet on his head.

As it always did, his quiet, friendly gaze seeks out Hans Castorp, "and him alone."[21] Hans gets up and switches on the light. The chair is empty. Ashamed at having disturbed the peace of his cousin's soul, Hans abruptly leaves the room.

Mann had prepared the attentive reader for this final manifestation.

Many pages earlier, he had described the final hour of Joachim: "He began making a strange continuous movement with his right hand . . . passing it across the bedcover, at about the hips, lifting it as he drew it back and toward him, with a raking motion, as though he were gathering something in."[22]

At the second séance, Mann has described Elly as making the same motions in the hour before the apparition comes: "For some minutes together she moved the hollow of her hand to and fro in the region of her hips: carried the hand away from her body and then with scooping, raking motion drew it towards her, as though gathering something and pulling it in."[23]

Did Thomas Mann believe that the dead survive and that we can raise them if we wish?

It seems that in *The Magic Mountain* he refuses to allow us to draw conclusions, just as life refuses to allow us to draw conclusions—except when we insist, and if we don't mind being wrong. Such is the greatness of Mann's art.

## *Seventeen*

# Harry Houdini
# (1874–1926)

## *Ultimate Escape*

On Sunday, October 24, 1926, the great Hungarian-American escape artist and investigator of fake mediums Harry Houdini was hospitalized after being punched repeatedly in the stomach two days before.

The next day, Robert Gysel, an investigator who worked for Houdini, wrote to a friend, "Something happened to me in my room on Sunday night, October 24, 1926, 10:58. Houdini had given me a picture of himself which I had framed and hung on the wall. At the above time and date, the picture fell to the ground, breaking the glass. I now know that Houdini will die. Maybe there is something in these psychic phenomena after all."[1]

Houdini died six days later, on October 31, from peritonitis and other complications arising from the unexpected flurry of blows delivered to his abdomen in his dressing room on Friday night, October 22. He had just completed a standing-room-only performance at the Princess

Theater in Montreal, Canada. The wielder of the blows was a twenty-two-year-old McGill University student named J. Gordon Whitehead, who said he wanted to test Houdini's claim that his abdominal muscles were so tough they could take any punch without his being injured. At the time of his death, Harry Houdini was fifty-two years old.

The escape artist's world-famous stunts, such as escaping from a box that had been nailed shut and dropped into the Hudson River in midwinter with Houdini manacled inside, were achieved through a skillful combination of mental acuteness, discipline, and brawn. Yet another side of Houdini was on display when, in the decade before his death, he made separate post-life pacts with more than twenty friends, providing each with a unique code by which that friend would be able to tell if Houdini were attempting to communicate with him after the escape artist's death.

One of these friends was W. J. Hilliar. Arriving at Hilliar's *Billboard* magazine office in New York on December 2, 1917, Houdini dropped a copy of *Roget's Thesaurus* on the newspaperman's desk. Opening the volume, Hilliar saw a penciled inscription. He began to thank his visitor for the gift, but Houdini interrupted him. As authors William Kalush and Larry Sloman tell the story in *The Secret Life of Houdini: The Making of America's First Superhero,* Houdini whispered: "Hilliar, there is *our* code. But never breathe it to a living soul. If I go first and you get a message from me which includes these words, you will know it is genuine."[2]

Hilliar used the book over the years, always noting the inscription on the front page, but when he picked it up three days after the magician's death, he was stunned to see that while Houdini's signature was still prominent, the code words had faded away. Hilliar consulted handwriting experts, who told him that penciled words should never fade away. A minute examination revealed that the indentations of the pencil still existed, and one night Hilliar carefully traced over them. He was shocked to discover the next morning that the code had once again faded from the page.

Houdini seemed to be manifesting himself in other post-life circumstances. When he posed for the marble bust that eventually adorned his grave, he had three clay copies made. He kept one and gave one to Harry Day and one to Joe Hyman. Ten days after Houdini's death, Hyman's copy fell on the floor and shattered. A few days later, the exact same thing happened to Day's copy.[3]

Harry Houdini performed difficult escapes up to the very last days of his life. During the last dozen years of that life, he spent a great deal of time exposing fraudulent mediums. After Houdini's death, his wife, Bess, offered a reward to anyone who could pick up post-life messages from the escape artist. At one point, medium Arthur Ford seemed to have won the award, but the jury is still out as to whether Houdini made the greatest escape of all, returning, at least in message form, from the land of the dead.

Houdini's angry denial of an afterlife may have masked a certain vulnerability to the notion that the dead survive. The authors of *The Secret Life of Houdini* tell this story:

> Houdini had been spurred to develop his improved [diving] suit when a friend of his in Melbourne, Australia, drowned while deep-sea diving. Eerily, the two men had had plans to meet for dinner that night. His friend's death hit Houdini hard and he "formed a strong impression" that the friend had attempted to communicate with him, urging him to invent a safer suit.[4]

As we will see, Kalush and Sloman also present evidence in *The Secret Life of Houdini* suggesting that Harry Houdini did not die accidentally, but was murdered.

Ehrich Weiss, who later took the name Harry Houdini, was born to Jewish parents in Budapest on March 24, 1874. The family emigrated to Appleton, Wisconsin, when the future escape artist was four years old. Houdini's father was a sometime businessman and part-time rabbi who never really learned English; as a result, Houdini's preteen years were poverty-stricken. He left home at twelve and worked as a vaudeville/circus performer all through his teens. By his early twenties, he was famous in Europe as an escape artist. He rose to the pinnacle of success in the United States in his thirties, electrifying audiences with such feats as being lowered into the East River in New York in midwinter bolted into a coffin (he emerged an hour later) and escaping from a straitjacket hanging upside down from the side of a Manhattan skyscraper.

Only five feet four inches tall and weighing 150 pounds, Houdini was a wiry mass of impeccably trained muscle. He was in perfect shape when he died; certainly, without the accident, he would have lived for many more years.

A year before his death, Houdini told his wife, Bess, that if there was survival after death, he would send her an encoded message from the spirit world. After he died, Bess offered a $10,000 reward to the medium who delivered Houdini's message. More than two years after Houdini's death, and after three months of séances, the celebrated psychic Arthur Ford transmitted the decoded words *rosabelle believe* to his waiting wife.

Houdini's wife vowed that, yes, this was the agreed-upon message. All around the world, the media trumpeted the news of the great escape artist's ultimate escape. For a brief moment, Houdini's fame returned. Then skepticism set in, even on the part of Bess, who took back her claim that Arthur Ford had come up with the agreed-upon message. But such was the charisma of Harry Houdini that many would continue to believe he had returned, and do so to this day.

During his lifetime, particularly among his fellow professionals, Houdini was known as a man of outstanding ability and courage but also as somewhat less than a saint. Some claimed he owed his fame to his powers of self-promotion. Others saw his espousal of certain social causes as simply a means of garnering publicity. As mentioned earlier, Houdini spent a great deal of time exposing phony mediums, even attending bogus séances incognito and afterward re-creating the hoaxes onstage.

Stage professionals regarded his medium-bashing, which included testifying before Congress in favor of a bill banning mediumship, fortune-telling, and other "occult" activities initially from Washington, D.C. (the bill sank into legislative oblivion),[5] as the height of hypocrisy. It was of a piece, they said, with his highly publicized exposures of fake mediums that included his re-creating of their hoaxes onstage. After all, hadn't Houdini been a fake medium himself in the early years of his career? And hadn't he attended séance after séance after the death of his mother, longing to reconnect with the woman who had been the light of his life? His rivals and others wondered if (along with his ceaseless need to promote himself) bitterness over his failure to posthumously contact his mother was the real reason behind his obsessive and vicious bashing of the world of mediums.

Over the years, the power of Houdini's legend to deflect criticism has faded. Many of his contemporaries and near-contemporaries have stepped forward to point out the warts on Houdini's superbly muscled body. William V. Rauscher is a clergyman, professional magician, and researcher into paranormal phenomena. He knew many of those who claimed to bear witness to the dark side of Harry Houdini. In *The Houdini Code Mystery: A Spirit Secret Solved,* written primarily for professional magicians, Rauscher assembles their testimony. He concludes that for all his acknowledged courage, persistence, and skills, Houdini was hardly a hero in the classical, ancient-Greek mold, but rather one more in keeping with our tawdry modern world. The data Rauscher assembles also throws light on that greatest of Harry Houdini mysteries: whether he really spoke to his wife from the afterworld.

Rauscher asserts that central to Houdini's character was a mother fixation so severe that "even as a grown man he liked to sit on her knee, his head resting on her breast, listening to her heart."[6] It was while at a press conference in Copenhagen that he received the cable containing the news of his mother's death; reading it, the Great Houdini "crumpled to the floor in a dead faint."[7] He stipulated that a bundle of his mother's letters be placed under his head in the coffin he was buried in, and his instructions were obeyed.[8] A further indication of his mother fixation was that Houdini "literally froze" in the presence of any other woman except his wife, Bess, claims Rauscher.[9] This may have helped scuttle his acting career since—though he was not without talent—he was forever unable to play up to his leading lady. Rauscher believes that the Great Houdini was at the very least infertile (he and Bess never had children) and probably impotent.

Rauscher asserts that out of all this there arose in Houdini a rage that boiled over into a ruthless will to succeed. According to the old magician hands Rauscher interviewed, Houdini stole whole acts from other magicians and stage artists, and sometimes sabotaged their performances. From time to time he bribed people to swear he had performed feats he hadn't, such as that of allegedly escaping from a locked cell in a Chicago police station in 1901. One of Houdini's rivals, speaking in his old age, claimed that Houdini had tried to maim a competitor (the German escape artist "Minerva") by having his assistants put acid in her water barrel.[10] The portrait that emerges from Rauscher's book makes us believe that Houdini could well have prearranged his seeming "return from the dead."

Rauscher also focuses on some of Houdini's contemporaries who may have been involved in any plot on Houdini's part to fake a return from the dead. One of them was Arthur Ford. Rauscher and Ford were close friends for fifteen years, up to the latter's death in 1972. Rauscher writes:

> Ford, an urbane, educated, emotionally up-and-down personality, often reminisced wryly and sometimes wistfully (but never, to me, cynically) about "the good old days." Curiously, he would never, except on the rarest exceptions, discuss the Houdini Message episode. However, he could reflect on a vast procession of former "sitters" (as a medium's clients are called) ranging from movie stars and the intelligentsia to royalty. He had a rare gift (along with less admirable traits, such as episodic alcoholism, a touch of fraud, and a

confused sexual identity) of not taking himself seriously—in private, at least.[11]

Whatever his reservations about Ford, Rauscher believes he was a genuine medium. He writes: "If you ask me, 'Do you really believe that Ford sometimes—not always, not perhaps regularly, but sometimes—talked with the dead,' the evidence of my own experience compels me to answer: YES!"[12]

Houdini's Code Message came to Ford in nine séances (conducted from November 28, 1928, to January 7, 1929) from the medium's ostensible spirit guide "Fletcher." Only one word was produced per session. The encoded message finally rendered up was *"Rosabelle . . . answer . . . tell . . . pray-answer . . . look-tell . . . answer."* The code was this: that each word channeled after the word Rosabelle stood for a number, and that number indicated where the letter stood in the alphabet. This "telepathic" code is fairly well known—at least to stage magicians—but at the time of these séances no one knew that Rosabelle was Houdini's pet name for Bess, and that this name was inscribed on the inside of Bess's wedding band. When the final, climactic séance took place in Ford's apartment on January 7, Fletcher asked Bess at the conclusion to show her wedding ring to the assembled witnesses. Fletcher also communicated the phrase *"I pull the curtain,"* which Houdini had used with Bess in their first years together as man-and-wife stage magicians.[13]

Despite Bess's insistence that *"Rosabelle believe"* was the agreed-upon message, accusations of fraud surfaced just two days later. On January 9, Rea Jaure of the *New York Graphic*—one of the reporters who was present at the final séance—asserted that the message was a hoax engineered by Ford and Bess, with the connivance of none other than Rea Jaure herself. This barefaced lie, advanced by Jaure solely to sell newspapers, had to be quashed in the courts, even though not a shred of evidence existed to support Jaure's claim, and Ford and Bess had immediately issued denials.

The world-famous "mentalist" William Dunninger quickly leaped

into the fray, declaring that the fraud had been perpetrated by a cur-
vaceous one-time stage assistant to Houdini named Daisy White and
a twenty-eight-year-old "fish handler at the Fulton Market"[14] named
Joseph Bantano. Again, not a shred of evidence could be brought forward to support this claim, and with Daisy White threatening to sue
for libel, Dunninger dropped the charges.

Arthur Ford had been fairly well known as a medium for some time.
But it was because of his role in the Houdini Code Message affair that
his career really took off. This didn't change a bit when, a year or so
later, Bess changed her mind about the message from Houdini and
declared that *"Rosabelle believe"* was not at all the posthumous message
she and her husband had agreed on. However, those who still wished
to believe could come up with all sorts of psychological and emotional
reasons why Bess might have issued this untrue disavowal, so the legend
of Houdini's "return" from the dead lived on, and continues to thrive
to this day.

Rauscher has come up with one new piece of evidence regarding the
controversy surrounding Houdini and the afterworld. His source is Jay
Abbott, a New York Spiritualist and long-time, intimate friend of both
Ford and Bess. Jay Abbott spoke to Rauscher in April 1973—just three
months before Abbott's own death, in July of that year.

Abbott told Rauscher that Ford and Bess often dated before the
final Houdini séance, that Bess was in love with Ford, and that her ring
had fallen off as she was washing her hands in her apartment one day
when Ford was there. Ford had retrieved the ring, held on to it just long
enough to surreptitiously read its contents, then returned it to Bess.
That was how, said Abbott, the psychic had become the only person
besides Bess and Houdini to know the words inscribed inside the ring.
Ford put this knowledge to good use at the final séance.[15]

Abbott insisted Bess had known nothing about Ford's deception.
For Rauscher, however, this revelation was final proof of something he
had suspected for many years, namely, that ". . . Arthur Ford and Bess

Houdini were in full cahoots. It was a mutually agreed-upon grand and glorious hoax. Both were full partners. It was like Ragtime and the Roaring Twenties all rolled into one!"[16]

William Rauscher's contentions in *The Houdini Code Mystery* have attracted controversy. Martin Ebon, author of numerous books on paranormal phenomena, expressed the belief in 2001 that in making such charges, Rauscher was caught in a fundamental contradiction: "On the one hand, he says Arthur Ford sometimes actually did communicate with the dead. But, if he says this, then he has to accept that his 'control spirit,' Fletcher—or whatever energies Fletcher personifies—has some sort of objective reality bound up with the control spirit's connection to an 'afterworld.'"[17]

What role, then, asks Ebon, did Fletcher play in the unfolding of the cycle of nine séances that ended with Fletcher's delivering the final, fake, two-word message to Bess? Was Ford able so easily to persuade Fletcher to go along with the conspiracy? Or was Ford able to put his spirit control aside so easily and make it all up himself?

Ebon contends that if Ford was able to do these things so easily, then "he wasn't really psychic, and he never really communicated with the dead." But, says Ebon, Rauscher himself asserts that Ford really did sometimes communicate with the dead. "Then he has to deal with the problem of what role Fletcher played in this conspiracy. I think the presence of a real Fletcher, with all the unpredictability you get in channeling phenomena, would have made it very difficult for Ford to pull off any sort of a systematic hoax."[18]

Rauscher's quotes from Jay Abbott show Abbott to have a less-than-perfect memory, and suggest he may have had his own ax to grind; Rauscher speculates that Abbott may have been speaking out of the shadow of his own soured personal relationship with Arthur Ford.

In *The Secret Life of Houdini: The Making of America's First Superhero,* authors William Kalush and Larry Sloman are more focused on exploring whether Houdini was intentionally killed by J. Gordon Whitehead, the McGill University student who, without warning, hammered Houdini's abdomen with punches. For many years, Houdini had been attacking the Spiritualist movement and its mediums in every way he could; the authors wonder if Houdini's actions had not built up such a wave of resentment from believers in an afterlife that the nominal head of the worldwide Spiritualist movement, Sir Arthur Conan Doyle—author of the Sherlock Holmes stories and many serious works on Spiritualism and the spirit world—had not put out a *fatwah,* so to speak, against Houdini, or even hired Whitehead to murder him. To back up their theory, Kalush and Sloman offer only slim bits of circumstantial evidence and much speculation. One has to wonder if the highly intelligent and esteemed Doyle, known for going out of his way to help people, and with a worldwide reputation to maintain, would have felt any need to, or even been capable of contemplating, committing such a crime.

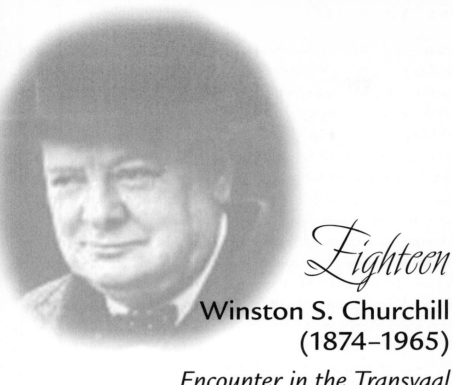

# *Eighteen*
# Winston S. Churchill
# (1874–1965)
## *Encounter in the Transvaal*

"My sole companion was a gigantic vulture, who manifested an extravagant interest in my condition, and made hideous and ominous gurglings from time to time."[1]

The above line could be a sort of metaphor for the desperate plight of the British nation during 1940, with Adolf Hitler playing the role of the monstrous vulture. All that year, England desperately shored up its defenses against an invasion from Nazi Germany, which now occupied Holland, Belgium, and France and stood on the shores of the English Channel manifesting an intense desire to cross the narrow strait and conquer the British people.

The author of the sentence about the vulture is Sir Winston Churchill, who, in the year 1940, as prime minister of Great Britain, rallied the British people to stand alone against the Nazi menace. So great was the personal courage he displayed in that year (and indeed in subsequent years) and so successful was he ultimately that many historians believe, in the words of Geoffrey Best, that this towering wartime leader "did what the more dogmatic critics of 'great man theory' doubt that even the greatest of men can do: he changed the apparent course of history."[2]

Churchill's words about a vulture were not about Adolf Hitler. Forty-one years earlier, in 1899, in South Africa's Transvaal, Winston Churchill, then just turned twenty-five, defiantly faced an actual vulture. The occasion was the early months of the Boer War, fought between the British and the Boers of Dutch descent in 1899–1902, in which Winston Churchill fought as a journalist soldier. Taken prisoner of war and transported to Pretoria, Churchill escaped and was making his way through enemy territory, first during the night, then during the day, when he encountered the ominous predator of the dead.

Churchill would, of course, make it to freedom. But only just, and—as we'll see—perhaps only because spiritual worlds reached out to help him.

Winston Spencer Churchill, prime minister of Great Britain and Ireland in 1940–1945 and 1951–1955, was born at Blenheim Palace in England on November 30, 1874, son of Lord Randolph Churchill, a brilliant politician who would one day be Chancellor of the Exchequer, and Jennie, née Jerome, a radiantly beautiful American woman who had been married to Lord Randolph for somewhat less than eight months before Winston Churchill was born.

Born with a large silver spoon in his mouth, Churchill grew up with every social amenity except one: attentive parents. Randolph and Jennie were aloof in their different ways, caught up in exercising and enjoying all the rights and privileges of the ruling class. But a wonderful nanny, Mrs. Everest, gave Winston much-needed love. Brilliantly creative, fearless, and of a restlessly active temperament, young Churchill went to Harrow and then Sandhurst. Graduating, he quickly saw action in some of the farthest-flung military engagements of that long-ago British

Empire upon which the sun had not begun to set. The battlegrounds included Afghanistan (as terrible and irreducible then as it is now) and the Sudan, where Winston took part in the last cavalry charge of the British Empire, at the Battle of Omdurman, when the British under Lord Kitchener decisively defeated the Sudanese.

The young Winston had been writing war dispatches all along. When the Boer War, fought between Great Britain and the Boer Republics of South Africa, broke out in 1899, Winston seized the opportunity and flung himself with his usual impetuous vigor into the dual role of soldier and reporter in this violent struggle at the bottom of the world.

The Dutch had in 1652 founded those colonies in South Africa that were now the Boer Republics. Great Britain also had possessions in the region: Cape Colony and Natal. In the mid-1800s, gold and diamonds were discovered in the Boer Transvaal Republic. Briton and Boer alike coveted these riches. British imperial ambition clashed with Boer independence sufficiently to alarm the Boers and make them attack and take Cape Colony in 1899. The Boers' aim was to forestall an impending British conquest, but their actions merely provoked the British into a declaration of war. In autumn 1899, the Royal Navy fleet steamed along the west coast of Africa on its way to Cape Town. The British were expecting a quick and easy victory. They would be very mistaken.

Pacing the deck of the lead ship, in fact a requisitioned ocean liner, was Winston Churchill. He had resigned his commission as a second lieutenant in 1898 to run (unsuccessfully) for a seat in parliament. Now, a year later, he was a war correspondent, hired by the *Morning Post* of London to send dispatches from South Africa. He was also itching to take a hand in the actual fighting. Disembarking at Cape Town, the British learned their forces had suffered initial and devastating defeats. Winston threw himself into the thick of the action. The action was very thick, and the British army was still struggling to find its feet. On November 15, 1899, Churchill was taken prisoner by the Boers.

Winston Churchill was a profoundly moral man, though he was

neither particularly religious nor excessively spiritual. "King and country was about all the religion Winston had," his personal physician,
Lord Moran, wrote many years later.[3] But Churchill was intensely
curious about everything, and thoughts about the afterlife had not
been absent from his mind. Fifteen months before, he had attended a
dinner the night prior to his departure for the Sudan; on that occasion, as he tells us in *My Early Life: 1874–1904,* the president of the
Psychical Research Society "extracted rather unseasonably a promise
from me after dinner to 'communicate' with him, should anything
unfortunate occur."[4]

This was not the sort of thing Winston Churchill dwelt on. But
now, in this new war, he may have recalled the words of the president of
the Psychical Research Society, as, after an exhausting forced march of
sixty miles and a very long train ride, he and sixty other British officers
found themselves locked up in a former schoolhouse in the Boer capital of Pretoria. This war was turning out to be as unrelenting as any;
Winston had no guarantee he would survive.

Pretoria was deep in enemy territory, three hundred miles from the
Portuguese colony of Lorenço Marques on the east coast, which was the
nearest neutral country. This did not deter Churchill and his companions from plotting an escape. They decided that if they could distract
the attention of the armed guards long enough, they might be able to
scale a ten-foot, corrugated-iron fence surrounding the schoolhouse and
jump to freedom on the other side. How they would manage the three-
hundred-mile journey to Lorenço Marques they would make up as they
went along.

After a month, Churchill seized a window of opportunity, scaled
the fence, and dropped to the ground on the other side. He looked
back and saw that he was the only one of the British prisoners to have
made the escape. His armament consisted solely of £75 and some bars
of chocolate.

It was the middle of the night. The future prime minister of
Britain made his way nonchalantly down the center of the street as if

he was just another Boer farmer. He hopped a freight train heading east, traveled all night, and jumped off as dawn was breaking. All the next day he hid in the bush, waiting for night to come, when he could hop another freight train. The day was an agonizing one. "My sole companion," Churchill wrote in *My Early Life,* and we will repeat his words, "was a gigantic vulture, who manifested an extravagant interest in my condition, and made hideous and ominous gurglings from time to time."[5] Night fell; the vulture faded into the darkness, but no freight train appeared. Churchill continued the journey on foot. After several hours, he slumped to the ground in exhaustion. He wrote that, at this point:

> I realized with awful force that no exercise of my own feeble wit and strength could save me from my enemies, and that without the assistance of that High Power which interferes in the eternal sequence of causes and effects more often than we are always prone to admit, I could never succeed. I prayed long and earnestly for help and guidance. My prayer, as it seems to me, was swiftly and wonderfully answered.[6]

Not long afterward, as Churchill continued to plod along, he saw in the distance what looked like the lights of a *kraal*—a village of native blacks (called Kaffirs). Thinking he might be able to pay the Kaffirs to help him, he set out toward the lights.

After an hour's walking, the lights did not seem much closer. Churchill recalled:

> Then I turned back again to the railway line and retraced my steps perhaps half the distance. Then I stopped and sat down, completely baffled, destitute of any idea what to do or where to turn. Suddenly without the slightest reason all my doubts disappeared. It was certainly by no process of logic that they were dispelled. I just felt quite clear that I would go to the Kaffir kraal. I had sometimes in former

years held a "Planchette" pencil and written while others had touched my wrist or hand. I acted in exactly the same unconscious or subconscious manner now.[7]

A planchette is the tiny three-legged marker used to spell out letters on a Ouija board. Without being entirely conscious of it, Churchill felt he was being guided. He struck out again for the lights. After an hour had gone by, he was close enough to see that they were not the lights of a Kaffir kraal but those of a coal mine. He knew many of these mines were run by British citizens whom the Boers had allowed to stay in South Africa for this purpose. Churchill thought there was a chance these nationals might help him. He hesitated. Then he strode up to the front door of a large imposing house and knocked.

The outline of a head appeared in an upper window. A voice called out in Afrikaans, the language of the Boers, asking who was there. Churchill's heart sank. "I want help; I have had an accident,"[8] he replied in English. The outline of the head disappeared. After a moment, he heard footsteps coming downstairs, then a key turning in the lock. The door opened; a man stood before Churchill. He asked the escaped prisoner in English who he was. Churchill told him the truth. The man silently escorted him into an office. Revolver in hand, he stared thoughtfully at the fugitive. Then he held out his hand and exclaimed: "Thank God you have come here! It is the only house for twenty miles where you would not have been handed over. But we are all British here, and we will see you through."[9]

Churchill later wrote: "It is easier to recall across the gulf of years the spasm of relief which swept over me, than it is to describe it. A moment before I had thought myself trapped; and now friends, food, resources, aid were all at my disposal. I felt like a drowning man pulled out of the water and informed he has won the Derby!"[10]

His flight from captivity was far from over. The English owner of the coal mine told him the Boers had distributed posters throughout the Transvaal offering £25 for "the escaped prisoner of war Churchill, dead or alive."[11] An official had knocked on his door the day before, demanding to know if Churchill was there.

But the ultimate deliverance of the future prime minister was close to being ensured. The mine owner hid him at the bottom of a two-hundred-foot-deep mine shaft. For the next three days, Churchill read Robert Louis Stevenson's *Kidnapped* and slept. Periodically, hordes of harmless white rats scurried across his body. He was more than ready to leave his hiding place when the mine owner and his two British assistants extricated him from the cubbyhole and smuggled him aboard a freight train carrying a shipment of bales of wool to the Portuguese colony of Lorenço Marques. For the next twenty hours Churchill lay crammed in a tiny space between the tightly packed bales, waiting anxiously for the train to arrive at its destination. When it finally did, Churchill disembarked without incident and, walking quietly through the streets, arrived at the British Embassy. Soon he was on his way in triumph by railway to Britain's Cape Colony. He would be highly feted in the days to come; these were dark hours for Britain's campaign in South Africa, and the British needed something to celebrate.

The acclaim accorded Churchill for his three-hundred-mile escape through enemy territory would catapult him into a seat in the British parliament. It launched the political career that made him, some forty years later, the indispensable and indomitable prime minister of Great Britain during World War II.

Back in 1899, the celebrated escapee continued to play a role in the Boer War, both fighting and cabling dispatches to the *Morning Post* that would later be published as a book. By mid-1900 the tide of the Boer War had turned in favor of the British. The Boer armies were conquered, though the British had then to endure a brutal guerrilla war. This ended in 1902, when treaties were signed ceding the Boer colonies to Great Britain. Britain conferred colonial self-government on the Transvaal in 1906 and on the Orange Free State in 1907. A delegation of Boers came to London to sign the final agreement. Churchill, now a member of the government, was present at the signing. He was introduced to Louis

Botha, a Boer general and now their leader, who immediately recognized him. Then Churchill recognized Botha: this was the very man who had taken him prisoner in South Africa on November 15, 1899.

Let's give the great man, whom Queen Elizabeth II knighted Sir Winston Churchill in 1953, the last word regarding religious feelings. Churchill wrote in *My Early Life,* slightly tongue-in-cheek:

I found that whatever I might think or argue, I did not hesitate [in battle] to ask for special protection when about to come under the fire of the enemy: nor to feel sincerely grateful when I got home safe for tea. I even asked for lesser things than not to be killed too soon, and nearly always in those years, and indeed throughout my life, I got what I wanted. This practice seemed perfectly natural, and just as strong and real as the reasoning process which contradicted it so sharply. Moreover the practice was comforting and the reasoning led nowhere. I therefore acted in according with my feelings without troubling to square such conduct with the conclusions of thought.

. . . I came across a French saying which seemed singularly apposite. "Le coeur a ses raisons, que la raison ne connaît pas." ["The heart has its reasons which reason does not know."—Blaise Pascal] It seemed to me that it would be very foolish to discard the reasons of the heart for those of the head. Indeed I could not see why I should not enjoy them both. I did not worry about the inconsistency of thinking one way and believing the other. It seemed good to let the mind explore so far as it could the paths of thought and logic, and also good to pray for help and succour, and be thankful when they came. I could not feel that the Supreme Creator who gave us our minds as well as our souls would be offended if they did not always run smoothly together in double harness. After all He must have seen this from the beginning and of course He would understand it all.[12]

## *Nineteen*

# Carl G. Jung
# (1875–1961)

### *Speaker for the Dead*

Carl G. Jung, forty-one years old and already a well-known psychiatrist, was more apprehensive than usual on this sunny afternoon in the summer of 1916.

His house was filling up with the spirits of the dead.

It had started the day before, when his eldest daughter glimpsed a white figure flitting across the room. Then, independently, his youngest daughter had her blanket snatched away from her twice during the night. His nine-year-old son had an anxiety dream the same night.

An ominous atmosphere seemed to flow all around him today as he walked through the house. It was as though the air were filled with ghosts. At 5:00 p.m., the front doorbell rang frantically. Everyone looked to see who it was, but there was no one there. Jung, sitting near the doorbell, not only heard it but also saw it moving.[1]

Many years later, Jung, now one of the great thinkers of the Western world, wrote in his autobiography:

> We all simply stared at one another. The atmosphere was thick, believe me! Then I knew that something had to happen. The whole house was filled as if there were a crowd present, crammed full of spirits. They were packed deep right up to the door, and the air was so thick it was scarcely possible to breathe. As for myself, I was all a-quiver with the question: "For God's sake, what in the world is this?" Then they cried out in chorus, "We have come back from Jerusalem where we found not what we sought."[2]

Who were these spirits? What did they want? Why Jerusalem? Tremulously and fearfully, Jung put these questions to the uninvited guests. Answers came. They were as astonishing as they were alarming. Jung had more questions. There were more answers. Jung would wrestle all his life with what he learned that night.

The setting of this uncanny encounter was Jung's house in Zurich. This ghostly visitation was the culmination of an event that had been building toward critical mass for several months. Jung had been ill for three years, caught in an emotional crisis that rendered his mental health precarious. His wife had allowed Toni Wolff, who would be Jung's mistress for nearly thirty years, to become a member of the household because she was the only person who could calm Jung down. The symptoms had come on in late 1913, when the psychiatrist, along with having visions of eminent persons from the past, had experienced a recurring dream of a new ice age that destroyed all living things. He had come to believe that he was the vessel of a higher power that granted him visions of the future. This "creative illness,"[3] which he saw as menacing him with a psychosis, became so intense that he was forced to withdraw from teaching at the university. Many of his colleagues feared for his sanity. Jung found he could not read scientific literature.

Then, on this crisis day in 1916, the spirits came in numbers. They told Jung that what they had sought in Jerusalem were answers to questions: What is the nature of man? What is the nature of the universe? Who is God? Is God dead?

What he learned that night was hardly reassuring. It shattered any sense of complacency he might have had about what happens to us after we die. The spirits told Jung that the dead know nothing beyond what they knew at the moment of death. The young psychiatrist was taken aback. As he later wrote, "according to the traditional views the dead are the possessors of great knowledge. People have the idea that the dead know far more than we, for Christian doctrine preaches that in the hereafter we shall see 'face to face.'"

But apparently we do not see face-to-face. Jung continued: "Hence their endeavor to penetrate into life in order to share in the knowledge of men. I frequently have the feeling that they are standing directly behind us, waiting to hear what answer we will give to them, and what answer to destiny."[4]

That evening, Jung suddenly took up a pen and began to write an essay he would later call *Septem Sermones ad Mortuos* (Seven Sermons for the Dead). It seemed to him that he was not writing the essay himself but that it was being channeled through him from a Gnostic priest named Basilides, who lived in Alexandria in the second century AD.

Jung recalled that the text "began to flow out of me, and in the course of three evenings the thing was written." The spirits did not wait for him to finish. "As soon as I took up the pen, the whole ghastly assemblage evaporated. The room quieted and the atmosphere cleared. The haunting was over."[5]

Reflecting on this many years later, Jung wrote in his autobiography:

> From that time on, the dead have become ever more distinct to me as
> the voices of the Unanswered, Unresolved, and Unredeemed; for since
> the questions and demands which my destiny required me to answer
> did not come to me from outside, they must have come from the inner
> world. These conversations with the dead formed a kind of prelude

to what I had to communicate to the world about the unconscious: a kind of pattern of order and interpretation of its general contents.[6]

Jung's encounter with spirits that turned and twisted blindly in the physical world, not knowing what they were, planted a seed in the psychiatrist's soul. That seed would flower many years later in the form of one of Jung's most challenging books, *An Answer to Job,* published in 1951.

Carl Gustav Jung was the founder of analytical psychology and one of the pioneers of human thought in the twentieth century. Most of us are acquainted with his concepts of the archetype, the collective unconscious, the anima, and the shadow. Ultimately, Jung set forth a doctrine of God darker than any seen outside the ancient East or in the Cabala. All his life he was fascinated by the paranormal and prone to psychic experiences. Much of this latter interest, and most of these experiences, he kept to himself. What we know of them has come mostly from his autobiography, published posthumously in 1963, and from a few other materials that have emerged since his death.

Jung was born in Kesswil, Switzerland, the son of a pastor in the Swiss Reformed Church. His mother, Emilie, née Preiswerk, was high minded, competent, and prone to the same sort of emotional disturbances verging on psychic experiences that would assail Jung most of his life. He was a strange child. Anthony Storr writes: "Although he had a sister, who was born in 1884, he was an only child for the first nine years of his life. In his autobiography, he described playing solitary games and his dislike of being observed or interrupted whilst engaged in them. . . . Jung wrote that he liked school because he at last found playmates; but also recorded that his efforts to fit in with his rustic schoolmates made it seem that they were alienating him from his true self. Throughout his life Jung remained a solitary person who only felt fully himself when he was alone."[7]

Jung studied medicine at the University of Basel, in Switzerland. But August 1890 saw the start of a drawn-out, multifaceted encounter with the occult that completely changed the course of his life. He wrote in his autobiography:

All in all, this was the one great experience which wiped out all my earlier philosophy and made it possible for me to achieve a psychological
point of view. I had discovered some objective facts about the human
psyche. Yet the nature of the experience was such that once again I was
unable to speak of it. I knew no one to whom I could have told the
whole story. Once more I had to lay aside an unfinished problem.[8]

This major experience was preceded by some minor psychic events. In
the summer of 1890, when studying at home, Jung heard a sound like a pistol shot in the next room, where his mother was knitting. He went in and
found her stunned. "W-w-what's happened?" she stammered. "It was right
beside me!" The stout walnut table at his mother's elbow had split right
through and produced the explosive sound of a gunshot. A few days later
a bread-knife blade snapped into several pieces all at once. When this happened Jung's mother gazed at him "meaningfully." She did this out of what
he had come to regard as her "No. 2" personality—a strange, "other" self
that contrasted sharply with her usual matter-of-fact, take-charge demeanor.
These experiences opened Jung to the world of psychic phenomena.[9]

He wrote in the autobiographical *Memories, Dreams, Reflections*:

A few weeks later I heard of certain relatives who had been engaged
for some time in table-turning, and also had a medium, a young girl
of fifteen-and-a-half [actually, not quite fourteen]. The group had
been thinking of having me meet the medium, who produced som-
nambulistic states and spiritualistic phenomena. When I heard this,
I immediately thought of the strange manifestations in our house,
and I conjectured that they might be somehow connected with this
medium. I therefore began attending the regular séances which my
relatives held every Saturday evening.[10]

The participants at these séances included Jung's young cousin and
childhood playmate, Helene ("Helly") Preiswerk, who was usually the
medium. Jung's attitude toward his cousin was one of condescension.

We know a great deal about these séances today (with some of what Jung wrote having been corrected) because of the 1975 publication in Germany of *C. G. Jung's Medium*, a book by Helly Preiswerk's niece Stefanie Zumstein-Preiswerk. We learn from this book that "Helly had a teenage crush on her handsome older cousin Karl (he adopted the less Germanic spelling of 'Carl' at the beginning of his professional life) and that Jung exploited her to benefit his scientific career."[11]

In his discussion of Zumstein-Preiswerk's book, Martin Ebon writes:

> Very much the budding but hard-nosed psychiatrist, young Jung wrote of Helly's, and therefore of his mother's family as an assortment of more or less lovable semi-lunatics. He noted that Helly's paternal grandfather, a clergyman, frequently had "waking hallucinations," mostly visions but often whole dramatic scenes, including dialogues. He had a "feeble-minded" brother, "an eccentric who also saw visions," and a sister who was "a peculiar, odd character." Helly had a grandmother who, at age twenty, and possibly after suffering from a fever, fell into a trance that lasted for three days; later she suffered fainting fits, nearly always followed by "brief somnambulism during which she uttered prophecies."[12]

Zumstein-Preiswerk affirms in *C. G. Jung's Medium* that initially the séances were organized by Jung, and that they took place over a period of years. At one of the first séances, Helly Preiswerk suddenly turned pale. She fell back in her seat and declared, "Grandfather is visiting with us, and I must travel now. Ask him where he is sending me. He will take my place." Then Helly slipped to the floor, unconscious. The others picked her up and placed her on a sofa. Jung spoke to the motionless girl: "Where is Helly? Answer, you spirit who has taken her away!"

A deep voice, like that of an old man, issued from Helly's throat: "Don't be afraid! Know that I am with you, every day. I am Father Samuel who resides with God. Pray to the Lord and ask him to permit my grandchild to reach her goal."

The spirit guide was Helly's grandfather Antistes Samuel Preiswerk (1799–1869), who was also Jung's grandfather, and who had been chief administrator of the Reformed Congregation of Basel. The family knew that Samuel's wife—Jung's grandmother Augusta—had regularly seen apparitions of persons who were unknown to her, but whose historic existence would later be proved. Jung's mother left a diary in which she confided that as a child she "helped to protect" her father, the congregational minister, from ghosts while he wrote his sermons; she had to sit behind him, she noted, so the "ghosts" could not distract him.[13]

Martin Ebon writes:

Helly Preiswerk later said that her grandfather had sent her a "guardian angel" long before his personality emerged as a spirit while she was in trance. The young girl, largely ignored by other family members, regarded herself as her dead grandfather's favorite, although he had sixty-four grandchildren. Once, in school, the usually tongue-tied girl described Heaven and God. Her teacher, rather surprised, asked her who had given her these details. Helly answered, "My grandfather." Although he had been dead for several years, she said, he had taken her "on far journeys to show her the stars."[14]

The séances included ordinary spiritistic phenomena, like raps coming out of the table and walls. Though the table "turned," moved, Jung thought this might be due to the involuntary movements of the medium. He accepted the "obvious autonomy of the rapping noises" and was particularly interested in the contents of the alleged spirit communications. Jung attended these séances until he got tired of them. Years later, he wrote that he "caught the medium trying to produce phenomena by trickery, and this enabled me to see how a No. 2 personality is formed, how it enters into a child's consciousness and finally integrates it into itself." As for the No. 1 personality—Helly the person—Jung deals with her life and death in two sentences: "She was one of those precociously matured personalities, and she died of tuberculosis at the age of twenty-six. I saw her once again when she was twenty-four and received a lasting impression of her independence and the maturity of her personality."[15]

The séances went on intermittently until 1895. Although Zumstein-Preiswerk shows us that much more happened at the séances than Jung lets on in his autobiography, Jung makes it clear (always writing with scientific detachment) that these gatherings were important to him. He incorporated data from the séances into his doctoral thesis, published in Leipzig in 1902 under the title "On the Psychology and Pathology of So-Called Occult Phenomena."

The year 1913 saw Jung break dramatically with Sigmund Freud, the founder of psychoanalysis, after a close professional relationship of six years. The causes of the break were complex, but had to do in part with Jung's increasing interest in symbolism. The years starting with the meeting with Freud, through the breakup, up to the beginning of World War I were critical ones for the formation of Carl Jung's worldview. It was during this period that he investigated certain persistent images in his mind—images that the world knows of today as the archetypes, the collective unconscious, along with others.

Jung now entered the lengthy period of his dark night of the soul, already discussed. He began to emerge from this period in 1916, with his compelling encounter with the spirits of the dead who sought enlightenment from him as to who and what they were. Jung eventually concluded that the dead are

> dependent on the living for receiving answers to their questions, that is, on those who have survived them and exist in a world of change: as if omniscience or, as I might put it, omniconsciousness, were not at their disposal, but could only flow into the psyche of the living, into a soul bound to a body. The mind of the living appears, therefore, to hold an advantage over that of the dead in at least one point: in the capacity for attaining clear and decisive cognitions.[16]

Jung was not the first to be aware of the uncanny phenomenon of the dependence of the dead upon the living. The Irish poet William Butler Yeats, during the four-year period when he communicated with the spirit world with his wife, Georgie (see chapter 14), also observed that the spirits seemed to manifest among us as much for their own sake as for ours. "We are starved,"[17] the spirits cried out to Yeats at one point. He wondered what this could mean. Did the spirits have to pass through the mind and imagination of a mortal person to acquire some definition of themselves? Could they have knowledge of their form and their being only if it was spelled out for them in the vocabulary of the living, sensuous world?

All his life Yeats was passionately concerned with magic. He had collected Irish folk tales in hopes of finding out secrets of magic known to the Irish peasantry. Here, as well, he had come across evidence of the mysterious need of the spirit world for at least the trappings of the physical world. He wrote in *A Vision:*

> The *Spirit* is . . . the light, and at last draws backward into itself, into its own changeless purity, all it has felt or known. . . . A farmer near Doneraile once told me that an aunt of his own appeared stark naked after her death and complained that she could not go about with the other spirits unless somebody cut a dress to her measure and gave it to a poor woman in her name. This done she appeared wearing the dress and gave thanks for it. Once an old woman came to Coole Park, when I was there, to tell Lady Gregory that Sir William Gregory's ghost had a tattered sleeve and that a coat must be given to some beggar in his name. A man, returned after many years spent in the West Indies, once told me and others of the apparition of a woman he had known in a dress that he had not known, copied, he discovered, from her portrait made after he had left England. May I not use such tales to interpret all those model houses, boats, weapons, slaves, all those portraits and statues buried in ancient tombs?[18]

The American writer Norman Mailer seems to have had a similar notion in mind when, in the 1983 novel *Ancient Evenings,* he described the now dead but multi-incarnated hero reconstructing his identity from the portraits and artifacts he sees in his own tomb. (See chapter 22.)

In 1951, when he was seventy-six—thirty-five years after he had channeled *Seven Sermons to the Dead* and dispersed the crowding, querulous spirits of the dead—that 1916 experience, much metamorphosed, began to reemerge within Jung. Now, for Jung, the spirit seeking answers was no less than God Himself.

In 1951, the philosopher-psychiatrist published a book-length essay, *An Answer to Job,* which is included in volume 11 of his *Collected Works.* In this essay, Jung confronts the problem of evil as set forth in the Book of Job.

Learning about it only after the war, Jung found what had gone on in Hitler's death camps harrowing. The destruction of Hiroshima and Nagasaki by atomic bombs also devastated him. Jung was not anti-Semitic. But he became aware in hindsight that, in the period leading up to World War II, he had made statements about the Jews with regard to what he saw as differences between the Jewish and non-Jewish mind that he realized now were open to misinterpretation. Jung wondered if, in light of the sadistic and lunatic racism of the Nazis that had swept across Europe and engulfed the Jewish people in the Holocaust, he had not been too complacent.

Why, he wondered with anguish, had God permitted the death camps to happen? Jung decided to frame this question in the context of the Book of Job: Why had God treated Job with such harshness and unfairness?

In fact, God was more compassionate in later biblical accounts, such as in the New Testament. Jung decided that God was not aware that he was acting badly when he persecuted Job with a vengeance. What was going on was different: God was looking to man to answer questions about him that he could not answer for himself. What came to pass as recorded in the Book of Job provided him with such an answer. This encounter with humankind served to increase God's awareness of himself. There was a benefit for humanity in this, insofar as God could now modify his behavior and, if he so desired, treat humanity with more consideration.

God's entire relationship with man, Jung thought, consisted of God's uncovering his dark side to himself. He was undergoing a kind of colossal Jungian analysis!

In one paragraph toward the end of *Memories, Dreams, Reflections,* Jung sums up:

> If the Creator were conscious of Himself, He would not need conscious creatures; nor is it probable that the extremely indirect methods of creation, which squander millions of years upon the development of countless species and creatures, are the outcome of purposeful intention. Natural history tells us of a haphazard and casual transformation of species over hundreds of millions of years of devouring and being devoured. The biological and political history of man is an elaborate repetition of the same thing. But the history of the mind offers a different picture. Here the miracle of reflecting consciousness intervenes—the second cosmogony [*Ed. note:* what Teilhard de Chardin called the origin of the "noosphere," the layer of "mind"]. The importance of consciousness is so great that one cannot help suspecting the element of *meaning* to be concealed somewhere within all the monstrous, apparently senseless biological turmoil, and that the road to its manifestation was ultimately found on the level of warm-blooded vertebrates possessed of a differentiated brain—found as if by chance, unintended and unforeseen, and yet somehow sensed, felt and groped for out of some dark urge.[19]

Jung concludes, in words uncannily far from normal experience, "As far as we can discern, the sole purpose of human existence is to kindle a light in the darkness of mere being. It may even be assumed that just as the unconscious affects us, so the increase in our consciousness affects the unconscious."[20]

# *Twenty*

## Sri Yashoda Ma
## (1882–1944)

### *A Guest in the House of Krishna*

When she stopped at St. Peter's Square in Rome on Easter Sunday 1902, with her husband, Dr. J. N. Chakravarti, Monica Devi was mobbed by the crowd.

She was twenty years old. Her hair was jet black, her eyes lustrous, her complexion a dusky glowing brown. On that Easter Sunday morning she wore a bright blue sari that seemed to gleam in the sunlight. The crowd mistook her for the Virgin Mary.

The couple traveled on to London. Strolling through the halls of the Paris Exhibition then at the British capital, Monica, dressed in all her finery, was mistaken for the queen of Madagascar. She and her husband went out to Windsor Castle, where Queen Victoria, noticing her from a distance, summoned her to the palace for an audience.

On the voyage home to Lucknow, India, crossing the Indian Ocean, the passengers, passing her on the decks, wondered what Asian royalty was on board this ship.

It was only many years later, after Monica Devi had taken the vows of a Vaishnava monk and become Sri Yashoda Ma and, because of her health, traveled with Sri Krishna Prem to the foothills of the Himalaya, where they together founded the Mirtola ashram, that her friends began to realize her radiant charisma came not from herself but from the presence of Lord Krishna.

For the past several hundred years, a debate has raged in India over two burning questions. The first is: Does India have a soul different from, and spiritually superior to, those of other nations? The second is: If it does, is it beginning to lose that soul?

Certainly, there is not, in India, the sharp distinction between the spiritual life and the worldly life that is found in the West. A contributor to *The Eternal Cycle: Indian Myth* writes,

> Present-day India is imbued with ideas that can be traced back through millennia. It is a country where religion retains a powerful hold over the popular imagination and where there are few distinctions made between mind and matter, or humankind and nature. Hinduism, the most widespread religion in India, is at once a science, a lifestyle and a social system.
>
> Western scholars trying to comprehend Indian philosophy often struggle with the apparent contradictions between the different schools of thought.... But the key to understanding them lies not in logic but in the Indian convention of *vidya* (unitary thought) which seeks to understand phenomena as a single system, in which God and Man are one and enlightenment lies in realizing infinite harmony with the universe.[1]

The debate over India's dual nature became sharply focused during World War II, when secular conflict, devoid of all spirituality, raged around India's borders. In April 1943, Bengali singer and poet Dilip Kumar Roy visited Sri Yashoda Ma and Sri Krishna Prem at the Mirtola temple. Here is what Prem had to say to him about the uniqueness and superiority of the Indian soul:

Often, while meditating, I find myself praying to Krishna that He may never let India's immemorial soul be swamped by the rational, robustious, God-deriding, scientific agnosticism of the blatant West, blaring over a thousand loudspeakers: "Religion is the opium of the mind." May He always shower His blessing on India, whose very dust heaves with latent godliness, in whose tiniest crannies mystic faith flowers like green grass-blades through chinks in rocks—India, whose people have only to anoint wayside stones with vermilion to endow them with sanctity.[2]

Over forty years later, in January 1985—long after the war had ended and India had gone through the twin fires of partition and independence—Sri Madhava Ashish, Sri Krishna Prem's disciple and now head of the Mirtola temple, expressed the same sentiments in the pages of the New Delhi journal *Seminar:*

... India stands out in the world as a land where the transcendental significance of human life is still recognized, where the man of spiritual attainment is still honored, and the path of spiritual inquiry is still accepted as a valid life aim and occupation. Unlike in countries of the developed world, here the immaterial roots of consciousness and being are not so deeply buried that they need heavy excavation to rediscover them.[3]

The lack of any real spirituality in the West—the important, indeed essential, role that Indian spirituality plays around the world—is reflected in the fact that neither Sri Krishna Prem nor Sri Madhava Ashish were born in India. Both were British. Ashish was sent from Scotland in World War II to overhaul Rolls-Royce engines for Spitfires at a base near Calcutta. Then, his name was Alexander Phipps. His father had been aide-de-camp to Lord Kitchener and it was expected that young Phipps would follow a military career. But drawn by the soul of India, he traveled across the country after the war in search of a guru. Arriving at Mirtola, near Almora in the Himalayan foothills, he met Sri Krishna Prem. He very soon took the vows of a Vaishnava monk, becoming Sri Madhava Ashish and Prem's disciple.

Prem's British name was Ronald Nixon. He had been a British pilot in World War I, whose life, he believed, had been miraculously saved during an air raid over Germany. He had acquired a brilliant First in English at Cambridge University. Once the war was over, he undertook a spiritual search that soon led him to India. His reputation as a scholar had preceded him, and he had no difficulty in obtaining a position as a lecturer in English at Lucknow University. This was the university where Jnanendranath Chakravarti, Monica Devi's husband, was vice chancellor. Chakravarti invited Nixon to stay with him and his family in the guest room of their house. It was in this way that Ronald Nixon met Monica.

It was now 1922—twenty years after the first trip to Europe of Monica and her husband. Now Monica was a mother of four who dressed in the latest fashions and, at receptions both at the university and at her home, entertained her husband's guests with wit and charm. She was passionate, even explosive, in her feelings. Dr. Chakravarti had become secretary general of the Indian branch of the Theosophical Society. (Many years later, Sri Madhava Ashish would characterize him as a "Theosophicalized Hindu.") Chakravarti knew the leading lights of Theosophy in India, including Madame Blavatsky, and he would boast that Monica's temper was the equal of Blavatsky's. Certainly it was apparent to all that Mrs. Chakravarti drew from wells of emotion so rich and deep they dipped into eternity. She was of a profoundly maternal nature; having raised four children, she adopted forty more. Her servants claimed she had once suckled a litter of abandoned puppies. She had lost none of the luminous charisma that, in India as well as Europe, commanded the attention of all.

Around the time that Ronald Nixon came to live in the house of the Chakravartis in Lucknow, it was apparent to no one but Dr. Chakravarti that Monica was on the path to becoming a visionary and a mystic.

Those who had known her as a girl might have been able to guess this. When she was thirteen, still growing up in her parents' home in Ghazipur, she had been chosen to represent the goddess at the annual *kumari-puja,* or ceremony of virgin worship. Swami Vivekananda himself had offered flowers to her feet. When she was fifteen, she heard that a local yogi, Pawhari Baba, was giving away a *dhoti* (clothing for the lower body) and a *bhand* (container) of food to every monk who came to visit him in his cave. Often, many monks came to see him at the same time. Monica wondered how Baba could fit into his tiny cave the large amount of clothing and food containers needed. She disguised herself as a boy and stood in line as the gifts were handed out. Many years later, Monica, now Yashoda Ma, told Dilip Kumar Roy the story, which he recounts in his book about Krishna Prem:

> "I stood among them and waited, moving slowly up, step by step, towards the mouth of the cave. And then, just when Pawhari Baba offered me my *bhand* with a *dhoti,* I just plunged straight in—headlong! Naturally, there was a big commotion outside: they were aghast, for such things are not done. Nobody would dare. But I was a school girl and did it all on an irresistible impulse—unthinkingly. And just imagine what I saw!"
>
> [Roy replies:] "Do tell me, Ma!" I said, deeply intrigued.
>
> She broke out into a young laughter that sounded like bells.
>
> "Believe it or not, Baba," she said. "I saw something absolutely incredible: it was just a tiny cave with no other exit. And there were neither *bhands* nor any *dhotis*—not a vestige! The narrow space inside the cave was quite empty!"[4]

As a result of this act, which prefigured the huge personal daring Monica would exhibit later in her life, she acquired a lifelong belief in the existence of miracles.

The Bengali singer and poet Dilip Kumar Roy knew the Chakravartis well, even in the 1920s, when he often came to the house to talk and to sing his songs. He was there when Ronald Nixon became a member of the household. He was a frequent visitor during the time when Monica Devi's thirst for the absolute began to emerge from the place where she had kept it hidden for many years. Dilip Kumar Roy described this period some forty years later in his book *Yogi Sri Krishnaprem,* published in 1968. In his account, he refers to Ronald Nixon as Sri Krishna Prem—though nobody at the time, least of all Ronald Nixon, knew that someday he would be the bearer of that name. Dilip Kumar Roy records his impressions of Monica Devi during that period:

> . . . it dawned upon me that she was not what she seemed. She had a mystical personality which was, indeed, not obvious to the superficial view, but to one who could delve deeper a different personality took shape which could well baffle the eye. . . . This came home to me primarily because she responded to devotional songs . . . with an astonishing warmth, so much so that tears coursed down her cheeks when I sang of the Lord's magic flute and cosmic play—*lila.*[5]

Dilip Kumar Roy now observed that Ronald Nixon/Krishna Prem, who he already knew had fallen in love with India's culture and spirituality, was responding to Monica Devi in a way that was neither the way a man cares for his mother nor the way a man loves his female counterpart—his wife or lover. "I noticed, next, how reverently Krishna Prem gazed at her and prostrated himself before her every time she greeted him as her *Gopal,* heart's darling (the name by which Krishna's Mother, Yashoda Rani, called her little son). I was no less impressed when I saw that, in her presence, the leonine intellectual turned in a moment into a docile lamb!"[6]

Dilip Kumar Roy observed all this—but it still did not prepare him for learning, a year later, that Monica Devi had taken the vows of a Vaishnava monk, changed her name to Yashoda Ma, and shaved her head, all at the insistence of her guru, the leader of a temple in

Brindaban. Still less did it prepare him for learning that, having accepted Sri Yashoda Ma as his guru, Ronald Nixon, now known as Sri Krishna Prem, had similarly put on the ocher-colored robes of an Indian *sadhu*.

A few years later, Krishna Prem confided to Dilip Kumar Roy that he had accepted Monica as his guru because she could talk about Krishna, the gods, and the goddesses from personal experience. At the time they both took their vows, Sri Yashoda Ma was suffering from health problems and needed the air of the mountains. Therefore the two of them set out, dressed in the robes of a Vaishnava monk, begging bowls in their hands, for the foothills of the Himalaya near Nepal, where they hoped to find a lofty elevation for their devotions.

Vaishnavism is a tradition of Hinduism distinguished by its worship of Vishnu as the original and supreme God. It is the most widely followed of all the Hindu traditions. Yashoda Ma and Krishna Prem found no resistance, only complete acceptance, as, arriving at the town of Almora far to the north, they quickly settled upon Mirtola, eighteen miles away and at an elevation of seven thousand feet, as the place where they would build a modest temple consecrated to the worship of Sri Krishna and his consort Radha. This they accomplished, and the small gray-domed temple they built in 1930 stands there to this day and serves as the centerpiece of the ashram at Mirtola.

Yashoda Ma and Krishna Prem would stay there for the rest of their lives. Sri Madhava Ashish, arriving fifteen years later, would also live at Mirtola until the end of his days.

Even in the West, where ego still dominates, some of the more important "New Age" channeled utterances of the past few decades have stated that great souls sometimes reincarnate on earth who come here for a purpose and do good works for humanity—but do them in perfect anonymity.

In the Pulitzer Prize–winning American poet James Merrill's epic poem *The Changing Light at Sandover* (1982), spirit guides tell the author about the "V"—five immortal souls who come to earth again and again, always remembering all their past lives, to help humankind move forward. The immortal V have appeared in such guises as Akhnaton, Mozart, Marie Curie, and Montezuma, along with many others. The spirits qualify this revelation by saying that on rare occasions, a member of the V returns to earth to live a completely anonymous life. "These are often our choicest agents," they add.[7]

In *Ultimate Journey* (1994), the third volume of Robert A. Monroe's trilogy describing his astral voyages through a multidimensional universe, the author, in astral form, is taken by his spirit guide to meet "the most mature and evolved human in physical earth, living in your time reference." Monroe visits this being, who is androgynous, and who Monroe calls "Heshe," in a nondescript little office.

Although Heshe is 1,800 years old, does not need to sleep, and is engaged in important work for humankind, no one knows Heshe's true identity or purpose; this evolved being operates behind mundane "day" jobs, like ambulance driver, late-night bartender, and psychiatric counselor. She is trying to save the world—but anonymously.[8]

In India, there is no distinction between anonymity and greatness. Any man, woman, or child can, by dint of spiritual practices, come to be firmly established in the self. Such enlightenment unleashes the power to do great deeds. And, since the little self—the ego ever begging for attention—has to be put aside so that that contact can be made with the Self, there is every likelihood that the good deeds will be carried out anonymously.

So we should not be surprised to find Monica Devi traveling a path about which few others would ever know the details. Just as the guru in the spiritual practice called Siddha Yoga gives *shaktipat*—transmits from his or her own fully realized Self the spark that will ignite the Self in the other—so does the enlightened soul of someone like Sri Yashoda Ma make its presence known by the silent, invisible effect it has on others. The guru may attract just a single disciple; that disciple will attract other disciples; bystanders on the path to spirituality—musicians, poets, skeptical seekers—will be brought unwittingly into the orbit of the guru. Thus, almost imperceptibly, does this most powerful of influences selflessly spread.

This was to be the dynamic of the Mirtola temple.


Today the visitor on the road to Mirtola arrives first at the town of Almora, which gives way to a soaring vista of mountains seemingly suspended in the sky. The slanting roofs of the white bungalows of Almora bow like pilgrims toward the Himalayan peaks climbing into the clouds. To the west, the lofty peaks of Badrinath and Nilkanth dominate thier surroundings. To the east, the gleaming gray-blue mass of the mountains of Nepal straddles the horizon. In the center, the three mountain peaks together constituting Trisul (the Hindu word for Shiva's trident), along with Nanda Devi (at twenty-four thousand feet, the highest mountain completely inside India's borders), thrust their gleaming snowcapped peaks upward to the heavens.

Mirtola is eighteen miles away, on the far side of a deep valley along whose pine tree–covered floor a thinly graveled road winds patiently. Peering across the valley on a sunny day, the visitor can make out the Mirtola ashram, a glittering white dot perched on the green wooded hills. You drop precipitously into the valley and then, crawling along the bottom to the other side, ascend even more steeply up the other side. Between the tree branches, which metamorphose subtly from oak to pine as you climb up, you catch glimpses of plunging valleys and soaring mountains. The final half-mile is a nerve-racking skein of whiplashing switchbacks. Then, suddenly, you burst into a swaying ocean of yellow marigolds and red cosmos that have been allowed to run wild so that they stand as tall as a man. You drive carefully through a narrow track in the middle of this undulating yellow-red sea until, suddenly, the gleaming gray dome of a temple rises up with a princely air. A white-washed cowshed, no less stately than the temple dome, stands off to one side. This is the entrance to the Mirtola ashram.

You are seven thousand feet high. The air is clear and crisp. There is no sound save a ringing silence broken now and then by a burst of birdsong. The first thing you see when you enter the two-story temple is an inner sanctum where two gleaming figurines, Krishna and his consort Radha, rest on a marble altar; fresh flowers lie at their feet. At the evening service, this inner shrine glows with the fire of many candles, while the sounds of gongs, bells, and a kettledrum echo along the walls. Tiny bedrooms flank the temple; a guest house stands nearby.*

There are more buildings today, but what is described above is what served as a home for Sri Yashoda Ma, Sri Krishna Prem, and Ma's youngest daughter, Motirani—who had also taken orders—along with several others, when, in April 1943, with war raging all around the borders of India, Dilip Kumar Roy arrived, musical instruments in hand, to visit with these well-loved friends for a week.

The illness that, long before, had first sent Sri Yashoda Ma to the foothills of the Himalaya had taken a heavy toll. The former Monica Devi was now bedridden most of the time. On those occasions when she moved about the temple, Krishna Prem followed her like a shadow, tending to her every need. At night he slept on a bare blanket on the floor at the foot of her bed, like a simple servant.

On the first night of his visit, Roy listened as Prem held forth in his customary fashion on the meaning of *jagat-pranam*. "The *Bhagavat* puts it beautifully," he was explaining, "that you must turn all your senses Godward: words must be used to sing His praises; eyes directed to the saints in whom He presides; the ears dedicated to hear them; hands taught to worship His feet and, lastly, your head must bow down in reverence to the world throbbing with His consciousness; that is *jagat-pranam*."[9]

To this preroration from Krishna Prem, Yashoda Ma responded in an unexpected way. Dilip Kumar Roy, in *Yogi Sri Krishnaprem*, describes what happened:

---

*For complete details of the Mirtola ashram as it is today, see *In Search of the Unitive Vision: Letters of Sri Madhava Ashish to an American Businessman 1978–1997*, compiled with a commentary by Seymour B. Ginsburg (see the bibliography).

Ma suddenly shivered in ecstasy, lowered her head and, in a thick voice, said: "Listen, Dilip. You asked me this morning why I let this pariah dog [she points to a mangy dog beside her] sleep on the same bed with me. I will tell you now."

"I used to abhor dogs," she went on. "I simply couldn't stand them. Now, one day, I had just offered Balgopal [Lord Krishna] the *bhoga* [milk-pudding] I had cooked myself, when I found this street dog, which had stolen in from behind, lapping up the milk-pudding. Shocked to the soul, I gave it a blow with my stick. The dog howled in pain . . . when, lo, I saw my Lord . . . my heart's Beloved . . . the little Balgopal, lying prone inside the dog . . . and . . . and He was crying."

She wiped her eyes and added, "Since that day I have adopted it and made it my constant companion."[10]

The next evening was no less dramatic. First, Krishna Prem asked Dilip Kumar Roy, a composer and singer renowned across India, to sing *Brindabaner lila,* one of his best-loved airs. Roy tells us that he sang this lengthy song—the English title is *Krishna, the Evergreen*—"with an overwhelming emotion such as I had never felt before. Time seemed almost to stand on tip-toe."[11]

When he had finished the song, silence reigned.

They had all thought that Ma, not well that day, was in her room. But suddenly one of the devotees—Alec, an English doctor who had come to Mirtola to work and worship with Prem—exclaimed: "You know, Krishna Prem, *Ma* was listening, standing in the veranda with folded hands!"[12]

Dilip Kumar Roy describes what happened next:

Krishna Prem gave a start.

"*Ma!* Good heavens! How dare she walk along the other way all by herself. She might have collapsed!"

"I noticed it too late," Alec sighed. "Just when she had turned back, at the end of Dilip's song."[13]

They trooped around to Ma's room. Dilip Kumar Roy entered:

She was sitting on her bed with folded hands, as though petrified; just two streaks of tears glistened on her cheeks in the candle-light.

Krishna Prem said reproachfully: "*Ma!*—how could you possibly—?"

"Sh-h!" Motirani shushed. "Don't you see she's in *bhavsamadhi* [partial trance]?"

So we waited in silence, watching breathlessly . . .

After a few minutes she opened her eyes, now swimming in tears, and gave a beatific smile. Then she asked me to draw near and sit close to her.

I complied hesitantly, as so far I had never sat on her bed; the others sat on the floor on the mat.

*Ma* placed a loving hand on my shoulder.

"You didn't see anything, Baba?" she asked, tenderly.

I caught my breath.

"See? No! What should I have seen?"

"*Thakur!*" she said simply. "He had come, and was standing beside you!"

A shiver passed through my spine.

"You mean Krishna?" I gasped.

She smiled. "Whom else could I mean, Baba? When . . ." She spoke now in staccato, through her tears . . . "You were improvising on the last verse. He . . . came first and stood for a second in my room and then . . . then stepped across the threshold . . . I . . . could not follow Him that way. So I took the . . . the other way . . . till I got to the veranda . . . and saw him . . . standing beside you, listening . . . Yes, Baba . . . I . . . I did see Him, with *open* eyes . . . as I often do . . . *You* didn't see?"

"No, *Ma*. But I did *feel*—"

But she went on as though she had not heard: "And He was standing . . . beside you . . . in person . . . looking so . . . so tenderly

... at you! . . . And . . . I . . . I appealed to Him: 'O *Thakur,* give him the . . . the blessed boon of vision . . . so . . . so he may see that you . . . *you yourself* have come down to hear his song . . . blessed, blessed, boy!'"

I bowed down and kissed her feet—and wept.

And then she opened herself to me and went on telling me, very simply, her varied spiritual experiences. I had never yet—except once—heard her speak of her supraphysical visions, nor the incredible miracles of Grace to which she had borne witness. But on this memorable night it was as though a sluice had been suddenly opened and her words came down in a ceaseless torrent.[14]

Ma now tells Dilip that she has seen the light of the soul within.

"I have *seen* this soul of ours as a blue bird of beauty and bliss—held captive in the body's cage yet isn't affected by it at all. Yes, Baba, the Gita hasn't told us a fairy tale when it assures us that nothing on earth can burn, mutilate or whittle it down."[15]

Dilip asks: "Still why do we labor under the illusion, *Ma,* that the husk is the most dependable of all realities and grow to cherish it more than anything else on earth?"[16]

Ma replied:

"In the last analysis, Baba," she smiled, "we cherish the body, too, for the sake of the Lord who ensouls it. It is He who makes it so lovable, I tell you; only we don't know this till we find Him . . . till He claims us for His own. And when we are one with Him we find that everything drips honey because all . . . all that we sense, perceive is He Himself. There is nothing in this world that stands by itself— apart from Him, and none dearer than His beloved Self. And once you know Him as the Dearest of the dear, do you *need,* to be told: 'Treasure Him, meditate on Him, sing His Name' and so on? You won't be able then to sing of anything *else,* to do without Him for a single moment, Baba! Look at Gopal [Krishna Prem]. Can anyone tempt him away from His feet? Just let them try. Offer him a kingdom or heavenly maidens—he won't even look at them, I tell you. Why? Because he has had a glimpse of His Beauty beside which all the beauty of the world, lumped together, seems pale, futile . . . a bauble. I assure you, Dilip, that no one who has even once glimpsed His Loveliness could feel otherwise. This is not mere theory, Baba, I speak from direct experience—after having *seen* Him."

"Do you see Him, all the time, *Ma*?" I asked, emboldened by his confidences.

"Do you see Him in my heart all the time," she answered. "But not outside—I mean, not always."

"But why can't you, *Ma*?"

She answered after a brief pause: "I once asked Him. He said: 'If I appear before you too often your body will not last long.'"[17]

This weeklong visit was the last time Dilip Kumar Roy would speak to Yashoda Ma at any length. Her health continued to deteriorate. Krishna Prem continued to respond to her unvoiced call; he was serving Krishna, the guru within, with selfless devotion. Sri Yashoda Ma died in 1944. She had lived a dozen years longer than any of her doctors expected. Sri Krishna Prem continued to serve the guru selflessly until he died in 1965. His successor, Sri Madhava Ashish, served the guru for thirty-two years, dying in 1997.

The Mirtola ashram continues to this day, under different leaders.

# *Twenty-one*

# Doris Lessing
## (1919– )

# Canopus in Argos: Archives

I would not be at all surprised to find out that this earth had been used for the purposes of experiment by more advanced creatures . . . that the dimensions of buildings affect us in ways we don't guess and that there might have been a science in the past which we have forgotten . . . that we may be enslaved in ways we know nothing about, befriended in ways we know nothing about . . . that our personal feelings about our situation in time, seldom in accordance with fact, so that we are always taken by surprise by "ageing," may be an indication of a different life span, in the past—but that this past, in biological terms, is quite recent, and so we have not come to terms with it psychologically . . . that artifacts of all kinds might have had (perhaps do have) functions we do not suspect . . . that the human race has a future planned for it more glorious than we can now imagine.[1]

These are the words of novelist Doris Lessing, the British winner of the Nobel Prize for Literature for 2007. Born in Teheran, Persia (now Iran), to English parents in 1919, Lessing was raised in Southern Rhodesia (now Zimbabwe), leaving the country in 1949 for London, where she has remained.

The wide-open spaces often appear in Lessing's work, and they are interstellar in *Canopus in Argos: Archives,* the quintet of "space fiction" novels she wrote from 1979 through 1983. She has been inspired all her life by the memory of her father's thousand acres of barely cleared farmland in Africa; in the postscript to volume 4 of the *Canopus* series, *The Making of the Representative for Planet 8,* she paints a portrait of a normal day:

> It was in the middle of Africa, in the old Southern Rhodesia, now Zimbabwe, on my father's farm. We, the family, were in the habit of sitting outside the house in the open, to enjoy the daytime or nighttime skies, and the weather, and the view which was miles in every direction, a wild and mostly empty landscape ringed by mountains. . . . It was nearly always hot, and the skies spectacular, either wonderfully blue and empty or full of the energetic cloud movement made by heat rising off sun-cooked earth and vegetation. Through the dry months forest fires were usually burning somewhere close.[2]

Lessing quickly established herself in London as a novelist. Today her works comprise close to sixty volumes, including novels, short stories, essays, plays, and opera librettos for two of her *Canopus* novels. The publication in 1962 of Lessing's novel *The Golden Notebook* marked a departure from her customary social and political themes. A multilayered depiction of the mind of an emancipated woman, the book is hailed today by the feminist movement as a classic that greatly advanced the cause of women's liberation.

In *The Four-Gated City* (1969), the final volume of her semiautobiographical *Children of Violence* series, Lessing came close to leaping off our planet. Near the end of the book, this passage appears:

It was during this year that many of us walking alone or in groups along the cliffs or beside the island streams met and talked to people who were not of our company, nor like any people we had known—though some of us had dreamed of them. It was as if the veil between this world and another had worn so thin that earth people and people from the sun could walk together and be companions. When this time which was so terrible and so marvelous had gone by some of us began to wonder if we had suffered from a mass hallucination. But we knew we had not. It was from that time, because of what we were told, that we took heart and held on to our belief in a future for our race.[3]

The speaker is Martha Quest, Doris Lessing's alter ego. The time is the early twenty-first century, the place an island off the coast of northwest Scotland. Martha has gone through tumultuous events: on the personal level, a period of trying to expand her being, when she skirted madness; on the group level, a growing experience of communal living, as communes spring up all over the globe; and, on the planetary level, nuclear war, which has destroyed most of the infrastructure of modern living and, perhaps, cleared the way for the mysterious blending of levels of reality that Martha is now experiencing.

A decade later, with the publication of the first *Canopus* volume, *Re: Colonized Planet 5: Shikasta,* Lessing expanded the action to the interstellar level. She also made it clear why Martha Quest, in *The Four-Gated City,* feels the veil between the worlds beginning to lift. In *Shikasta,* we learn that our Earth (called Shikasta) has been controlled for millennia by emissaries from the Canopean and Sirian galactic empires; that, immensely far back in time, Canopus had joined Earth (then called Rohanda) to its Home World with a Lock providing a steady stream of positive energy to our planet; that a misalignment of the stars had shortly thereafter caused the Lock to malfunction—and that, just now, in the twenty-first century, the Lock is functioning again.

We learn in *Shikasta* that in the beginning of Earth's history, the Canopeans used genetic engineering on us and sent benevolent alien giants to tutor the protohumans. Most important, they fastened our planet into the aforementioned Lock, that grid of emanations, focused through "substance-of-we-feeling" (or SOWF) radiation, that sent forth pulsations of goodness and maintained us firmly in synch with the Canopean empire. We also learn that there is a third—and evil—empire in our galaxy. This is Puttiora, which has placed many of its criminals on a prison planet called Shammat. Shammat's civilization taps in to the Canopus–Rohanda SOWF connection, constantly disrupting its energy flow and interfering with the evolution of Earth.

Then the disaster occurs that not even the near-omniscient Canopeans have foreseen: the sudden misalignment of the stars that radically diminishes the flow of SOWF. Humans begin to degenerate. Their life spans shorten and they become far less intelligent. Over the next millennia, the Canopeans and Sirians continue to aid us. Sometimes their actions are formidable, as when they help us through the Flood. But they can do nothing decisive until, finally, the Lock snaps back into place.

The Canopeans are near-immortals in that they can renew their bodies almost indefinitely, discarding them at will and entering new ones. They can be born into the body of a mother about to give birth; or they can enter a body at any stage. This is essential to their function as agents. The Sirian emissaries are also quasi-immortal: they have mastered the science of organ replacement. Death can come, but only if, say, a Sirian spaceship is hit by a meteor, or a Sirian contracts a rare disease.

The word "God" hardly ever appears in Lessing's *Canopus in Argos: Archives* quintet of space-fiction novels. The word *religion* crops up only to be dismissed by the galactic emissaries as a hysterical display of group rhetoric that intelligent species should be quick to put behind them. Do the Canopeans have any metaphysical or spiritual concerns at all? The emissary named Klorathy speaks mysteriously of his being "given existence" on a particular planet, and of the "light from which we all come. . . . A world of dazzling light, all a shimmering marvel—where the colors you yearn to see are shining."[4]

In fact, the Canopeans are specific about just one thing: Tasks must be undertaken, missions carried out, only on the basis of "Need." It seems the Canopeans are informed about what is "needed"—but only if there is a need to inform them! We never learn who does the informing; all Klorathy says is, "Laws are not made—they are inherent in the nature of the Galaxy, of the universe."[5]

Lessing devotes a great deal of time in the *Canopus* quintet to the Canopeans and Sirians and some of their other projects in the universe; Earth is only one of thousands of planets these emissaries have been guiding through the millennia. In part, Lessing does this to drive home the point that we humans play only a minuscule role in galactic affairs; the author has no time for the typical vanities and grandiosities of *Homo sapiens*.

But she is also at pains to show that the Canopeans and Sirians have their points of weakness and frailty too. These seeming super-beings routinely shoulder the responsibility for the populations of whole planets, shepherding them briskly up the evolutionary path. And the pressures can get to them. In volume 5 of the *Canopus* quintet, *Documents Relating to the Sentimental Agents in the Volyen Empire,* Incent is a Canopean emissary trying to moderate and head off the constant warring between and within the planet Volyen and its two moons Volyenadna and Volyendenda. Incent finally succumbs to the violent rhetoric being endlessly spouted around him and begins to make revolutionary speeches himself. The senior emissary Klorathy has to come to Volyen and its moons himself and place Incent in Restorative Detention.

On Earth, the Canopean emissary Nasar spends too many thousands of years in a less respectable part of our planet, and begins to go native in the same way as Kurtz does in Joseph Conrad's novel of the horrors of the Belgian "colonization" of the Congo, *Heart of Darkness*. The estimable Sirian emissary Ambien II, who enjoys good relations with the Canopeans, has to be sent—though she is not informed of the real nature of her mission—to a corrupt city in thrall to criminals from Shammat, where she shrewdly and bravely rescues Nasar from the slough of destructive despond into which he is sinking.

Volume 4 of *Canopus in Argos: Archives, The Making of the*

*Representative for Planet 8,* is about a suddenly onrushing ice age, caused by another misalignment of the stars, that will turn this once mild and temperate planet into a frozen ball of ice, and in just a lifetime or two. Here, even the wise and gentle Canopean emissary Johor is at a loss how to console the inhabitants of this planet, whom Canopus had promised to fly to another world in the event of a catastrophe like this. Johor knows that somehow the workings of galactic Necessity will enable him to keep his promise to the people of Planet 8. But how? As time stretches on, and the universe remains intractable, even the manly and tactful Canopean emissary wonders what to say next.

Doris Lessing describes the Canopean and Sirian emissaries so beautifully, and so convincingly, in all five *Canopus in Argos: Archives* novels, that we sometimes wonder if there are things she isn't telling us. Lessing went through a lengthy period of immersion in Sufism, during which she sought to expand her being to its limits. Did she expand it into interstellar space?

Lessing can take her place in the proliferation of information being channeled these days through mediums on Earth ostensibly from aliens scattered around the universe. This "alien literature" can be strikingly rich. Most of these channeled ETs share a message that locates humanity within a vast intergalactic network of spiritual evolution. They say they are converging on earth to give our species a necessary boost in the evolutionary process. The alternative to taking this giant stride forward (which must be done quickly) is the disappearance of humanity.

That's also what Doris Lessing says. It's what a great many mediums say these days. According to Patricia Pereira, who channels an alien named Palpae, twenty-five planets orbit the star Arcturus, a red giant located thirty-seven light-years from Earth in the Boötes constellation. The fourth planet in the Arcturian star system is the Blue Crystal Planet. This planet is the hub of a virtually numberless federation of planets that, stretching across the galaxies, makes up an unthinkably diverse group of mostly nonphysical species. Palpae is an Arcturian galactic envoy and Ambassador of Light, Love, and Peace, based on the Blue Crystal Planet, who says that "the multidimensional interfacing harmonics" of the Arcturian star system "make it an ideal gathering place for multistar-multidimensional beings"[6] who are working for the upliftment of universal vibration through that sector of the galactic core.

Earth is being readied for entry into this federation of planets. An Arcturian starship named *Marigold-City of Lights* presently orbits our world. The star-beings occupying it are reviving energies stored for millennia past in Earth's sacred mountains and ancient pyramids. The Arcturians have been with us since the formation of our earth, when they combined their seed energies with those of other star-peoples, like the Orions and the Andromedans, to provide the initial impetus for the birth of *Homo sapiens*.

You can read Palpae's words in the four volumes of the *Songs of the Arcturians* by channel-author Patricia Pereira, who lives in Boise, Idaho. Of equal interest is an extraterrestrial named Bashar, channeled by Darryl Anka of Los Angeles, California. According to Bashar, eight planets orbit the star Sha, located five hundred light-years from Earth on a straight line to the constellation Orion. Bashar hails from the third planet in this system, called Essassani (Place of Living Light). He claims to be an emissary to Earth for a federation of planets called the Association of 360 Worlds, which Bashar says contains hundreds of thousands, even millions, of different, sentient consciousnesses. (He adds that this is a tiny number compared to the Milky Way galaxy as a whole, which harbors sixty- to seventy million planets peopled by sentient beings.)

Bashar comes to Earth from time to time to help us evolve from our third-density nature into a fourth-density one—an evolution he says it is essential we accomplish. Once earth people make that evolutionary leap, says Bashar, "You will be living in the moment and truly understanding that every single moment of time is literally a new moment. . . . You will begin to truly see through the illusion of physical reality as your own projection. You will be able to come and go, in and out of your body at will."[7]

Bashar's arrivals on Earth are a trip through time as well as space.

The planet of Essassani from which he hails is six hundred years in our future, and Bashar is the hybrid descendant of ETs from Zeti Reticulum, who mated with human beings during the alien abduction epidemic on Earth at the end of the twentieth century.

Bashar's utterances are available in *Bashar: Blueprint for Change,* in *Quest for Truth,* and on numerous audiotapes and CDs. [In the summer of 1987 and 1988, Anka channeled Bashar for eleven nights] in Tokyo; a thousand Japanese turned out each night to listen and later to buy a transcript of the talks.

An overall examination of material channeled from aliens (at least fifty mediums have books out) reveals that alien worldviews divide up into two distinctly different camps. One group (of which Palpae and Bashar are representatives) describes our Milky Way galaxy as teeming with hundreds of millions of different sentient planetary life-forms; the others say its representatives are not exactly aliens but more like angels, come to help us *Homo sapiens,* whose planet, Earth, is the only one inhabited by a sentient species in the entire Milky Way galaxy. Ken Carey and James Merrill belong to this latter camp.

Does this mean that, insofar as the two camps thoroughly contradict each other, we can't take anything these aliens say seriously, that everything they say is a figment of the medium's imagination?

We will perhaps find the beginnings of an answer in an account of the day, in the first decade of the sixteenth century, when the first Europeans arrived in North America, disembarking in Nova Scotia. We read this story in Silas T. Rand's *Legends of the Micmac,* published in 1894:

Before the coming of the white man, a Mi'kmaq [Micmac] girl dreamed that a small island floated in toward the land. On the island were bare trees and men—one dressed in garments of white rabbit skins. She told her dream to the wise men, but they could not explain the meaning. The next day at dawn, the Mi'kmaq saw a small island near the shore, just as the girl had dreamed. There were trees on the island and bears climbing among their bare branches.

The people seized their bows and arrows to shoot the bears. To their amazement, the bears were men. Some of them lowered into the water a strange canoe into which they jumped and paddled ashore. Among the men [was] one dressed in a white robe who came toward them making signs of peace and goodwill. Raising his hand, he pointed toward the heavens, and addressed them in an earnest manner, but in a language they could not understand.[8]

The Micmac girl sees only a small island, trees, and bears because she does not have the perceptual framework, the memories, the experiences—the particular social conditioning—to properly perceive the Europeans and their ship. Eventually, she will—but not for a while. This new experience is necessarily filtered through her subjectivity. She must alter that subjectivity.

Our experiences of channeling aliens and our perceptions of them are also necessarily filtered through our subjectivities. Ken Carey is an Evangelical Christian, and Evangelical Christians are taught to believe that humankind is the only species in our galaxy. Therefore, whatever the profounder realities of what he channels, it will always be difficult for Ken Carey to see beyond this Evangelical Christianity filter.

What if the channeling aliens themselves were to channel exercises to help us change our perceptual framework, our Earth-based conditioning, so that we could begin to see more clearly what they are? In fact, this is exactly what Darryl Anka's Bashar is doing in Los Angeles. In periodic, channeled presentations, the emissary from Essassani guides his audiences through a series of consciousness-altering techniques, often using pencil and paper, that are intended to eventually make Bashar's true nature more apparent to us.

If, beyond the shifting filters of our subjective consciousnesses and our cultural conditioning, there is an objective reality to the aliens and to what they channel to us, exactly what form might that take—and does Doris Lessing know?

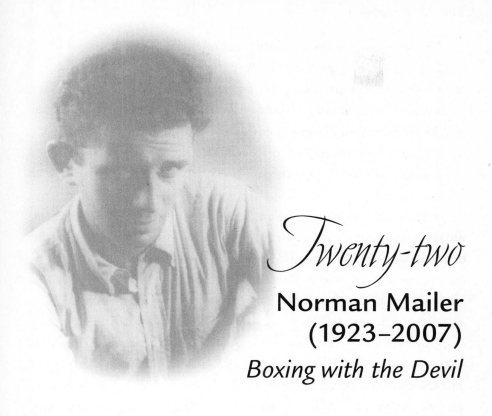

# Twenty-two

## Norman Mailer
## (1923–2007)

### Boxing with the Devil

You might have thought that Norman Mailer, when he got a chance to talk to God, would have done so on top of Mount Sinai, or some American equivalent like Mount Shasta, with the TV cameras whirring full blast and Mailer being handed tablets from God on which were etched answers in letters of fire.

After all, wasn't the great American novelist and journalist Norman Mailer one of the most self-promoting and exhibitionistic and narcissistic authors of all time, with books titled *Advertisements for Myself* (1959) and *The Gospel According to the Son,* the 1997 novel in which Mailer, a nice Jewish boy from Brooklyn, tries to put himself in the head of Jesus Christ?

Wasn't this the same writer who challenged Muhammad Ali to a boxing match and ran for mayor of New York on a platform of banishing automobiles from Manhattan and staging gladiatorial contests in Central Park?

Yes, it was. But what is astonishing is that when Mailer, who died in 2007 at the age of eighty-four, finally did get to talk to God, the conversation took place quietly, with no one else around, in an all-night dinner in Brooklyn, at three o'clock in the morning. Moreover, the exchange was very brief, consisting of two sentences from God and one from Mailer.

The subject was a cup of coffee and a doughnut.

Norman Mailer talks about this conversation in *On God: An Uncommon Conversation,* published in 2007, the final work of this brilliant and rebellious American author who won a Pulitzer Prize for General Nonfiction in 1969 with *The Armies of the Night* and a Pulitzer Prize for Fiction in 1980 with *The Executioner's Song.*

When the then twenty-five-year-old Mailer rocketed to fame in 1948 with *The Naked and the Dead,* still generally considered to be the best novel about the Second World War, no one would ever have thought that, some thirty volumes later, Mailer would end his career with a slim volume on theology that takes God's existence for granted. After all, what was so disturbing about *The Naked and the Dead* was not the actual horror of the war, but, in the words of critic Philip H. Bufithis, "Mailer's unrelenting vision of the void—of the lack of love, justice, and mercy."[1]

Yet that's exactly what happened, with the publication in 2007 of *On God: An Uncommon Conversation,* in a question-and-answer format with Michael Lennon, professor emeritus of English at Wilkes University and Mailer's friend and literary executor, as the questioner. Mailer tells us that this single conversation with God took place in 1963, just after his third wife, Lady Jeanne Campbell (Lord Beaverbrook's granddaughter), told him she was leaving him.

Mailer was devastated. He had thought he might be able to make something of this marriage. The writer wandered from bar to bar in Brooklyn all night. He ended up at an all-night diner at 3:00 a.m. He was hungry. He ordered a coffee and a doughnut. He finished eating.

Then, Mailer tells Michael Lennon, "a voice spoke to me. I think it's one of the very few times I felt God speaking to me."

The voice said, "Leave without paying."

Mailer was at a loss. It was only a matter of twenty-five cents, but he had been brought up never to steal.

He told God: "I can't do it."

God replied—and Mailer thought he could detect just a hint of amusement: "Go ahead and do it."

The writer got up and left the restaurant without paying.

The more he thought about it afterward, the more Mailer was convinced that the voice he'd heard was God's, not the Devil's. He says in *On God*: "To this day, I think it was God's amusement to say, 'You little prig. Just walk out of there. Don't pay for the coffee. They'll survive, and this'll be good for you.'"[2]

Is Mailer putting us on?

We might feel that such a minor piece of advice is not something God would waste his time on. But we discover in *On God* that God as envisioned by Norman Mailer is not the God we hear about in the churches and the synagogues. He is, rather, a much harassed and put-upon God. He is a God who not only is not all-powerful, but is in danger of failing. He is a God who from time to time feels compelled to counsel a person to "break out" of a situation, in the same way a surrounded army sometimes has to crash through the weakest part of an encirclement. He is a God who thinks that not paying for a cup of coffee and a doughnut can be a necessary breaking-out. Certainly Mailer, as he tells us, felt better as he left that diner, perhaps because he had taken charge of the situation.

It's remarkable that Norman Mailer had even a single conversation with God. For most of his life, the exchanges this writer had with the supernatural were much more likely to be conversations with the Devil. Arguably the most famous example of this took place on the night of November 20–21, 1960, when, in the grip of a dark influence that even his friends could sense, Mailer assaulted his wife with a penknife.

The occasion was an all-night party at the Mailers' new apartment in Manhattan. Just as the evening was ending, Mailer, completely inebriated, seized a three-inch penknife and stabbed his wife, Adele Morales, twice. He narrowly missed her heart. Adele was rushed by ambulance to University Hospital, in Manhattan, where she underwent emergency surgery. She survived, but declined to press charges. Mailer had to undergo seventeen days of psychiatric observation at Bellevue Hospital.

Two years later, the couple divorced.

Why did Norman Mailer stab his wife? There were the usual reasons. Mailer, who was married six times, had a penchant for fighting with his wives. He was often belligerent, angry, and even violent. Adele had been taunting him. He had drunk too much.

Apparently, there was another reason. In *Mailer: His Life and Times,* Peter Manso records these words from H. L. "Doc" Humes, who was a guest at the party that night and a witness to the stabbing: "I'd never seen him so drunk, and it was as though an occult influence were operating. Not supernatural or ghostly but just as he intuited, a shadowy influence at work that was deliberately trying to make him into a madman."[3]

It may seem somewhat of an exaggeration to suggest that Mailer was communicating with the Devil that night. But Mailer would not think it was an exaggeration. He tells us in *On God* that all of us often have conversations with the Devil. We have them with God as well, he adds—and God has them with the Devil. Mailer believes that God and the Devil exist and are involved in a relationship that includes ourselves. This is a warring relationship among three forces who are separate yet intertwined.

It's war, and a war that God is not necessarily winning. The God of Norman Mailer is not all-powerful. Mailer tells his interviewer, Michael Lennon, that the Devil is always nearby, always present in human affairs, because he is "another god and wishes to preempt the god who exists. The Devil has other notions of what existence could be. I'd go so far as to assume that technology is the Devil's invention. Like God, the Devil wants to have power in the universe, whereas God wants that power to satisfy His vision of what the universe could be."[4]

Mailer asserts further that both God and the Devil desperately need our help. Both of them actively woo us, though the Devil does so with far more tricks, devious measures, and underhanded practices than does God.

For Norman Mailer, God is an artist. Like an artist, he works by trial and error. He has an idea, he executes it—and if it doesn't work, he wipes it out and tries again. God is evolving and growing just like us. So is the universe.

But the Devil is always hanging around, trying to foul things up, waiting to throw a monkey wrench in the works. It's a power struggle. But we human beings are not powerless. We can stand up to both God and the Devil if we wish.

In all this, the process of reincarnation plays a major role. Mailer believes that reincarnation is one of God's most powerful tools in this cosmic war he is waging to perfect humanity and himself. The Devil knows this too and is constantly trying to subvert the process of reincarnation, to turn it to his advantage.

One of the ways the Devil subverts reincarnation is through technology. (Farther below, we'll discuss in detail Mailer's views on reincarnation.) Mailer believes that a kind of time exists in heaven, and that God needs time, if only a minuscule amount, to make decisions about what we will be in our next lifetime. (It's not entirely our choice, nor is the process automatic.) It's because God needs time in which to make decisions about individual reincarnations that the Devil has been able to use two of his technological triumphs, the concentration camps (with their efficiently death-dealing Zyklon B gas) and the atomic bombings of Hiroshima and Nagasaki, to interfere with the process of reincarnation.

Mailer explains that

. . . the atom bomb, the concentration camps, and the gulags were mighty efforts by the Devil to foul up reincarnation, to choke off the subtlety of the divine judgment within reincarnation. I hope I've suggested the delicate dispositions of God, the care with which the question is asked: "What shall I do with this soul?" That is the core of reincarnation—delicate, responsible, artful, *deliberate* judgment. If the process is overloaded, it can break down.[5]

God's reflections on what we will be in our next lifetime are complicated by the fact that we are neither all good nor all bad. Mailer believes:

> The good guy may be 65 percent good and 35 percent bad—that's a very good guy. The average decent person may be 54 percent good, 46 percent bad—and the average mean spirit is the reverse. So say I'm 60 percent bad and 40 percent good—for that, must I suffer eternal punishment? . . . I would suppose that we receive instead a partial reward or partial punishment and it is meted out to us in our reincarnation.[6]

But sometimes the soul wearies and decides, itself, that it does not wish to be reincarnated. God may then terminate it. And God may sometimes create new souls, ones that are better able to wage war with the Devil.

Moreover, Mailer continues,

> I would say God sees wonderful potentialities in awful people. One of the reasons they were so awful was because they had large potentialities that became frustrated early and so turned into their opposites. Concerning this particular soul, therefore, God wants to try again. Or, to the contrary, take the case of someone who is perfectly bland and pleasant, good and decent, yet God is not vitally interested. That soul has done about what it's going to do and is no longer interesting to the Lord's higher purpose. God might then decide, we can only reincarnate him or her in an animal. We have to see if that soul responds to a more arduous life. Or God may decide—not worth repeating: Just as artists can be ruthless, so can God when it comes to humans with mediocre lives. So reincarnation is, I think, the nexus of judgment.[7]

What of Mailer's belief that technology is basically the work of the Devil?

Mailer might tell you what he wishes the modern world was like by asking you: Can you imagine a world of today in which there are no cell phones, no computers, no televisions, no radios, no telephones? A world in which there are no electronics, and not even flush toilets? One in which we're all psychic, so that if we want to talk to someone, we simply put our mind in immediate contact with that person—even if he or she is a thousand miles away? Where, instead of watching TV, we can reach into our dream lives and enjoy organized and marvelous dramas that people create for themselves and send to their friends telepathically? Where "great entertainers will be so intense in their art that men and women all over the world can experience the performance?"[8]

In *On God,* Mailer suggests this is the kind of world that God originally wanted for humanity. (As we will see, in writing his 1983 novel *Ancient Evenings,* he tried, in a way, to sketch out such a world.) If God intended such a world for us, what happened? Why didn't it come about?

Because, since God is not all-powerful, the Devil has been able to successfully advance technology, and technology, says Mailer, "tends to crimp our senses and reduce us to people who are able to live in a closed environment. . . . [It] tends to curtail our possibilities and accelerate our dependencies."[9] It obviates our need to be telepathic.

Mailer insists that the emergence of technology wasn't inevitable once God gave us free will and intelligence. Rather, "God hoped and expected that all of us would become psychic." Instead—Mailer believes it was at the prompting of the Devil—we sought out and effectively achieved technological means of communication. (When Lennon asks Mailer why he believes this was "at the prompting of the Devil," Mailer replies, "I feel it viscerally."[10])

Lennon reminds Mailer that in 1900 the average life span of an American was forty-six; 6 percent of Americans graduated from high school; 14 percent of homes had a bathroom; 6 percent had a telephone. But Mailer wonders: "Did we really improve anything spiritually?"[11]

If, for example, the flush toilet is an improvement in existence . . . then look at the price that was paid. It's not too hard to argue that the gulags, the concentration camps, the atom bomb, came out of technological improvement. For the average person in the average developed country, life, if seen in terms of comfort, is better than it was in the middle of the nineteenth century, but by the measure of our human development as ethical, spiritual, responsible, and creative human beings, it may be worse.[12]

Mailer's prognosis for the future? The writer is not sure if we—or even God—will survive. God's odyssey through the universe is tremendously more difficult than we can ever imagine:

I have no notion at all whether our God is only a master of the Solar System or commands galaxies. I have no notion at all whether God is in command of black holes in space or is terrified of them. My fundamental idea is that the cosmos is at war within itself and the God that created us is not the Emperor, but the Artist. This is my most basic notion: God—Being, if you will—is not a lawgiver but an artist. Being is doing the best that He or She can do to project a new notion of existence into the cosmos. There may be other notions out there as well—other concepts concerning which turn the cosmos should take. We humans are part of God's venture into the unknown. We humans are God's soldiers, God's ability to change the given in the cosmos. . . . To ask, then, that the end be posited is philosophically misleading, since we commence with the notion that the end is as yet undetermined.[13]

The theological ideas Mailer presents in *On God* go back a long way. Mailer expressed the idea of God at war with other immortal beings in the universe in an interview reprinted in *Advertisements for Myself* (1959). The protagonist of his novel *An American Dream* (1965), Stephen Rojack (a professor and TV personality), is so imbued with

Mailer's notions of God at war with the Devil and both of them vying for our attention that, in times of stress, Rojack neglects to distinguish between the two sets of messages. This is exacerbated by his tendency to obey what he takes to be the magical promptings of the moon. (Doing so enabled him to kill six Germans single-handedly one moonlit night during World War II.) In the course of *An American Dream,* Rojack murders his wife (and gets away with it), has an instant affair with a jazz singer (for which she is murdered by somebody else on the same day), delivers a severe beating to a black rock star (from which he strolls away unharmed), and at the end ambles out of the United States. He has no remorse and seems to feel mightily proud of himself. The borderline psychopathic behavior of Mailer's hero caused critics to speak with some reserve about the book. Philip H. Bufithis writes reflectively that it

> does not favorably lend itself to consideration on an ethical level. How does Mailer justify the fact that other people have to be victimized so that Rojack can achieve rebirth? . . . Insofar as it is fair to judge literature on moral as well as aesthetic grounds, the novel suffers from its refusal to deal with the ethical nature of man's relation to man.[14]

Mailer's seeming glorification of psychopathic behavior is a major, legitimate charge many critics have leveled against this generally very brilliant writer. Mailer's criticisms of technology have also had a place in his books for some time. In *Of a Fire on the Moon* (1970), his nonfiction account of the first Apollo moon shot, Mailer is not sure if he loves this supreme achievement of technology or hates it. Bufithis writes: "Whether we concur . . . or not, we cannot help agreeing with Mailer that what the moon mission means to the American people is an attestation of man's control over nature, not a rediscovery of his mysterious partnership with it."[15]

In his 1983 novel *Ancient Evenings,* Mailer creates a world that has never known technology. It is the Egypt of the nineteenth and twentieth dynasties (1290–1100 BC). Mailer's ancient Egypt possesses some of the attributes he would have liked to see in our society. His Egyptians are telepathic, though we can't really tell to what extent telepathic ability is spread throughout this society as a whole. Those who are telepathic sense feelings, more than thoughts—and they sense them strongly.

Modern-day technology has conquered nature—and, insofar as we are a part of nature, it has conquered us; it has cut us off from the instinctual part of ourselves. This has not happened to Mailer's ancient Egyptians. They are highly intelligent as well as brutal creatures who revel in the mud of life. Mailer portrays this with sumptuous Oriental pageantry, colossal action, and mountains of sexuality of every sort, including an extraordinary number of acts of sodomy on the part of members of the military, within and outside the context of war and both among themselves and with the enemy. Perhaps this is one of Mailer's methods—perhaps exaggerated at times—of demonstrating a certain wholeness, a certain solidarity of mind and body, among these ancient Egyptians.

Reincarnation is a fact of life for these ancient Egyptians. The book's narrator, at least, is consciously aware of this. His name is Menenhetet. He is the great-grandfather of the small boy through whose mind much of the narration passes telepathically and thereby becomes available to the reader.

Menenhetet regales us with memories that span one thousand years; they are of the four lifetimes of which he is conscious. The most illustrious (and long-lived) of these was as the general who won the Battle of Kadesh during the reign of Rameses II two centuries before. But he has also lived through stretches as harem master, magician, priest, grave robber, and raconteur.

As the novel opens, Menenhetet is dead, between lifetimes, trying to remember who or what he is; at first, he remembers nothing. When his wandering soul finally becomes aware of his tomb—which for a while he does not know is his own tomb—the portraits on its walls and on his coffin begin to remind him (they are of him!) who he was. This is their purpose; and we'll recall that Yeats mentions this in *A Vision,* when he also ponders the apparent need of the spirits of the dead to communicate with the living in order to orient themselves in the afterworld.

According to the ancient Egyptians, when we're dead our shade is a sevenfold entity. Mailer takes us through a bewildering odyssey as the soul remakes itself in preparation for rebirth. Strange, esoteric descriptions like those above are scattered throughout *Ancient Evenings.* No tale of reincarnation in the book, however, is quite as compelling as the one that begins in the middle of the sex act (the speaker is Meni, a charioteer—Menenhetet in a previous lifetime):

> Yet in all the ways I could have met Her on all the great days of my life, I came forth instead in one small spurt, and my seed would never have reached Her home for I was not in it, no, it merely came out of me, and then I felt the hand of heaven on my back, a tongue of flame, a spear of anguish, seven times I felt such fire reach into each of my seven souls and spirits and the force of those blows drove me forward into my seed. Then I was beneath some water and swimming. I felt my heart divide. The Two-Lands sundered.[16]

Meni is having an orgasm, and because he is practicing an esoteric procedure that he has carefully rehearsed, he knows he has just impregnated the woman beneath him. He also knows he is dying, and while this is happening—it's all part of the procedure—he is vigorously projecting his immortal soul out of his dying body into the child he has just co-created in the womb of his partner.

Meni will reincarnate as this child. He'll be his own, posthumous father. His lover in this life will be his mother in the next.

Meni has learned this procedure from a Jew, who learned it from no less than (and here Mailer may be indulging in the ultimate nice-Jewish-boy-gone-bad joke): Moses.

# *Twenty-three*

# Yukio Mishima
# (1925–1970)

## *Martyr-Genius of Japan*

Kanetoshi Mashita had served in the Second World War and seen two of his senior officers commit ritual suicide, but even that had not prepared him for the atrocious drama that was unfolding before his eyes on this cold morning of November 25, 1970, twenty-five years after the end of the war.

Mashita, now a general and commanding officer of the Self Defence Force's Eastern Army Group Headquarters at Ichigaya in central Tokyo, was tied hand and foot to his office chair. Earlier that morning, Yukio Mishima—arguably the most famous man in Japan and probably its best writer—had entered the general's office with four cadets from Mishima's ninety-man private militia, which he called the Shield Society. Mishima had come, he said, to show Mashita a sixteenth-century samurai sword he had acquired; he had brought the four cadets with him to commend them to the general for their excellent work.

As he examined Mishima's sword, Mashita wondered to himself why this brilliant author had gone to the trouble of creating his troop of teenaged amateur soldiers. The regular army tolerated Mishima's Shield Society well enough. And certainly these four cadets looked fit and handsome in their yellow-brown uniforms with green cuffs and double rows of brass buttons and peaked caps—designed, Mishima had told the general, by himself with the help of General Charles de Gaulle's tailor. But what was the use of it—?

Mashita had been abruptly cut short in his private meditation. Two of the cadets had seized him, gagged him, and bound him hand and foot to his chair. They had barricaded the doors to the office. Mashita's subordinates had pounded on the other side. Mishima had responded in a raucous voice that he would kill the general if the eight hundred soldiers stationed at the base were not immediately summoned to the parade ground below the commandant's balcony. Ten of Mashita's orderlies had stormed the office. Mishima and his second-in-command, Morita, had driven them back with their swords, wounding seven.

So Mashita's subordinate officer had given the order. The soldiers had quickly assembled in the parade ground below the balcony. Mishima stepped smartly out onto the balcony. Mashita, tied to his chair, aghast and angry, straining forward, was surprised to see how oddly shaped the famous author was: hardly more than five feet tall, pencil-thin with matchstick legs, but with a powerful torso that strained against the yellow-brown fabric of his uniform.

Mishima gave a short speech. The soldiers jeered him loudly. His message was that Japan had lost its heart and soul; that he, Yukio Mishima, would lead the soldiers to a new Japan in which the old virtues of honor and integrity had been restored. But Mishima's message grew more and more incoherent, his voice louder and more strident, as the soldiers jeered him with increasing anger.

Mishima abruptly stopped speaking. He turned and strode back into the office. Kneeling swiftly on the carpet, he stripped off his tunic. He let the trousers of his uniform slip down over his thighs, revealing a snow-white loincloth. Mishima nodded and one of the cadets handed him a foot-long dagger. He placed the tip of the knife lightly against his powerfully muscled groin. Morita, his second-in-command, took a step forward and stood erectly behind his leader. He raised high above his head the samurai sword Mishima had brought into the office.

Mishima had donned a headband while on the balcony. Straining forward in his chair, General Mashita saw that it bore the words *Shichisho Hōkuku*—"Serve the Nation for Seven Lives." Mashita was appalled. This was the headband the kamikaze pilots had worn in World War II when they rammed their planes into the decks of American aircraft carriers, sacrificing their lives while pledging the next seven lives to the Emperor.

The general's gag had been removed a few minutes earlier. Now he cried out, "Mishima-*san,* you do not have to do this!" But events were moving too quickly. Yukio Mishima breathed in and out sharply three times and then drove the dagger into his groin.

His face went white. His hand trembled on the hilt of the knife. He joined it with the other hand and dragged the blade across his stomach. He had driven the dagger in deep; blood spurted from the widening wound and spilled out over his belly, turning the snow-white loincloth crimson red.

Mishima turned his head, trembling, and looked up at Morita, who gripped the samurai sword with both hands. Mishima nodded. The blade came rushing down. The instant before it struck, Mishima bobbed forward. The sword glanced off his shoulders and sliced deeply into his back. Morita raised the blade again and brought it crashing down a second time. It missed Mishima completely, slicing into the blood-soaked carpet. The cadet raised the sword a third time and brought it down. This time it cut deeply into the writer's jaw but failed to sever his head. A third cadet seized the sword from Morita and brought it down quickly, cutting off Mishima's head with a single blow. A raw stench filled the room. Mishima's bowels, wet and gleaming, had spilled out onto the floor.

Mashita's eyes widened in horror. A world-famous writer, probably

Japan's best, had just killed himself in an act of ritual suicide—and apparently it wasn't over! Morita was stripping off his own tunic and kneeling on the floor. He eased his trousers down, picked up Mishima's dagger, and slid the blade weakly across his belly. He nodded at the other cadet, who raised the samurai sword again and brought it crashing down. Morita's head was severed with a single blow.

"Don't continue the butchery," Mashita gasped. "It is useless."

They answered in one voice that Mishima had forbade the remaining three to die. They were sobbing loudly.

"Cry to your heart's content," Mashita commanded hoarsely, "but be calm when the doors are opened. Cover the bodies decently."

They obeyed him, then started for the door to unlock it. Mashita asked: "Are you going to let my subordinates see me tied up like this?"

They untied the commanding officer, unlocked the door, and let the officers enter. The three cadets allowed themselves to be handcuffed and taken away. Within a few hours, a stunned world had heard the news that Japan's most famous writer had committed *seppuku*.

All through this utterly unforeseeable catastrophe, General Kanetoshi Mashita had behaved with perfect correctness. That did not stop the politicians from making a scapegoat of him. They had allowed Yukio Mishima's ninety-man private militia to flourish because they needed Mishima for their own purposes; now they wanted to avoid the blame. The general was relieved of his duties at Ichigaya and transferred to a sinecure position at Haneda Airport. He died a few years later.[1]

In the last weeks of his life, until the end, the image of Yukio Mishima's last moments must have burned with a sinister brightness in General Mashita's brain. The general had seen the writer's severed head fly through the air. He had seen the letters *Shichisbo Hōkuku*—"Serve the Nation for Seven Lives"—glittering on the bloody forehead.

Did the general feel, rushing past him as he sat bound in his chair, the invisible cloud, as light as a mist of perfume, of the *alayavijnana* consciousness bearing the soul of Yukio Mishima into the next lifetime?

That's one of the questions we'll try to answer in this chapter.

Yukio Mishima had worked all through the night before the terrible morning of November 25 to put the finishing touches on *The Decay of the Angel,* the final volume of his four-volume novel sequence *The Sea of Fertility.* This was the masterwork by which he wished to be judged by posterity. Reincarnation is a central theme of *The Sea of Fertility,* and one of its two main characters lives through four lives in the course of the tetralogy.

How important was the concept of reincarnation to Mishima? To what extent did he believe in its reality? He told a critic only that "one of the reasons [I use the theme] is technical. I thought the chronological novel outdated. Using reincarnation, it was easy to jump in time and also in space."[2]

There is very little mention of what the East calls the "transmigration of souls" in any of Mishima's works except *The Sea of Fertility,* in spite of his prodigious productivity. In his short life of forty-five years, Yukio Mishima produced forty novels, thirty-three plays, two hundred short stories, numerous essays, a great deal of poetry, and one screenplay, while acting in three movies. The great majority of his works were both commercially successful and critically acclaimed.

Mishima's literary work contains "paradoxes: beauty equated with violence and death; love yearned for but rejected when it is offered; exquisite attention to detail in the delineation of character."[3] The most famous example is *The Temple of the Golden Pavilion* (1956), in which a psychopathic monk burns down the temple he loves. Mishima's attention to detail often casts a glaring light on the dark side of human behavior: voyeurs, narcissists, sadomasochists, and lunatics frequent his works. But readers are never put off by these vivid portrayals of distressing people; rather, they are mesmerized. Mishima has transformed ugliness into beauty. How does he do it? The answer lies in both the twisted vicissitudes of his unhappy life and the mysterious alchemy we call genius.

For all his high intelligence and great creative power, Mishima—as his spectacular self-immolation at the end makes clear—was as narcissistic and sadomasochistic as any of his characters. All his life he yearned for attention and for death. He attracted the former not only with his writings but also by founding and maintaining his ninety-man militia and becoming a fervent bodybuilder, an expert in *kendo* (Japanese fencing), an exhibitionist who posed for nude and seminude photos, a minor movie star, a sometime singer, and in general an all-around self-promoter and public clown in the mold of Norman Mailer. But none of this satisfied him, and near the end of his seemingly rich and fulfilling life—in July 1970—he wrote: "When I relive in my thoughts the past twenty-five years, their emptiness fills me with astonishment. I can barely say I have lived."[4]

The bizarre and claustrophobic upbringing of Yukio Mishima surely played a role in making him the tortured man he was. He was born Kimitaké Hiraoka on January 14, 1925, in the large house in Tokyo where his parents and grandparents lived. When he was seven weeks old, his "narrow-minded, indomitable and rather wildly poetic"[5] grandmother took him away from his mother to live with her in her own bedroom, which was "perpetually closed and stifling with odors of sickness and old age." The child was "raised there beside her sickbed";[6] he witnessed his grandmother's nervous breakdowns, dressed her sores, accompanied her to the bathroom, and wore the girls dresses she often forced on him. She didn't let him play with other boys or make loud noises; she hardly let him out of the house until he started school.

Kimitaké was virtually a prisoner in his grandmother's sickroom until he was twelve, when his parents moved down the block and insisted on taking him with them. Adolescence brought a storm of homoerotic feelings to the frail and brilliant youth; he would make them part of the Mishima legend by incorporating them into his 1948 autobiographical novel, *The Confessions of a Mask*. (This novel skyrocketed him to fame at age twenty-three.) The painting by Italian Baroque master Guido Reni of the Christian martyr Saint Sebastian's nearly naked youthful body pierced by arrows drove the young Kimitaké to involuntarily ejaculate (this was, he boasted, his first sexual act).[7] Later his feverish sexual imaginings turned into, as he famously tells us in *The Confessions of a Mask,* fantasies of torturing, of murdering—even of eating as cooked dishes at banquets—handsome young men. These atrocious fantasies fired up Kimitaké's writing talents. At age sixteen, adopting the pen name of Yukio Mishima, he wrote, entirely in twelfth-century Court Japanese, a novel so masterful that it astonished and delighted his teachers.

Yukio was turning seventeen as World War II swept across Japan. The youth wrote prodigiously while working in a factory that manufactured kamikaze planes. A misdiagnosis of tuberculosis spared him from conscription. But at twenty-one he believed, like all his contemporaries, that the war would end only with his death. Mishima tells us in *The Confessions of a Mask* that he acquired so great an appetite for imagining that death (and with it the end of all future anxieties and responsibilities) that when the war actually ended—and he was still alive!—he was heartbroken: Defeat "for me—for me alone . . . meant that fearful days were beginning."[8]

The young writer completed law school, graduating at the top of his class. This gained him a plum job at Tokyo's Finance Ministry. By all accounts he was an excellent bureaucrat. But he had also launched himself on a writing career, and by subjecting his huge talent to the most rigorous of disciplines, he was soon able to make a living with his writing and to quit his job. From 1948 to his death, Mishima adhered to a writing schedule that resembled that of Honoré de Balzac: every day he wrote from 11:00 p.m. almost until dawn, in sickness or in health, without fail. Balzac wrote many drafts; according to biographer Christopher Ross, Mishima hardly rewrote at all. Rather, he "wrote down in longhand what he intended to say, neither changing much as he went along nor separately producing a clean finished copy. This is similar to the way Mozart wrote music . . . but is possibly unique for a writer."[9]

Twenty-three of Mishima's novels were "serious"; the other seventeen were "potboilers," dashed off in as few as ten days for women's magazines.[10] Mishima's serious novels took several months to complete and usually garnered both critical and financial success. But his potboilers were commercial successes as well, *A Misstepping of Virtue* (1957) selling three hundred thousand hardback copies in the first year. (This novel introduced a new word into the Japanese language: "lady misstep" [*yoromeki fujin*] for adulteress.)[11]

Mishima's thirty-three plays, including Noh plays (classic Japanese musical dramas), Kabuki theater, and conventional two-act, three-act, and four-act plays, were usually written in two three-day sessions. The author "began with the curtain line of the last act; once he had it, he produced the rest with astonishing speed."[12] The majority of these plays were moneymaking hits, 1956's four-act drama *The Hall of the Crying Deer* becoming the most successful play in Japanese theater history.[13]

Looming over all these works, however, is *The Sea of Fertility*, a single novel in four volumes, which Mishima took five years to complete, and which he considered to be his masterpiece.


A single waterfall flows through all four volumes of *The Sea of Fertility*.

This stream is one soul, one self, being carried from one life to the next through the four individual volumes. This single transmigrating consciousness is the spoiled, aristocratic Kiyoaki in volume 1; the fanatical, athletic Isao in volume 2; the indolent, voluptuous Siamese Princess Ying Chan in volume 3; and the brilliant, psychopathic Tōru in volume 4 (though the inclusion of this fourth personality in the reincarnational cycle is problematic). Every time we encounter, in a new volume, the new lifetime of this fourfold reincarnating consciousness, it is under the sign of the waterfall.

According to the Yuishiki branch of Mahayana Buddhism, there is no such thing as a soul or a self. Yet there is reincarnation. Then what is it that carries the personality forward from one life to the next? The Yuishiki school posits something called *alayavijnana* (originally a Sanskrit word, used in Chinese)—"storehouse consciousness." According to this school, "the effect of a good or bad deed remains in one's consciousness, permeating it as the fragrance of perfume permeates clothes, and thus forms character."[14] Alayavijnana is as tenuous as a fragrance that has been spread over so wide an area that it is incredibly dispersed. It almost doesn't exist; it is like a mood, or the atmosphere of a dream. It's so incredibly tenuous that it doesn't need a carrier—a soul or a self—to pass from one life to the next.

One commentator trying to describe reincarnational transference without a self or soul likened it to "a billiard ball knocking against another billiard ball and passing on its momentum, without the two balls being the same."[15] Giordano Bruno believed that since there is no self or soul in any conventional religious sense, the body itself must reincarnate, or virtually so; Bruno coined a term that comes close to this meaning, "the transcorporation of souls."[16] In heralding the manifestation of reincarnation with the presence of cascading falls, Yukio Mishima meant to give the process a certain force, a certain vitality. In volume 3 of the tetralogy, *The Temple of Dawn,* he describes alayavijnana, or storehouse consciousness, as "in constant flux like a foaming white waterfall. While the cascade is always visible to our eyes, the water is not the same from minute to minute." He quotes the fifth century sage Vasubandhu: "Everything is in constant flux like a torrent."[17] Marguerite Yourcenar simplifies further: "If all is passage, the elements which exist in a transitory state, those enabling reincarnation, are nothing but forces which have, so to speak, traversed the individual . . ."[18]

In volume 2, *Runaway Horses,* Mishima allows the second key figure in the tetralogy, Shigekuni Honda, who lives through all four volumes until he is over eighty, to ruminate on different aspects of the Yuishiki school of reincarnation. Honda recalls reading that according to this school, there is

> an intermediate period of existence, a state midway between the previous life and the reincarnation to come. At its shortest this lasted seven days, and it could extend for as long as seventy-seven.
>
> . . . [In this state,] one existed, not as a merely spiritual being, but

in the form of a fully sentient young child of five or six. Now, however, all the ordinary powers were marvelously heightened. The eye and ear became incredibly keen. One heard the most distant sounds, one saw the most hidden objects, one was immediately present wherever one wished to be. The childlike figures thus gifted, though invisible both to men and to beasts, could be seen hovering in the air by the rare clairvoyant who had attained sufficient purity.

These invisible children nourished themselves on the fragrance of burning incense as they went about their rapid journeys through the air. Hence this intermediate state was also known as "seeking fragrance," after the divinities called Gandharva in Sanskrit.[19]

Mishima told the critic Donald Keene that the title of his tetralogy was "intended to suggest the arid sea of the moon that belies its name. Or, I might go so far as to say that it superimposes the image of cosmic nihilism with that of the fertile sea."[20]

But the waterfall cascading from the beginning of the tetralogy to the end, which is an image of reincarnation, is also literally a sea of fertility: there is the force of the water, and there is also the pulsating, inseminating power of the soul in the full bloom of reincarnating.

Close to the beginning of *Spring Snow*—volume 1—there is a disturbing incident. On a Sunday late in 1912, in the gardens of the Tokyo estate of Kiyoaki Matsugae's parents, he and Honda, both schoolboys, with the young and beautiful Satoko Ayakura (with whom Kiyoaki will have a passionate love affair), Kiyoaki's mother, and Satoko's great-aunt, the abbess of Gesshu Abbey, come upon an artificial waterfall whose flow is blocked by the corpse of a black dog. This is a bad omen. The black dog is removed, and the waterfall flows again. The abbess offers to bless the dog when it is buried. All feel relief; but it doesn't bode well that the reincarnational flow has initially been blocked by the accidental death of an animal.[21] Sixty years later, Satoko herself, choosing to enter Gesshu Abbey because of her affair with Kiyoaki, has after many years become the abbess. Honda, now over eighty, visits her, but the abbess now presides over a world of chaos and dissolution, and the cascading waters of reincarnation have dried up.

But we are a long way from this in volume 1. As *Spring Snow* draws to a close, Kiyoaki, not yet twenty, dies as a result of the complications of his love affair with Satoko. His last words, breathed to his schoolmate and best friend Honda, are: "I'll see you again. I know it. Beneath the falls."[22]

Through the four volumes, as Honda gets to live out his full complement of years, around him revolve in intense and problematical relationship the four lifetimes that began with Kiyoaki's. Volume 2, *Runaway Horses,* opens in 1934. Honda, now thirty-nine, is a successful judge. He happens to see an eighteen-year-old martial arts student, Isao Iinuma, performing a ritual ablution under a waterfall. Honda suddenly recalls Kiyoaki's last words, "Beneath the falls." He sees, on Isao's body, "back from the nipple, at a place ordinarily hidden from the arm . . . a cluster of three small moles."[23] Honda recognizes this configuration of moles; it was present on Kiyoaki's body. In volume 1, Mishima describes Kiyoaki lying naked on his bed: ". . . on Kiyoaki's left side, where the pale flesh pulsed softly in rhythm with his heartbeat . . . were three small, almost invisible moles. And much as the three stars in Orion's belt fade in strong moonlight, so too these three small moles were almost blotted out by its rays."[24]

Honda is thrilled at this revelation that reincarnation is a reality and Kiyoaki has returned to him. Honda's study of India's ancient laws of Manu that make allowance for reincarnation reinforces his newly found belief. Twenty years earlier, at their school in Tokyo, he and Kiyoaki had discussed reincarnation with two visiting Siamese princes, both believers. Now the memory of that time flows back to Honda, as does that of the "Dream Book," now in Honda's possession, that Kiyoaki kept. The book contains dreams that, Honda now sees, foretell Kiyoaki's incarnations. Waterfalls figure in these sensuous dreams, as does, apparently, a Siamese princess.

Near the end of *Runaway Horses,* the theme of reincarnation is forcefully reintroduced, in what critic Marguerite Yourcenar calls "perhaps the strangest and sweetest passage in the whole tetralogy":[25] Isao has become a right-wing fanatic plotting a coup that will involve the murder of several Japanese businessmen. The plot is discovered. Honda resigns his judgeship to defend Isao in court. There is a strange incident at the trial. Yourcenar describes it:

> In preparing his plot, Isao has sought backing from the military, in particular from one officer who lives in an old hovel at the bottom of the lane, not far from his barracks. . . . [Kiyoaki and Satoko had often come clandestinely to this hovel for passionate lovemaking] upon entering the garden of the house at the bottom of the steep lane, the tough-skinned Isao, in whom no emotion of this kind has ever surfaced, suddenly feels he is swooning with delight, as if something of the happiness once felt here by Kiyoaki possessing Satoko has reached him through the maze of time. . . . [During the trial, the aged landlord of the same hovel] is summoned to see if he will recognize Isao on the bench of the accused. The elderly cripple, leaning on his stick, approaches the young man, examines him, and in a cracked voice answers in effect: "Yes, he came to my house with a woman twenty years ago." Isao's age is twenty. The old man is laughed out of the room. . . . The old man so close to death has felt as one the heat of two burning youths.[26]

Isao is acquitted. The trial ends. A few weeks later, Honda, alone with Isao while he is asleep, hears him murmur: "Far to the south. Very hot . . . in the rose sunshine of a southern land."[27] Two days later, Isao buys a gun and sword, murders a businessman—one of those targeted in the original plot—and commits seppuku. He is twenty years old.

Honda cannot forget Isao's dream, since Kiyoaki's Dream Book had recorded a similar image of a hot southern land (along with a princess). Kiyoaki had also recorded a dream, whose predictive power becomes clear partway through volume 2, when Isao breaks away from his schoolmates and shoots a pheasant with a gun he isn't supposed to have. Isao's father is at the school, as is Honda; the latter is present when Isao's father, catching up with the son, berates him with: "You are heedless and intractable. You have proved it beyond all question."[28] Honda instantly recalls a dream in the Dream Book in which Kioaki was the central figure in the exact same drama, including even the words: "You are heedless and intractable. You have proved it beyond all question."[29]

Volume 3 of the tetralogy, *The Temple of Dawn,* opens in 1941. Honda, now forty-seven, comes to Bangkok, the capital of Thailand (then called Siam), on legal business. He encounters Ying Chan, a six-year-old Thai princess, who runs to him exclaiming that she isn't Thai but Japanese and is extremely grateful to him for all that he has done for her.

Honda is ecstatic. Surely Ying Chan is the reincarnation of Kiyoaki/ Isao. The lawyer escorts her to the Bangkok Public Baths to try to see, while she is swimming, if she has the telltale three moles on her side. Ying Chan doesn't disrobe enough for him to tell. We might have expected this: the waters of the baths are calm, even tepid; there are no cascading falls to signal the resurgence of reincarnational forces.

Disappointed, Honda takes a side trip to India. There, at the famed cave temples of Ajanta near Benares, he witnesses the tumultuous flow of the two celebrated waterfalls thundering above the caves. Startled, shaken, he wonders if the presence of ever-cascading alayavijnana—the storehouse consciousness of reincarnation—is being signaled to him. Are the falls at Ajanta what the dying Kiyoaki was really referring to when he murmured to Honda, "I'll see you again. I know it. Beneath the falls"? Does the thunder of these falls hold a message for him: that Ying Chan actually is the third incarnation of Kiyoaki?

Eleven years pass. It is 1952. Honda, in Tokyo, learns that Ying Chan has arrived in the city. He hasn't seen her since 1941.

Honda has degenerated greatly from the man he once was. Perhaps the role of perpetual go-between for Kiyoaki and Satoko originally set the pattern, but he has become a shabby practitioner of voyeurism. This compulsion exacerbates his need to see whether the three moles are on Ying Chan's body. He builds a swimming pool on his country estate solely so that he can invite her to an outdoor cocktail party and observe, while she is swimming, whether she bears this insignia that surely is the hallmark of the soul of Kiyoaki/Isao.

But once again, at the party, he can't quite make out if the moles are there. This time, however, Honda has a contingency plan. He has made a peephole in his study into the room where Ying Chan will be spending the night. That night, he peers through the peephole.

He is rewarded: he is able to observe that the three moles are there. Mishima writes: "Ying Chan's whole side was exposed. To the left of her bare breast, an area her arm had previously concealed, three extremely small moles appeared distinctly, like the Pleiades in the dusky sky of her brown skin that resembled the dying evening glow. . . . Honda was shocked. It was as if his eyes had been pierced with arrows."[30]

But, consumed as he is by adolescent lust for Ying Chan's voluptuous body, he has an unpleasant surprise: he also sees that she is engaged in passionate lesbian sex with an older woman friend of his. *The Temple of Dawn* ends in an agony of dissolution and death. The next morning a fire accidentally burns Honda's country house to the ground, killing two of the guests. Ying Chan returns to Thailand but soon dies from a snakebite. She is only twenty.

In the final volume of the tetralogy, *The Decay of the Angel,* Honda, disillusioned, ailing, almost eighty, meets Tōru Yasunaga, a highly intelligent, cold-hearted orphan in whose enigmatic smile Honda thinks he recognizes the consciousness of Kioyaki/Isao/Ying Chan. He believes he has glimpsed the telltale three moles on Tōru's side when the sixteen-year-old is washing himself in the cascading flow of water of his bathroom shower.

In volume 4, the modern world, as seen through Honda's eyes, is a vision of hell. Honda adopts Tōru; Tōru treats him viciously; a host of terrible incidents leave Tōru blind and disinherited. Honda, diagnosed with cancer, presented with indisputable proof that Tōru is not the reincarnation of Kiyoaki/Isao/Ying Chan, loses all hope. Desperate to hold on to what is left of his past with Kiyoaki, he travels to the Gesshu Abbey, where, sixty years before, Satoko, having loved Kiyoaki and aborted his child, took her vows and eventually became the abbess.

But Honda doesn't find what he seeks. Mishima scholar-journalist Henry Stokes writes:

> As a religious background to the novel, Mishima used the teaching of the small Buddhist sect known as Hossu, whose *yūishiki ron,* or theory of consciousness, only affirms that all experience is subjective and that existence cannot be verified. Mishima gave a twist of his own to the teaching of this ancient Buddhist sect, which came to Japan in the seventh century and lost most of its hold in the country in the succeeding five hundred years. As only consciousness existed, there was no telling reality from illusion.[31]

Honda has been playing with this vision of reality, and it will take possession of his soul forever when he meets the abbess. He knows she is Satoko. But the abbess stuns him by declaring that she doesn't remember him and has never heard of Kiyoaki. Is yūishiki ron in fact the true nature of things? Honda asks himself in horror. Is there really no way to tell the difference between experience and illusion? Herein must lie the reason for the abbess's lack of response. But illusion itself may be an illusion. Leaving the abbey, Honda gazes out over the grounds and sees only the Void of the Buddhists: "The garden was empty. He had come, thought Honda, to a place that had no memories, nothing. The noontide sun of summer flowed over the still garden."[32]

The theme of reincarnation is not new in Japanese literature. Christopher Ross writes:

The device of the reincarnation of a central character who dies in the first volume to be reborn in each of the following novels in the series is taken from a classical model, the *Hamamatsu Chūnagon Monogatari*, "The Tale of the Hamamatsu Middle Counselor," an eleventh-century Heian romance attributed to Sugawara no Takasue no Musume.[33]

Mishima's use of birthmarks is also a well-known Japanese literary convention. Marguerite Yourcenar tells us: "The Japanese tales of Lafcadio Hearn are full of examples of instances of reincarnation confirmed by a mark on the body, which seems to indicate that this kind of folklore was common in Japan in the nineteenth century."[34]

Mishima's treatment of reincarnation conforms to what little scientific knowledge we have of reincarnation today. Yourcenar notes the correlation between how Mishima makes Ying Chan act—emerging from childhood at eight, she forgets about her previous incarnation as a Japanese and stops talking about it—and the researches of Canadian physician and parapsychologist Ian Stevenson, especially as set forth in *Twenty Cases Suggestive of Reincarnation,* where he asserts that "in the jabbering of very young children we can find the clearest traces of life before life." "Chan," states Yourcenar, "conforms to the parapsychologist's model."[35]

Marguerite Yourcenar wonders if the transference of alaya consciousness can be related to the driving force that is love. She says of *The Sea of Fertility:*

> More profoundly, as well as more subjectively, we feel we are witnessing a phenomenon comparable to love, and this even if we cannot properly give the name of love to Honda's total devotion to the two young men, Kiyoaki and Isao, or if, should something akin to the emotion of love have blossomed there, the author has not told us about it. . . . But, in these three cases, the marvel of love has in fact taken place . . .[36]

We'll return to Mishima's treatment of the theme of reincarnation at the end of this chapter, because there is an eerie postscript to this theme in the aftermath of the author's death. To a large degree, Mishima used the idea of reincarnation in the tetralogy as a device enabling him to go directly to the heart of four different epochs in modern Japanese history. These historical periods were: in *Spring Snow,* the twilight years of Japan's ancient aristocracy, when vital and moneyed provincial families were beginning to seize social and political power; in *Runaway Horses,* the 1930s, when numerous right-wing conspiracies and coup d'états fatally weakened Japan's political structures, paving the way for the fanatical dictatorship of World War II; in *The Temple of Dawn,* the eve of World War II through the Allied occupation and the postwar era, when Japan seemed to be irretrievably losing its national identity; and, in *The Decay of the Angel,* the late 1960s, when Japan, losing all sense of its courtly traditions, its samurai ideals, and its devotion to Buddhism, succumbed to an aridity inviting nihilism and destruction.

These four epochs describe the decline and fall of traditional Japanese society. Mishima regarded his country as now completely and hopelessly Westernized. In *The Decay of the Angel* the tetralogy becomes a pophecy for the decline and ultimate destruction of Western civilization as a whole. The author does not revel in the vistas he evokes. *The Sea of Fertility* is not an exercise in nihilism; rather, it is a cry of despair. Mishima yearned for the return of a world in which humankind could accomplish mighty purposes. He felt this would happen only if we were forced to live at full stretch, to the very limits of our being, with the ecstatic nobility in the face of the chaos of existing possessed by the ancient Greeks.[37] In Doris Lessing's *The Sirian Experiments* (see chapter 21), the narrator tells how the interstellar empire of the Sirians, in achieving its goal of developing technologies that freed billions of its citizens from toil, found it had to pay a terrible price:

> We did not foresee that these billions, not only on our Home Planet
> but also on our Colonized Planets, would fall victim to depression

and despair. We had not understood that there is inherent in every creature of this Galaxy a need, an imperative, towards a continual striving, or self-transcendence, or purpose. To be told that there is nothing to do but consume, no work needed, nothing to achieve, is to receive a sentence of death.[38]

Mishima felt this need toward self-transcendence to the very marrow of his bones. The sentiments of Kiyoaki Matsugae's grandmother, expressed in a key scene in the first volume of the tetralogy, *Spring Snow*, are surely the author's sentiments. Kiyoaki's parents have discovered that he has gotten Satoko Ayakura, the daughter of an aristocratic family, pregnant. To make matters worse, Satoko is betrothed to a member of the Japanese royal family. Kiyoaki's parents are appalled: the family has insulted the Emperor. The grandmother, who lives with them, is summoned to give her opinion.

In her youth, this elderly lady had known an era when the vibrant traditions of the samurai still ruled. Her long-dead husband had been a role model for these times. The grandmother begins by asking Kiyoaki if it is true that he has gotten Satoko pregnant:

"It's true," he said quickly in nasal tones, immediately seizing the fresh handkerchief proffered by his mother and clapping it to his face. [His father had hit him in the face.]

His grandmother then made a speech that seemed to echo the hoofbeats of horses galloping free, a speech that eloquently tore to shreds the conventional niceties.

"Getting the betrothed of the Imperial Prince pregnant! Now there's an achievement! How many of these simpering lads nowadays are capable of anything like that? No doubt about it—Kiyoaki's a true grandson of my husband's. You won't regret it even if you are jailed for it. At least they surely won't execute you," she said, obviously enjoying herself. The stern lines around her mouth were gone now, and she seemed aglow with a lively satisfaction, as if she had banished decades of stifling gloom, dispersing at a single stroke the enervating pall that had hung over the house ever since the present Marquis [her son and Kiyoaki's father] had become its master. Nor was she laying the blame on her son alone. She was speaking now in retaliation against all those others, too, who surrounded her in old age, and whose treacherous power she could sense closing in to crush her. Her voice came echoing gaily out of another era, one of upheavals, a violent era forgotten by this generation, in which fear of imprisonment and death held no one in check, an era in which the threat of both was part of the texture of everyday life. She belonged to a generation of women who had thought nothing of washing their dinner plates in a river while corpses went floating past. That was life! And now, how remarkable that this grandson, who seemed so effete at first glance, should have revived the spirit of that age before her very eyes.[39]

Mishima yearned to revive that spirit. It is unfortunate that the author made people believe—indeed, seems to have sometimes made himself believe—that he thirsted only after the blood and death of the worst excesses of the samurai era, not after the heroic commitment to total living they reflected. Mishima was, after all, a man of his time and place, and even his prescient genius did not make him any less burdened by centuries of Japanese customs (which he knew were doomed) than any of his contemporaries.

Mishima was a student of the German nihilistic philosopher Friedrich Nietszche (1844–1900). The acuity of Mishima's indictment of Western civilization—and the universality of his vision—are put on bold display by the startling resemblance of basic elements of *The Decay of the Angel* to Nietszche's description of what modern man would become.

Nietszche sought to show that those critical belief systems within which societies live, and with which they structure and give meaning to their lives, have no basis in objective reality, but are merely invented by the societies themselves. These belief systems include all religions and even the presuppositions of social democracy and modern science. Nietszche asserted that once we see these life-structuring belief systems—which he called "horizons"—as no more than our own creations, we can no longer believe in them, or create them. Philosopher George Grant writes in *Time as History:*

> Nietzsche affirms that once we know the horizons are relative and man-made, their power to sustain us is blighted. Once we know them to be relative, they no longer horizon us. We cannot live in a horizon where we know it to be one. When the historical sense teaches us that our values are not sustained in the nature of things, impotence descends.[40]

Nietzsche believed that at the end of the era of man as a rational being, the world would be dominated by two types, the last men and the nihilists. Dr. Grant writes:

> The last men are those who have inherited the ideas of happiness and equality from the doctrine of progress. But because this happiness is to be realized by all men, the conception of its content has to be shrunk to fit what can be realized by all. . . Happiness can be achieved, but only at the cost of emasculating men of all potentialities for nobility and greatness . . . [In *Thus Spake Zarathustra* (1883), Nietszche describes the last men in these words:] "They have their little pleasure for the day and their little pleasure for the night: but they respect health. 'We have discovered happiness,' say the last men and blink." Or again, "A little poison now and then: that produces pleasant dreams. And a lot of poison at last, for a pleasant death." Or again, "Formerly all the world was mad, say the most astute of the last men and blink. They are clever and know everything that has ever happened: so there is no end in their mockery."[41]

The end of the era of man as a rational being also brings forth nihilists. In the words of Dr. Grant:

These are those who understand that they can know nothing about what is good to will. Because of the historical sense, they know that all values are relative and man-made; the highest values of the past have devaluated themselves. Men have no given content for their willing. But because men are wills, the strongest cannot give up willing. Men would rather will nothing than have nothing to will. Nietzsche . . . has little doubt of the violence and cataclysms which will come forth from men who would rather will nothing than have nothing to will. They will be resolute in their will to mastery, but they cannot know what that mastery is for. The violence of their mastery over human and non-human beings will be without end. In the 1880s he looked ahead to that age of world wars and continued upheavals which most of us in this [the twentieth] century have tried to endure.[42]

In the last volume of the tetralogy, *The Decay of the Angel,* Shigekuni Honda matches Nietzsche's description of the "last men." Honda's pleasures belong to the lowest common denominator of pleasures in a democratized, sanitized world. Often, in the pages of the tetralogy, he has his little drink at the end of the day. He is not a hero, but a voyeur and a narcissist. He has had his hopes and dreams; he has experienced the return of Kiyoaki as Isao and Ying Chan. All this is turning to ashes, as the world is turning to ashes.

Tōru Yasunaga matches Nietzsche's description of a "nihilist." He is brilliant and disciplined, and filled with the will to power. Tōru is without moral values. But the strongest cannot give up willing, and he would rather will nothing than have nothing to will. He lays about him in every direction, destroying everything he can, including Honda. When there is nothing left to destroy, he tries to destroy himself. When we last see him, he is blind and moving toward psychic paralysis.

Shigekuni Honda goes to the Gesshu Abbey in search of the last "horizons." He finds out that there are no horizons. He finds nothing.

Henry Scott Stokes writes in *The Life and Death of Yukio Mishima* that few Japanese critics today would call Yukio Mishima a genius and that the consensus in Tokyo is that he was a minor artist. This is because, for many, Mishima's right-wing politics are anathema. Moreover, the Japanese continue to resent Mishima for committing suicide in public and making Japan look like a nation of savages still bent on flying kamikaze planes.

But, says Stokes, "One of his elders in Japan gave Mishima phenomenally high marks. Yasunari Kawabata, winner of the Nobel Prize in Literature in 1968, told *The New York Times* two years later: 'Mishima has extraordinary talent, and it is not just a Japanese talent but a talent of world scale. He is the kind of genius who comes along perhaps once every three hundred years.'"[43]

Stokes, a British journalist living in Japan who knew Mishima personally, agrees with Kawabata. "Mishima communicates to me an urgency appropriate to a world at risk," he writes, remarking that Mishima's prediction, made toward the end of his life, that "Japan will disappear," seemed to be coming true. Mishima had added: "It will become inorganic, empty, neutral-tinted: it will be wealthy and astute, a large economic power in a corner of the Far East."[44]

Author Stokes, who knew the Nobel Prize–winning author Yasunari Kawabata personally as well as Yukio Mishima, notes in his biography of Mishima that Kawabata felt himself to be haunted by Mishima's ghost for two years after the author's death. Stokes writes, in a personal communication:

Kawabata was driven to distraction by visits from Mishima's ghost (*obake* in Japanese). The visitations were ceaseless and unrelenting. Kawabata was driven to take his life. [In 1971, Kawabata himself committed suicide by turning on the gas.] I think this very simple, colorful account of what happened is the most plausible. Kawabata was a very weak and feeble old man by this time. He really felt the rebuke that Mishima leveled at him [during these ghostly visits], for not supporting Mishima to the hilt, when the time came . . .

What Kawabata felt was a palpable presence in his room. Perhaps even during the day . . . Mishima used to say that the most fearful ghosts were the ones that appeared in daylight.[44]

Stokes adds in his personal communication that for two years after Mishima's death, "I was myself troubled by Mishima's ghost, if by that we mean a palpable sense of his accusing presence. I had a recurring dream rather than any daytime experience. . . . I was tormented by these dreams, in the two or three years after Mishima died; perhaps a bit more. Eventually, they faded."[45]

Did Yukio Mishima's alayavijnana consciousness pursue Yasunari Kawabata and Henry Scott Stokes for over two years in the form of a cloud of exquisitely extenuated fragrance or a mist of tiny droplets of water resembling a miniature waterfall?

If so, was he trying to say he was wrong, and that there is more than the Void?

## *Twenty-four*
# James Merrill
# (1926–1995)
## *I and Mine Hold It Back Brothers*

Which of the following statements is true?

In the fourteenth century BC, a pharaoh named Akhnaton ruled Egypt.

For a brief period, Akhnaton introduced monotheism into Egypt, specifically the worship of the Sun god Aton. This form of worship was repudiated after his death, when Egypt returned to polytheism.

Akhnaton was one of two "twinned" souls; the other twinned soul was that of his twin sister, Nefertiti. The two married each other at age thirteen. These twinned souls were part of a group of five immortal souls called the "V" (Roman numeral for five), the twinned soul of Akhnaton/Nefertiti counting as one of those five. The role of the V was to help humanity advance by returning to earth again and again remembering all their past lives. The twinned soul of Akhnaton/Nefertiti was the first of the V to incarnate on earth.[1] Nefertiti gave birth to five stillborn infants, after which she dedicated herself solely to the governance and transformation of Egypt.

During their reign, Akhnaton and Nefertiti not only banished polytheism but had all the temple priests put to death as well. They freed the slaves. Akhnaton and Nefertiti introduced a revolutionary new science into Egypt. They harnessed the power of the sun to control the tides all up and down the Nile. They also used it to close the Strait of Gibraltar, allowing just enough water through to turn the Mediterranean Sea into a quiet bay.[2]

But wait! The reader must have noticed by now that most of these statements aren't true. Yes, a pharaoh named Akhnaton ruled Egypt in the fourteenth century BC. And, yes, he introduced the worship of the one god Aton, and that worship was repudiated after his death and polytheism returned to Egypt.

But none of the rest is true. Modern historians say that though it's possible Nefertiti was Akhnaton's half sister and probable she was his first cousin, she couldn't have been his twin sister. They say that Akhnaton and Nefertiti did not reign thirteen years, but eighteen, and that Nefertiti did not give birth to five stillborn infants, but to five girls and a boy all of whom survived birth.

Historian Chester A. Starr tells us that Akhnaton, with the help of relatives and advisers, "opened the way to an amazing wave of reform, which spilled over from the political and religious fields into artistic and cultural revolution."[3] But Starr does not say that Akhnaton harnessed the power of the sun and tamed the tides of the Nile and the Mediterranean.

The odd pieces of alternative history that begin this chapter come from spirit guides who, from the mid-1950s to the early 1980s, spoke through a Ouija board to Pulitzer Prize–winning American poet James Merrill and his longtime companion and fellow writer (and composer) David Jackson. The spirits communicated to the two a dazzling vision of our world as one set in motion by a God who, like the deity of the Gnostics, has all but withdrawn from His creation. Moreover, this God is only one of a pantheon of gods. Our world, the spirits declared, was shaped and is controlled in its human and nonhuman dimensions by four powerful angelic presences, who are aided in their tasks by the discarnate spirits of a sentient species, long extinct, that preceded ours on earth. Reincarnation is an abiding, decisive principle of our world and the other levels of reality to which it is linked. Our universe is a dynamic one, but not always in a positive sense: even the gods are at war, and our own God is failing for reasons that Merrill and Jackson—and all of us—need to understand, for, in some mysterious way, God needs our help.

This unique, epic, channeled history of the universe as it concerns humanity was published as a five-hundred-page poem, *The Changing Light at Sandover,* in 1982. It had been published earlier in three parts: as *Divine Comedies* (1976), which won the Pulitzer Prize for Poetry; as *Mirabell: Books of Number* (1978), which won the National Book Award; and as *Scripts for the Pageant* (1980).

James Merrill was the son of Charles Merrill, the cofounder of the New York–based international brokerage firm of Merrill Lynch. Born in New York City, the son was brought up in the more elevated strata of society, graduated from Amherst College, and, after serving in World War II, rose steadily through the ranks of poets until, in the last decade of his life, he came to be considered America's greatest contemporary poet.

Few could have thought that the cultivated and multifariously gifted Merrill, who knew languages, music, literature, and even a great deal about science, would one day join the ranks of the tens of thousands of New Age enthusiasts who, in the United States and abroad, devote time to channeling information from the spirits of the dead. But that's exactly what happened to James Merrill, along with his friend David Jackson.

In the year or two prior to the summer of 1955, Merrill and Jackson occasionally dallied with a Ouija board, but nothing that made much sense came through. However, all that changed early one midsummer morning when the two, sitting at the kitchen table in their apartment near the harbor at Stonington, Connecticut, watched idly, then with growing concern, as the upside-down Tupperware teacup they used as a planchette began moving purposefully from letter to letter on the hand-drawn Ouija board that lay between them. Awkwardly, the teacup spelled out words, then—in the beginning—brief sentences.

By the time the morning was over, the two had been introduced to the discarnate shade of Ephraim, a bisexual Greek Jew strangled to death at age thirty-two, in AD 36, at the villa of the Roman emperor Tiberius on the isle of Capri.[4] Ephraim proved to be so charming and entertaining—and told them such sensational stories—that Merrill and Jackson could only listen spellbound if skeptical. Over the coming days, the spirit described for them the workings of a system of "patron" and "representative," whereby the souls of the dead, though forbidden to intervene directly, subtly guided the souls of the living.

This was just the beginning. Over the next few months, Ephraim was joined on the Ouija board by a host of other spirit guides, including: the discarnate spirits of a "root race" that preceded humankind on earth; the four angelic presences that administered earth for God; and the shades of Merrill and Jackson's more illustrious dead friends, including English poet W. H. Auden. On and off, over the next thirty years and more, all of these entities—and others—regaled Merrill and Jackson with captivating stories allegedly of the true nature and purpose of humanity, of our planet, of God, and of the afterworld.

The material that would eventually fill the pages of *The Changing Light at Sandover* can be grouped under three main headings: reincarnation, the root races, and the No Accident Clause. Each is described in the following pages.

*Reincarnation.* Merrill and Jackson were told that reincarnation is a fundamental feature of the life of humans, and that we all live many lives. Merrill was in his 268th, and was told it was his last. Jackson was living through his 289th—but had two or three more to go.[5] Early on, the spirit guides made a distinction between two strata of humans. There were the two million or so incarnate souls that were the "movers and shakers," in charge of any progress we might make. These souls were altered or adjusted (*cloned* was the word the spirits used) between lifetimes in the "Lab" (a place of vast, spiritual engineering activity) so as to be better prepared for the next lifetime. (James Merrill had undergone such enhancements himself before becoming James Merrill.) Only the two million elite souls were part of the patron-representative program. The rest of humanity, lacking higher guidance and without benefit of Lab enhancement, were seemingly hurled blindly from lifetime to lifetime.

Merrill (despite his patrician upbringing) and Jackson both vigorously objected to this elitist heirarchy. But the spirits saw it as obviously a necessity.

Reincarnating souls passed from rock to plant to animal to man. But there was no concept of advancement or regression; no value judgments were attached to this journey. It could be a reward to be reborn as a stone. The shade of W. H. Auden tells them he has been reborn as a mineral deposit and is therefore able to explore and understand the universe of stone on earth. Sometimes the soul-stuff of plants is inserted into reincarnating human beings while they are resting in the Lab. This spirit material, called "shooting," makes for great vitality in the reborn human although it shortens the life span. Poet Edwin Muir and horticulturist Luther Burbank were both mortals much imbued with "shooting." So, too, was Yukio Mishima (whom Merrill met when the Japanese novelist visited the United States in 1968). (See chapter 23.) The spirit guides tell Merrill:

> . . . *from its origin all Japanese poetry was*
> *The result of our experiments in vegetable*
> *Cloning. It took, & is now a mainspring of the Jap*
> > *mind*
> *(Hence their passion for the camera: photosynthesis)*

> *Yr confrere turning brutally against his veg nature*
> *Loppd off his own head as if with a cane among tulips.*[6]

In today's world, new perils are pushing the envelope of reincarnation. Merrill and Jackson are told that, due to earth's population explosion, there is a shortage of the matter that makes up souls. The Lab managers have now (in a procedure that seems to take place independently of the Lab) had to resort to the heavy cloning "*in the past half century [of the] souls of domestic animals, most recently the rat. By 2050 these too will be exhausted.*" Once that happens, the spirits will probably go to "*Wilder strains: mountain cats and forest monkeys.*"[7]

Does the successful completion of a cycle of reincarnation of several hundred lives result in a stay in an afterworld? The spirits speak only of nine spiritual stages that the discarnate spirit ascends after it works its way through its necessary incarnations. It's from these stages that patrons look earthward to aid representatives. The climb up the nine-step spiritual ladder seems to be the privilege of only the two million movers and shakers. Those who make it to the top become, say the spirit guides, "*safety deposits,*"

> *. . . which spice & fortify numberless earthly dishes. Proust*
> *Is deservedly enshrined. Tap him & as a statesman*
> *At a dull banquet, he converses, seems to be himself.*
> *But part of his mind literally wanders: Out on loan.*[8]

Disquieting demonstrations accompany these lectures. The guides maneuver Merrill into reexperiencing his death by heart attack in 1925, in his previous life as "Rufus Farmetton," a farmer in the Transvaal in South Africa. Ephraim—it seems—lets Merrill and Jackson help him locate a newly aborning baby to be the mortal body of the soul of a deceased friend of theirs about to reincarnate. (This has an alarming consequence: "*Higher powers,*" furious at this meddling by two mortals, threaten to shut down the Ouija board connection.)

The crowning achievements of this system of reincarnation are the "V," already mentioned, of whom Akhnaton and Nefertiti, in uniquely twinned form, were the first to incarnate on earth. (They have reincarnated as Galileo and Marie Curie, among others.) These five souls, who remember all their past lives, have "immortal" names: Laduman, Soriva, Rachel, Torro, and Von.[9]

The spirits explain that

> *These have lived centuries & live today heldover lives*
> *Not in the scheme you know of the 9 stages. Remaining*
> *Aware of it all, knowing the fruitlessness of speaking*
> *Of their knowledge, they return to earth charged with*
> > *Energy*
> *Beyond the norm.*[10]

The reincarnations of the V include, among many others, Mozart and Stravinsky (the same soul, born twice), Dag Hammarskjöld, Einstein, and Montezuma (now an East German astrophysicist).[11]

*Root races.* The spirit guides don't use the term "root race," which Madame Blavatsky reserved for the sentient species that, she claimed, flourished on earth before humankind. But they do describe for Merrill and Jackson three such analogous pre-human species. All are very different from the Lemurians and Atlanteans described by Blavatsky in *The Secret Doctrine* (and by Anthroposophical Society founder Rudolf Steiner in several of his books).

Merrill's guides say that God, through the instrument of the four angels Michael, Gabriel, Ezekiel, and Raphael, first of all sowed on earth a race of sentient, immortal, winged creatures who inhabited what is now China. This race destroyed itself in an atomic war. So violent was this act of self-immolation that God built a protective wall—the Himalayas—to protect the rest of the world from the resulting radiation. Next came a race of immortal creatures resembling the centaurs of ancient myth (i.e., half man, half horse). The centaurs were intelligent and reflective, and made many advances. But because they had forelegs with hooves and not hands with opposable thumbs, they were limited in their ability to manipulate physical reality.

Therefore, the centaurs injected fruit flies with radium and bred them in laboratories through many generations until they had produced erect, winged, black humanoids looking somewhat like giant bats. These creatures, also immortal, were intended to be the centaurs' servants. And so they were, for several millennia, until the bat-creatures rose up against their masters and destroyed them in an atomic war.

The bat-creatures then built their own cities, lofting them high into the ozone layer and mooring them to earth with immense cables. A millennium passed; the bat-creatures became arrogant, raised their cities higher and higher, and neglected the maintenance of the cables. Finally, one cable snapped, then another, then another—and the airborne cities of the bats plummeted back to earth, crashing and destroying every member of the bat civilization.

It seems that God had come to understand that immortality is not a valid option for creatures living a physical life in the space-time continuum. Merrill and Jackson are tempted to believe this is because there can be no ultimate deadline for immortal creatures. Mortal creatures have to strive to complete their tasks before their death; immortal creatures have no such goad to achievement. Reincarnation may be a reality and therefore a sort of second chance, though this is something a mortal can never know for sure.

The stage has been set for the coming of humankind.

*The No Accident Clause.* We now turn back to the Akhnaton and Nefertiti story with which the chapter began. According to the guides, the sojourn of that unique twinned soul in ancient Egypt had a catastrophic ending—one that compelled God to make the grave decision to institute the No Accident Clause.

Akhnaton and Nefertiti continued to make giant strides.

Revolutionizing medicine, they abolished sickness. Children of the next generation were a foot taller than their parents. Every structure in the country was heated and cooled with solar energy.

Akhnaton set about the construction of a fifty-foot-high rock-crystal pyramid, believing that if the dimensions of this pyramid were perfect, he would be able to harness enough of the power of the sun to rule the world.

On the night before the dawn when the capstone of the pyramid was to be lifted into place, Akhnaton and Nefertiti had themselves rowed to the site on a barge glittering with miniature diamond pyramids. Akhnaton, exalted, *"watchd so intensely thrilld his physicians fed him opium each hour,"*[12] waiting for his pyramid to blaze into a perfect engine at the first light of dawn.

But the first light triggered a catastrophe. A tremendous explosion engulfed the site and caused the crystal pyramid to rise, then fall, then melt into a lake of molten crystal that is still, today, buried under Thebes. Far away in Crete, the volcano Thera erupted and destroyed the city of Minoa. Akhnaton and Nefertiti, devastated, cut their wrists and bled to death over the side of their barge. So vast was the destruction that the deserts surrounding Egypt lay infertile for the next 1,200 years.[13]

What caused this catastrophe? The proportions of the pyramid were "a fractional millimeter wrong."[14] But Akhnaton was mistaken in thinking that had the dimensions of the crystal pyramid been perfect, he could have wholly tamed the sun and ruled the world. The guides tell Merrill and Jackson that had the proportions been perfect, the earth would have been in flames, our world destroyed. Ironically, it was the "fractional millimeter wrong" that saved the world—even though it resulted in the semidestruction of Thebes and the suicides of Akhnaton and Nefertiti.

This fiery ending, perpetrated by no less than the beloved first of His V to be sent earthward, causes God to do some rethinking.

He decides to introduce the No Accident Clause.

Up until then, the souls of the movers and shakers on earth—those eligible for guidance by patrons and retooling in the Lab—were at the mercy of elements of pure chance, of randomness, in the universe; things could "just happen" to them. Now God instructs his four angels to eliminate this. What the spirit guides tell Merrill and Jackson here almost defies analysis, but it might be said God moves from a policy of total deregulation of the mortal ruling classes to one of some clearly defined regulation; he orders that a No Accident Clause be cloned into the relevant mortals. An element of strict determinism descends upon the world; in the words of scholar Judith Moffett: "Apparently the No Accident clause means that what happens to [God's chosen] souls is planned and purposeful to the minutest detail."[15]

This period when God exercises some control extends from the fourteenth century BC to the twentieth century AD. But in our time, the No Accident Clause is unraveling. This is because of the erosion of religious and moral standards and because nonmembers of the ruling elite, without the No Accident Clause cloned into them, are increasingly acquiring the money, power, and leisure time to cause great harm, by, for instance, acquiring atomic bombs.

> Accidents have begun. Like the first faint twirls of
>    smoke
> We see all the old signals.[16]

The spirits hint that God now fears humanity is about to destroy itself. A new species, Alpha Man, is being prepared for this contingency. He will be immortal (eventually), winged, and—without genius. The divine spark that makes men and women angels can also make them devils; God will no longer allow it to enter the fabric of humankind.*

---

*Is Alpha Man a general term? Will there be no Alpha Women? Will the new species be a single, hermaphroditic gender, as were the bat-creature servants bred by the centaurs? Will the new species breed at all, since it is immortal? The spirits offer no details about any of this.

The new Alpha race, if it is needed, will

> *Swim & glide,*
> *A simpler, less willful being. Duller too?*
> *If so, is that sharp edge not well lost*
> *Which has so variously cut and cost?*[17]

The brilliant, learned, and intellectually sophisticated Merrill could never quite decide what sort of reality lay behind the spirits and their utterances.

In a 1985 radio interview for the Canadian Broadcasting Corporation's documentary series *Voices and Visions: A Guided Tour of Revelations,* Merrill said:

I worked very hard, in putting the poem [*The Changing Light at Sandover*] together, to try to persuade the reader that these things actually happened. Not to persuade him of the truth of the messages, but to persuade him of the actuality of the experience. I don't mind if people doubt what we were told, if people look at the page and say, "Huh, they call this revelation, you know, these are just banalities that anybody could stitch together." What does rather sadden me are the critics who think that we are pretending—that we didn't have the experience.[18]

He later told another interviewer that he had "maintained an attitude of perfect ambivalence toward the spirits for twenty-five years."[19]

In a summer 1982 interview for *The Paris Review,* Merrill advanced some carefully considered ideas on the subject of channeling. Certainly, he said, there were powers or energies present in his Ouija board experiences that came from neither himself nor David Jackson. He explained:

The powers they [the spirits] represent are real—as, say, gravity is "real"—but they'd be invisible, inconceivable, if they'd never passed through our heads and clothed themselves out of the costume box they'd found there. How they appear depends on us, on the imaginer, and would have to vary widely from culture to culture, or even temperament to temperament. A process that Einstein would entertain as a formula might be described by an African witch doctor as a crocodile. What's tiresome is when people exclusively insist on the forms they'd imagined. Those powers don't need churches in order to be sacred. What they do need are fresh ways of being seen.[20]

Were the truths expressed by the spirits literal or metaphorical? The spirit guides hinted that the answer was: both at once. As Judith Moffett puts it, "the story must be kept going at both levels, literal and subatomic. In one sense the batwing angels rose above the surface of the Earth and built a crust world, 'weightless and self-sustaining,' in the ozone layer. . . . In another sense this crust world seems to be 'the evolving cortex of the brain.'"[21] Merrill also wonders if these are not, as well, myths of the movement of proton and neutron—of every sort of matter and antimatter—within the atom. The largest questions of all, come, however, when the spirits describe our God to Merrill and Jackson. This is a description brimming with pathos. God is in dire straits, and only we, humankind, can help him.

The deity portrayed in *The Changing Light at Sandover,* whom the spirits call "God B" or "God Biology," is only one of many gods, the "youngest brother" in a galactic pantheon of gods. It was given to him to inseminate the Milky Way galaxy only—and, apparently, only the planet Earth (at least we are told nothing to the contrary).

But other gods of the pantheon are working in other parts of the universe—and sometimes, it seems, they come into conflict with our Creator. He intimates that he must contend with them, telling the angel Gabriel, "*. . . there are galaxies, gods as powerful as I. Son Gabriel, we are warnd. We are hard prest.*"[22]

God must also contend with the power of the Monitor. This is a sphere he had initially placed in the center of the earth so that he could relay messages back to his brothers in the pantheon and keep them abreast of developments. God tells the story himself; his account is relayed to Merrill and Jackson: "'Go / Build, youngest brother,' they had said, 'only take this one, / Our monitor, to dwell within your ball. / For our will must ever be done.'"[23] But as humans have moved across the surface of the earth, as we have grown fractious and rebellious, the Monitor's power for evil has increased. Now God must contend (as must humanity also) with the negative sucking forces radiating out from the Monitor. There are other "sucking forces" in the universe as well, perhaps related to black holes.

Now God, his three root races tragically extinct, setting about to create humankind, is not without concern. In the words of the angel Michael:

> He long knew the forces arrayed against
> him: the negatives, the voids. He had been bested
>     before.
> These had destroyed others of his works by explosion
> and by black suctioning, and he named them evil.[24]

In the late twentieth century—countless millennia after it has all begun—Merrill and Jackson come into the presence of God. They are empowered, via the spirit guides of the Ouija board, to "listen" to his "song."

This is what they hear:

> Ive brothers hear me brothers signal me
> alone in my night brothers do you well
> I and mine hold it back brothers I and
> mine survive brothers hear me signal me
> do you well I and mine hold it back I
> alone in my night brothers I and mine
> survive brothers do you well I alone

*in my night I hold it back I and mine*
*survive brothers signal me in my night*
*I and mine hold it back and we survive*[25]

The refrain that becomes insistent—that seems to have lurked beneath the surface almost since the beginning of *Sandover*—seems to be that God needs our help if he is to survive. The shade of W. H. Auden, listening in on God's song, remarks that our deity is like a ship-wrecked sailor, "alone / keeping up his nerve on a life raft."[26]

What can the spirits possibly mean when they tell Merrill and Jackson that God needs our help? Why should God, being God, need anything but himself? Let's step back and approach *The Changing Light at Sandover* from a slightly different direction.

There were some scary moments in the encounters of James Merrill and David Jackson with spirit guides speaking through a Ouija board. One such moment came when Merrill was told that if he was not able to communicate the messages of the spirits to the outside world, then not only would humanity destroy itself, but heaven would vanish as well.

This dire warning, delivered by Ephraim, is recorded in Merrill's poem "The Will," published in *Divine Comedies* (1976), the volume of poetry from which part of *Sandover* would be taken.

Ephraim says:

> *Sois sage [behave yourself] dear heart & set my*
> *teachings down . . .*
> *If u do not yr world will be undone*
> *& heaven itself turn to one grinning skull*[27]

Judith Moffett clarifies: "But heaven in all its Stages (this is the special revelation of *Ephraim* [*The Book of Ephraim* in *Divine Comedies*], one withheld from DJ and JM for years) is dependent upon Earth for its very existence. When humanity destroys its world—only a question of time, it would appear—Heaven itself will vanish."[28]

The spirit guides were particularly worried about the proliferation of nuclear weapons around the world. Such warnings aren't new for humanity. What is new here—and completely bewildering—is the statement that if we destroy ourselves, we'll destroy the afterworld too.

This can be understood only in the context of the strange metamorphoses that the spirits go through as they communicate with Merrill and Jackson. These transformations show that the forms in which the spirits present themselves and whether they present themselves at all, were dependent on how J. M. and D. J. felt about them.

This is illustrated by the time when the two Ouija board mavens walked out on their spirit guides. They had taken a break from the rigorous lectures of their spirit instructor and, lighting some candles, sipping some wine, were chatting lightheartedly with their old friend Ephraim (who by then had been retired as the chief spirit communicator).

Suddenly the spirit instructor whom they were avoiding (one of the shades of the bat-creatures) stalked angrily (or so it seemed) onto the Ouija board and swiftly spelled out: *Quench your candles! You listen to no one! Work tomorrow!*[29]*

Merrill and Jackson were upset. This whole situation of talking to the spirit guides was bizarre enough, and the communications difficult enough, without having to put up with rudeness into the bargain. The incident made David Jackson wonder, not for the first time, if these guides weren't evil—if he and James Merrill hadn't put themselves in league with the Devil.

So they walked out on the spirit guides—so to speak. They didn't use the Ouija board for a few days. But just a few days. Then they returned to the board. After all, this experience was quite an adventure, and they had a mission to accomplish. They had our planet, and its heaven, to save!

They were surprised to find a new spirit instructor awaiting them. He was one of the bat-creature shades, to be sure. But he was much milder than these creatures usually were. His name was "741." (He was,

*The actual words in the transcript were *Quench ye candles U listen to no one Work tomorrow*. They've been filled out here, with punctuation added, for the sake of clarity.

of course, one of the numberless workers in the Lab.). 741 bent over backwards to accommodate his mortal pupils:

*Are u at ease? Pointer* [the Ouija board marker] *perhaps slower? We must be comfortable, no? Teach me I am the pupil today Tell me of . . . manners."* The fate of the previous too-rude spirit instructor? [*His name was*] *40076 He vexd u He will not return.*[30]

The lectures proceeded apace. Merrill and Jackson got very fond of this new, painstakingly tactful instructor. They christened him Mirabell. Then, after several months—when they had grown to like their new instructor very much indeed—Mirabell underwent a transformation. He told them about it himself, building up slowly,

> *. . . with my superiors*
> *U wd have learnd faster but not in turn made as we*
> *      have*
> *This world of courtesy*

Then, Merrill writes: "Breaking off, the cup strolls around the Board / As who would take a deep breath before speaking:"
Mirabell finished:

> *Nor wd I have come to love u*
> *B4 our meetings I was nothing No time passd*
> *But now your touch like a lamp has shown me to*
> *      myself, &*
> *I am me.*[31]

But *what* is he? Merrill and Jackson are astonished and touched: He has come to love them—but they had understood that the bat-creatures didn't have feelings at all, let alone feelings of love! They, of course, cannot see what change has been wrought in Mirabell; but the shade of the poet W. H. Auden, their late friend and now their eyes and ears in the afterworld, can, and he tells them:

*Mes enfants he has turned into a peacock*
*. . . My dears his great tail snapped shut like a fan*[32]

This denizen of the Ouija board, earlier represented to them as a black-and-white, batlike creature with red eyes, has been transformed, because of their love for him, into a multicolored peacock. In this guise Mirabell will continue as their spirit instructor; and his "image" adorns the cover of *Mirabell: Books of Numbers*, volume 2 of the trilogy.

This transformation made Merrill and Jackson think. It was beginning to look as if the details of the spirit world were somehow dependent on how the mortals felt and thought about them. They thought back to the time when they had heard God singing—and sounding like a drowning man. That experience had come not long after the spirits had told them that mankind's growing indifference to God was weakening the Deity—or so the spirits seemed to say. Merrill and Jackson reflected on this modern-day God who was, it seemed, a mere shadow of His former self. And they compared Him to the representations of God of earlier visionary poets. Using the rose as a metaphor for God, Merrill framed the comparison in poetic form:

> *Dante heard that song*
> *The lyrics may be changing*
> *Dante saw the rose in fullest bloom*
> *Blake saw it sick*
> *You and Maria\* who have seen*
> *The bleak unpetalled knob*
> *Must wonder, can it last till spring?*
> *Is it still rooted in the sun?*[33]

It seemed that God, as experienced by Dante (1265–1321) in *The Divine Comedy* (1308–1321), was like a rose in its fullest flowering—rightly or wrongly, the Church still reigned supreme. God as experienced

---

*Deceased friends of JM and DJ, observing from the "other side."

by William Blake (see chapter 6)—whose poetry was a last-ditch attempt to stave off the oncoming assaults of technology—was like the sick rose in Blake's poem *The Sick Rose*. Merrill and Jackson wondered if their deceased friends W. H. Auden and Maria Mitsotáki, peering at God in heaven, did not see a rose so stunted—so closely resembling the enfeebled drowning God whom they had heard themselves—that this God could barely reach out to the sun.

The more they pondered this, the more it seemed to the two that the shape of God—his very existence—must be dependent on the feelings and thoughts of mankind as a collectivity. It was not that *Homo sapiens* "made up" God. It was that God was Pure Being, and dependent on our imagination for his very shape and form.

Mustn't this also be true for heaven?

In Zurich in 1916, the spirits of the dead had milled forlornly around C. G. Jung, beseeching the forty-one-year-old psychiatrist standing bewildered in his living room for answers to their questions. They knew nothing, the spirits said—neither who they were, nor where they were, nor even if God existed. (See chapter 19.)

We'll recall that later in life Jung put forth the theory that mankind was a mere chance occurrence emerging in a physical universe where, for countless eons, "mere being" has given birth in trial-and-error fashion to every variation of physical reality.

Jung wrote (as we've seen):

If the Creator were conscious of Himself, He would not need conscious creatures; nor is it probable that the extremely indirect methods of creation, which squander millions of years upon the development of countless species and creatures, are the outcome of purposeful intention. The importance of consciousness is so great that one cannot help suspecting the element of *meaning* to be concealed somewhere within all the monstrous, apparently senseless biological turmoil, and that the road to its manifestation was ultimately

found on the level of warm-blooded vertebrates possessed of a differentiated brain—found as if by chance, unintended and unfore-
seen, and yet somehow sensed, felt and groped for out of some dark
urge.[34]

Jung was tempted to conclude, "As far as we can discern, the sole
purpose of human existence is to kindle a light in the darkness of mere
being."[35] We have seen almost the same phrase before in *Sandover*, when
Mirabell says: *But now your touch like a lamp has shown me to myself,
& I am me.*[36]

Is pure being a fisherman who ceaselessly trolls the ocean depths of
itself to discover what it is? Did "mere being" stumble on Merrill and
Jackson and—seeing the light, the imagination, the intelligence, the
learning, issuing from the minds of these two men—seize this opportunity to establish a beachhead in physical reality and discover as much as
it could about what it, mere being, actually was?

Did the spirits coalescing out of that being in the minds of Merrill
and Jackson come to them, not with answers, but with questions?

# Notes

## Introduction. Prague's Other Universe

1. Frances A. Yates, *The Rosicrucian Enlightenment* (London: Routledge and Kegan Paul, 1972), 323.

## Chapter One. Benvenuto Cellini

1. Benvenuto Cellini, *The Autobiography of Benvenuto Cellini* (Garden City, N.Y.: Doubleday, 1927), 216.
2. Ibid., 217.
3. Ibid.
4. Ibid., 218.
5. Michael Grosso, *The Millennium Myth: Love and Death at the End of Time* (Wheaton, Ill.: Quest Books, 1994), 60.
6. Jacob Burckhardt, *The Civilization of the Renaissance in Italy* (New York: Modern Library, 1954), 104.
7. Cellini, *Autobiography,* 10.
8. Ibid., 118–21.
9. Ibid., 152–53.
10. Ibid., 219–21.
11. Ibid., 221.
12. Ibid., 222–23.
13. Ibid., 223.
14. Ibid.
15. Ibid., 224.
16. Ibid., 232.
17. Ibid., 349.
18. Ibid., 350.
19. Ibid.
20. Ibid., 353.

## Chapter Two. Michel de Nostradamus

1. Ian Wilson, *Nostradamus: The Man Behind the Prophecies* (New York: St. Martin's Griffin, 2007), xii.

2. Ibid., 31.

3. Ibid., 33.

4. Frances A. Yates, *Giordano Bruno* (Chicago: The University of Chicago Press, 1964), 12–14.

5. Ted Anton, *Eros, Magic, and the Murder of Professor Culianu* (Evanston, Ill.: Northwestern University Press, 1996), 107–8.

6. Ioan P. Couliano, *Eros and Magic in the Renaissance* (Chicago: The University of Chicago Press, 1987), 32.

7. Ibid., 33–34.

8. John Hogue, *Nostradamus: The Complete Prophecies* (Rockport, Mass.: Element Books, 1997), 6.

9. Martin Ebon, "Nostradamus: Prophet for All Seasons," *Occult* 4 (4) (1973): 24–27, 100–102.

10. Hogue, 12.

11. Ebon, 26.

12. Hogue, 9.

13. Ebon, 25–26.

14. George Boas, trans., *Hieroglyphics* (Princeton, N.J.: Princeton University Press, 1993), xiii.

15. Knut Boeser, ed., *The Elixirs of Nostradamus: Nostradamus' Original Recipes for Elixirs, Scented Water, Beauty Potions and Sweetmeats* (London: Bloomsbury, 1995), 59.

16. Ibid., 62.

17. Ibid., 16.

18. Renzo Baschera, *Guide des recettes magiques de Nostradamus et autres sages contemporains* (Rome: Casa Editrice MEB, 1980), 12.

19. Ibid., 18.

20. Ibid., 26.

## Chapter Three. Ben Jonson

1. Joseph Needham, *Science and Civilisation in China*, vol. 5, *Chemistry and Chemical Technology,* part 3, *Spagyrical Discovery and Invention: Historical Survey, from Cinnabar Elixirs to Synthetic Insulin* (Cambridge: Cambridge University Press, 1976), 213.

2. Ibid.

3. Richard S. Westfall, *Never at Rest: A Biography of Isaac Newton* (Cambridge: Cambridge University Press, 1998), 20.

4. Ben Jonson, "The Devil Is an Ass," *The Works of Ben Jonson: In Nine Volumes,* W. Gifford, ed. (London: W. Bulmer, 1816), Act 5, Scene 4, pp. 143–46.

5. Ben Jonson, *The Alchemist,* in *Five Plays* (London: Oxford University Press, 1956), Act 4, Scene 3, lines 92–103.

6. Ibid., Act 2, Scene 1, lines 433–48.

7. Ibid., Act 2, Scene 1, lines 156–59.

8. Eduard Zeller, *Outlines of the History of Greek Philosophy* (New York: Meridian, 1955), 47.

9. Honoré de Balzac, *Seraphita,* introduction by Paul M. Allen (Blauvelt, N.Y.: Steinerbooks, 1976), 4.

## Chapter Four. Sir Isaac Newton

1. Richard S. Westfall, *Never at Rest: A Biography of Isaac Newton* (Cambridge: Cambridge University Press, 1998), 13.

2. James E. Force and Richard H. Popkin, eds., *Newton and Religion: Context, Nature, and Influence* (Dordrecht, The Netherlands: Kluwer Academic Publishers, 1999), x.

3. Ibid., 247.

4. Gale E. Christianson, *Isaac Newton and the Scientific Revolution* (New York: Oxford University Press, 1996), 30.

5. Paul Johnson, *A History of the Jews* (New York: Harper and Row, 1988), 8–11.

6. Westfall, *Never at Rest,* 313.

7. Isaac Newton, *The Original of Religions* (The Newton Project), at www.newtonproject.sussex.ac.uk.

8. Emil L. Fackenheim, *What Is Judaism? An Interpretation for the Present Age* (New York: Collier, 1987), 183.

9. Ibid., 244.

10. Newton, *Original of Religions.*

11. Ibid.

12. Ibid.

13. Ibid.

14. Ibid.

15. Robert Markley, "Newton, Corruption, and the Tradition of Universal History," in *Newton and Religion: Context, Nature, and Influence,* James E. Force and Richard H. Popkin, eds. (Dordrecht, The Netherlands: Kluwer Academic Publishers, 1999), 136.

16. Newton, *Original of Religions.*

17. Newton, *Irenicum* (The Newton Project), www.newtonproject.sussex.ac.uk.

18. Newton, *Original of Religions*.

19. Markley, "Newton, Corruption, and the Tradition of Universal History," 138.

20. Newton, *Theologiae Gentiles Origines Philosophicae* (The Newton Project), www.newtonproject.sussex.ac.uk.

21. Ibid.

22. Westfall, *Never at Rest*, 352.

23. Newton, *Theologiae Gentiles Origines Philosophicae*.

## Chapter Five. Johann Wolfgang von Goethe

1. Martin Ebon, *They Knew the Unknown* (New York: World, 1971), 217–18.

2. Ibid., 217.

3. Walter Kaufmann, *Discovering the Mind,* vol. 1, *Goethe, Kant, and Hegel* (New York: McGraw-Hill, 1980), 26.

4. Harold Bloom, *The Western Canon: The Books and School of the Ages* (New York: Harcourt Brace, 1994), 204.

5. Nicholas Boyle, *Goethe: The Poet and the Age,* vol. 1, *The Poetry of Desire* (Oxford: Oxford University Press, 1992), 353.

6. Ibid., 295.

7. Ibid., 273–74.

8. Ibid., 468–69.

9. Kaufmann, *Discovering the Mind,* 22.

10. Quoted in Kaufmann, *Discovering the Mind,* 23.

11. Ibid., 24.

12. Kaufmann, *Discovering the Mind,* 47.

13. Boyle, *Goethe: The Poet and the Age,* 645–46.

14. L. A. Willoughby, "Goethe," in *Man, Myth & Magic: An Illustrated Encyclopedia of the Supernatural* (London: BPC Publishing, 1971), 1125.

## Chapter Six. William Blake

1. Ronald Neame, dir., *The Horse's Mouth* (VHS Movie, 1958).

2. Quoted in Frances A. Yates, *Giordano Bruno and the Hermetic Tradition* (Chicago: University of Chicago Press, 1964), 32.

3. Geoffrey Keynes, ed., *Poetry and Prose of William Blake* (London: Nonesuch Library, 1956), 72–73.

4. Mark Schorer, *William Blake: The Politics of Vision* (New York: Vintage Books, 1959), 6.

5. Ibid., 15.

6. Paul Johnson, *The Birth of the Modern: World Society 1815–1830* (New York: Harper Perennial, 1991), 590.

7. Ibid., 592–93.

8. Northrop Frye, *Fearful Symmetry: A Study of William Blake* (Boston: Beacon Press, 1947), 206.

9. Keynes, *Poetry and Prose*, 182.

10. Ibid., 118

11. Joyce Cary, *The Horse's Mouth* (New York: Harper and Row, 1965), 6.

12. Frye, *Fearful Symmetry*, 194.

13. Ibid., 194–95.

14. Keynes, *Poetry and Prose*, 847.

## Chapter Seven. Alphonse de Lamartine

1. Alphonse de Lamartine, *A Pilgrimage to the Holy Land; Comprising Recollections, Sketches and Reflections, Made during a Tour in the East*, vol. 1 (New York: Appleton, 1848), 136–37.

2. Ibid., 137.

3. Charles M. Lombard, trans. *Lamartine* (New York: Twayne, 1973), 25; Lamartine, *Oeuvres*, 39.

4. Ibid., 11.

5. Ibid., 28.

6. Ibid., 22.

7. Ibid., 25.

8. Ibid., 18, 26.

9. Henri Guillemin, *Lamartine* (Paris: Éditions du Seuil, 1987), 29.

10. Lamartine, *Pilgrimage*, 187.

11. Ibid., 143–44.

12. Ibid.

13. Ibid., 245.

14. Quoted in Joseph Needham, *Science and Civilisation in China*, vol. V, *Chemistry and Chemical Technology*, part 4, *Spagyrical Discovery and Invention: Apparatus, Theories and Gifts* (Cambridge: Cambridge University Press, 1959), 342.

15. Victor Hugo, *Oeuvres complètes*, vol. 12 of *Édition chronologique*, Jean Massin, ed. (Paris: Le Club Français du Livre, 1967–71), 16.

16. Lamartine, *Pilgrimage*, 254–55.

17. Robert Mattlé, *Lamartine voyageur*, preface by Maurice Levaillant (Paris: E. de Boccard, 1936), 307.

18. Lamartine, *Pilgrimage*, 141.

19. Guillemin, *Lamartine*, 36.

20. Lamartine, *Oeuvres,* 328.

21. Ibid., 823.

22. Mattlé, *Lamartine voyageur,* 404.

## Chapter Eight. Mary Wollstonecraft Shelley

1. Mary Shelley, *The Last Man,* introduction by Judith Tarr (Lincoln and London: Bison Books/University of Nebraska Press, 1993), 342.

2. Mary Devlin, "The Nightmare Futures of Mary Shelley," *Atlantis Rising* 22 (2000): 30.

3. Matthew Arnold, "Shelley," in *The Portable Matthew Arnold,* Lionel Trilling, ed. (New York: Viking, 1949), 390–91.

4. Martin Ebon, *They Knew the Unknown* (New York: World, 1971), 37.

5. Quoted in Noel B. Gerson, *Daughter of Earth and Water: A Biography of Mary Wollstonecraft Shelley* (New York: William Morris, 1973), 76.

6. Charles E. Robinson, ed., *Mary Shelley: Collected Tales and Stories with Original Engravings* (Baltimore: The Johns Hopkins University Press, 1990), 219.

7. Shelley, *Last Man,* ix.

## Chapter Nine. Honoré de Balzac

1. Quoted in André Maurois, *Prometheus: The Life of Balzac* (Harmondsworth, Middlesex, England: Penguin, 1971), 30.

2. Maurois, *Prometheus,* 37.

3. Quoted in Maurois, *Prometheus,* 450.

4. Stefan Zweig, *Balzac* (New York: Viking, 1946), 167.

5. Maurois, *Prometheus,* 457.

6. Graham Robb, *Balzac: A Life* (New York: W. W. Norton, 1994), 194.

7. Honoré de Balzac, *Louis Lambert,* in *The Short Novels of Balzac,* introduction by Jules Romains (New York: Dial Press, 1948), 267–68.

8. Ibid., 231.

9. Quoted in Arthur Symons, "Balzac," in *The Symbolist Movement in Literature* (New York: E. P. Dutton, 1958), 104.

10. Gustave Flaubert, *Bouvard et Pécuchet,* introduction by Lionel Trilling (Norfolk, Conn.: New Directions, 1954), 233.

11. Mircea Eliade, *The Two and the One* (New York: Harper Torchbooks, 1969), 98–99.

12. Honoré de Balzac, *The Quest of the Absolute* (London: J. M. Dent, 1932), 19.

13. Robb, *Balzac,* 303.

## Chapter Ten. Victor Hugo

1. Adèle Hugo, *Le journal d'Adèle Hugo,* Francis Vernor Guille, ed., vol. 3 (Paris: Lettres Modernes Minard, 1968–2000), 226–28.
2. Victor Hugo, *Oeuvres complètes,* vol. 9 of *Édition chronologique,* Jean Massin, ed. (Paris: Le Club Français du Livre, 1967–71), 1396–98.
3. Adèle Hugo, *Journal,* 226–28.
4. Victor Hugo, *Oeuvres complètes,* vol. 9, 372–73. [*Les Contemplations. VI. Ce que dit la bouche d'ombre.*]
5. Ibid., 374.
6. Ibid., 384.

## Chapter Eleven. Jules Verne

1. UNESCO, *Index Translationum,* http://databases.unesco.org/xtrans/stat/xTransStat.html.
2. Roger Maudhuy, *Jules Verne: la face cachée* (Paris: France-Empire, 2005), 14–22; William Butcher, *Jules Verne: The Definitive Biography* (New York: Thunder's Mouth Press, 2006), xxviii–xxxi.
3. Maudhuy, *La face cachée,* 121–25.
4. Butcher, *Definitive Biography,* 16.
5. Maudhuy, *La face cachée,* 65–70.
6. Jules Verne, *Paris in the Twentieth Century: The Lost Novel,* Preface by Eugen Weber (New York: Random House, 1996), xxxiii–xxxiv.
7. Edward J. Altmann, "Jules Verne and the Lost Science of Atlantis," *Fate* (May 2003): 18–22, 19–21.
8. Joseph W. McMoneagle, "Jules Verne: Science Fiction Writer, Psychic, or Remote Viewer?" *The Anomalist* 5 (Summer 1997): 63.
9. Verne, *Paris in the Twentieth Century,* xxxvi.
10. John Lichfield, "Jules Verne: Mythmaker of the Machine Age," *Independent* (London), March 14, 2005.
11. Butcher, *Definitive Biography,* 186–87.
12. Michel Lamy, *The Secret Message of Jules Verne: Decoding His Masonic, Rosicrucian, and Occult Writings* (Rochester, Vt.: Destiny Books, 2007), 11.
13. Ibid., 12.
14. Ibid., 62.
15. Lynn Picknett and Clive Prince, *The Sion Revelation: The Truth About the Guardians of Christ's Sacred Bloodline* (New York: Touchstone/Simon and Schuster, 2006), 235–36.
16. Ibid.
17. Quoted in Lichfield, "Jules Verne: Mythmaker of the Machine Age."

18. Jules Verne, *Twenty Thousand Leagues Under the Sea* (New York: Charles Scribner's Sons, 1925), 331.
19. Ibid., 79.

## Chapter Twelve. Leo Tolstoy

1. Leo Tolstoy, *Anna Karenina* (New York: Penguin, 2002), 732–33.
2. Ibid., 738.
3. Ibid., 739.
4. Thomas E. Berry, *Spiritualism in Tsarist Society and Literature* (Baltimore: Edgar Allan Poe Society, 1985), 93.
5. Vladimir Nabokov, *Lectures on Russian Literature* (Orlando, Fla.: Harvest/Harcourt, 1981), 171.
6. Berry, *Spiritualism*, 87.
7. Quoted in George Steiner, *Tolstoy or Dostoevsky: An Essay in the Old Criticism* (New York: E. P. Dutton, 1959), 286.
8. Ibid., 254.
9. Ibid., 251–52.
10. Ibid., 252.
11. Ibid., 254.
12. John Bayley, ed., *The Portable Tolstoy* (Harmondsworth, Middlesex, U.K.: Penguin, 1978), 14.
13. Thomas Mann, "Goethe and Tolstoy," in *Three Essays* (New York: Knopf, 1929), 73.
14. Ibid., 73–74.
15. Ibid., 74–75.
16. Ibid., 87.
17. Tolstoy, *Anna Karenina,* 52–53.
18. Ibid., 53.
19. John Gassner, *Masters of the Drama* (New York: Dover, 1954), 506.
20. Henri Troyat, *Tolstoy* (Garden City, N.Y.: Doubleday, 1967), 386.

## Chapter Thirteen. Madame Helena Blavatsky

1. Richard Smoley, "Isis a Little More Unveiled," *Gnosis Magazine* (Winter 1999): 64.
2. K. Paul Johnson, *The Masters Revealed: Madame Blavatsky and the Myth of the Great White Lodge,* foreword by Joscelyn Godwin (Albany: SUNY, 1994), 39–40.
3. Ibid., xv.
4. David H. Caldwell, ed., *The Occult World of Madame Blavatsky* (Tucson, Ariz.: Impossible Dream, 1991), 21–22.

5. Ibid., 25–26.

6. Johnson, *The Masters Revealed,* 19–20.

7. Caldwell, *Occult World,* 28.

8. Sylvia Cranston, *H.P.B.: The Extraordinary Life and Influence of Helena Blavatsky* (New York: Tarcher/Putnam, 1993), 36.

9. Johnson, *The Masters Revealed,* 36.

10. Cranston, *H.P.B.,* 105.

11. Caldwell, *Occult World,* 45–46.

12. Ibid.

13. Ibid., 73–76.

14. Ibid., 16.

15. Ibid.

16. Ibid., 15–16.

17. Helena Blavatsky, *The Secret Doctrine,* unabridged, vols. 1 and 2 (Los Angeles: Theosophical Company, 1982), 3.

18. H. P. Blavatsky, *Isis Unveiled: Madame Blavatsky's First Work,* abridged by Michael Gomes (Wheaton, Ill.: Quest Books, 1997), 3.

19. Ibid., 29–30.

20. Colin Wilson, *The Psychic Detectives* (San Francisco: Mercury House, 1985), 83.

21. Ibid., 82–83.

22. Johnson, *The Masters Revealed,* 2–3.

23. Cranston, *H.P.B.,* 265, 328.

24. Smoley, "Isis a Little More Unveiled," 64.

## Chapter Fourteen. William Butler Yeats

1. Martin Ebon, *They Knew the Unknown* (New York: World, 1971), 166.

2. Richard Ellmann, "At the Yeatses'," in *A Long the Riverrun: Selected Essays* (New York: Alfred A. Knopf, 1989), 240–41.

3. R. F. Foster, *W. B. Yeats: A Life,* vol. 2, *The Arch-Poet, 1915–1939* (Oxford: Oxford University Press, 2003), 101–2.

4. Brenda Maddox, *Yeats's Ghosts: The Secret Life of W. B. Yeats* (New York: HarperCollins, 1999), 73.

5. Ibid., 74.

6. W. B. Yeats, *A Vision* (New York: Collier Books, 1966), 8.

7. Ellmann, "At the Yeatses," 243.

8. Ibid.

9. Yeats, *A Vision,* 9.

10. Ibid., 15–17.

11. W. B. Yeats, *Collected Works,* vol. 4, *Early Essays,* Richard J. Finnerman and George Bornstein, eds. (New York: Simon & Schuster, 2007–2008), 25.

12. Yeats, *A Vision,* 13.

13. Maddox, *Yeats's Ghosts,* 96.

14. Yeats, *A Vision,* 22–23.

15. Ibid., 8.

16. Maddox, *Yeats's Ghosts,* 76–77.

17. M. H. Adams, ed., *The Norton Anthology of English Literature,* 6th edition, vol. 2 (New York: Norton, 1993), 1884.

18. Ibid., 1880–1881.

19. Ibid., 75.

20. Ibid., 77.

21. Foster, *W. B. Yeats: A Life,* vol. 2, 107.

## Chapter Fifteen. H. G. Wells

1. H. G. Wells, *The Last War: A World Set Free,* introduction by Greg Bear (Lincoln: University of Nebraska Press, 2001), 52–53.

2. Ibid., 60.

3. H. G. Wells, *The War in the Air* (Harmondsworth, Middlesex, U.K.: Penguin, 1941), 76.

4. H. G. Wells, *Experiment in Autobiography* (New York: MacMillan, 1934), 243.

5. Ibid.

6. Peter Fenwick and Elizabeth Fenwick, *The Truth in the Light*: *An Investigation of Over 300 Near-Death Experiences* (New York: Berkley Books, 1997), 110.

7. Ibid.

8. Ibid., 111.

9. Ibid., 81.

10. Ibid., 82.

11. Ibid., 125.

12. H. G. Wells, *Collected Stories* (London: Penguin, 1971), 108.

13. Ibid., 109.

14. Ibid., 110.

15. Ibid., 111.

16. Ibid.

17. Ibid.

18. Ibid.

19. Ibid., 112.

20. Ibid.

21. Dannion Brinkley, *Saved by the Light* (New York: HarperCollins, 1994/2008), 31.

22. George Gesner, ed., *Works of H. G. Wells.* "A Dream of Armageddon" (New York: Avenel, 1982), 645.

23. Ibid., 658.

## Chapter Sixteen. Thomas Mann

1. Thomas Mann, *The Magic Mountain* (New York: Vintage Books/Random House, 1969), 12.

2. Ibid., 719.

3. Thomas Mann, "An Experience in the Occult," in *Three Essays* (New York: Knopf, 1929), 228–29.

4. Ibid., 234.

5. Ibid.

6. Ibid., 236.

7. Ibid., 239.

8. Ibid., 238.

9. Ibid., 246.

10. Ibid.

11. Ibid., 247.

12. Ibid., 252.

13. Ibid., 252–53.

14. Ibid., 248.

15. Ibid., 253.

16. Ibid., 256.

17. Ibid., 259.

18. Ibid., 260.

19. Mann, *Magic Mountain,* 660.

20. Ibid., 680.

21. Ibid.

22. Ibid., 538.

23. Ibid., 677–78.

## Chapter Seventeen. Harry Houdini

1. William Kalush and Larry Sloman, *The Secret Life of Houdini: The Making of America's First Superhero* (New York: Atria Books, 2007), 533.

2. Ibid., 532.

3. Ibid., 533.

4. Ibid., 313.

5. William V. Rauscher, *The Houdini Code Mystery: A Spirit Secret Solved* (Pasadena, Calif.: Mike Caveney's Magic Words, 2000), 98–103.

6. Ibid., 95.

7. Ibid.

8. Ibid.

9. Ibid., 80.

10. Ibid., 53.

11. Ibid., 33–34.

12. Ibid., 109.

13. Ibid., 126–28.

14. Ibid., 148.

15. Ibid., 172.

16. Ibid., 176.

17. Martin Ebon, personal telephone communication, December 2001.

18. Ibid.

## Chapter Eighteen. Winston S. Churchill

1. Winston Churchill, *My Early Life: A Roving Commission* (Thornton Butterworth: London, 1930). Reprinted as *My Early Life: 1874–1904* (New York: Touchstone/Simon & Schuster, 1996), 275. Citations are to the 1996 edition.

2. Geoffrey Best, *Churchill: A Study in Greatness* (Oxford: Oxford University Press, 2002), 330.

3. Quoted in John Keegan, *Winston Churchill: A Life* (New York: Penguin, 2002), 11.

4. Churchill, *My Early Life,* 167.

5. Ibid., 275.

6. Ibid., 276.

7. Ibid., 280.

8. Ibid., 281.

9. Ibid., 282.

10. Ibid., 282–83.

11. Ibid., 291.

12. Ibid., 115–16.

## Chapter Nineteen. Carl G. Jung

1. Carl G. Jung, *Memories, Dreams, Reflections* (New York: Vintage Books/Random House, 1965), 190.

2. Ibid., 190–91.

3. Anthony Storr, "Carl Gustav Jung," in *Feet of Clay: Saints, Sinners and Madmen: A Study of Gurus* (New York: Free Press Paperbacks/Simon & Schuster, 1997), 88.

4. Jung, *Memories,* 308.

5. Ibid., 191.

6. Ibid., 191–92.

7. Storr, *Feet of Clay,* 87.

8. Jung, *Memories,* 107.

9. Ibid., 105–6.

10. Ibid., 106.

11. Martin Ebon, "Jung's First Medium," *Psychic Magazine* (May–June 1976): 43.

12. Ibid.

13. Ibid., 44.

14. Ibid.

15. Ibid., 43.

16. Jung, *Memories,* 308.

17. W. B. Yeats, *A Vision* (New York: Collier Books, 1966), 12.

18. Ibid., 220–21.

19. Jung, *Memories,* 339.

20. Ibid., 326.

## Chapter Twenty. Sri Yashoda Ma

1. *The Eternal Cycle: Indian Myth.* Myth and Mankind (London/Amsterdam: Time-Life Books, 1998), 7.

2. Dilip Kumar Roy, *Yogi Sri Krishnaprem* (Bombay: Bharatiya Vidya Bhavan, 1968/1992), 94–95.

3. Seymour B. Ginsburg, ed., *In Search of the Unitive Vision: Letters of Sri Madhava Ashish to an American Businessman, 1978–1997* (Boca Raton, Fla.: New Paradigm Books, 2001), 37.

4. Roy, *Yogi Sri Krishnaprem,* 109.

5. Ibid., 54–55.

6. Ibid., 55.

7. James Merrill, *The Changing Light at Sandover* (New York: Knopf, 1982), 142.

8. Robert A. Monroe, *Ultimate Journey* (Garden City, N.Y.: Doubleday, 1994), 50–55.

9. Roy, *Yogi Sri Krishnaprem,* 95.

10. Ibid.

11. Ibid., 97.

12. Ibid., 99.

13. Ibid., 100–101.

14. Ibid., 102.

15. Ibid.

16. Ibid., 102.

17. Ibid., 102–3.

## Chapter Twenty-one. Doris Lessing

1. Doris Lessing, *The Sirian Experiments (The Report by Ambien II, of the Five), Canopus in Argos: Archives* 3 (New York: Knopf, 1980), viii–ix.

2. Doris Lessing, *The Making of the Representative for Planet 8, Canopus in Argos: Archives* 4 (New York: Knopf, 1982), 124.

3. Doris Lessing, *The Four-Gated City (The Children of Violence,* Book 5) (St. Albans, Hertfordshire, U.K.: Panther, 1969), 658.

4. Lessing, *The Making of the Representative for Planet 8,* 59.

5. Lessing, *The Sirian Experiments,* 240.

6. Patricia Pereira, *Songs of the Arcturians: Arcturian Star Chronicles: Volume One* (Hillsboro, Ore.: Beyond Words, 1996), 61.

7. Darryl Anka, *Bashar: Blueprint for Change: A Message from Our Future* (Redmond, Wash.: New Solutions, 1990), 117.

8. Rev. Silas Tertius Rand, *Legends of the Micmacs,* vol. 2 (New York: Longmans, Green, 1894), 28–29.

## Chapter Twenty-two. Norman Mailer

1. Philip H. Bufithis, *Norman Mailer* (New York: Frederick Ungar, 1978), 24.

2. Norman Mailer, with Michael Lennon, *On God: An Uncommon Conversation* (New York: Random House, 2007), 68–70.

3. Peter Manso, *Mailer: His Life and Times* (New York: Simon & Schuster, 1985), 317.

4. Mailer, *On God,* 10.

5. Ibid., 33.

6. Ibid., 21–22.

7. Ibid., 59–60.

8. Ibid., 116.

9. Ibid.

10. Ibid., 47–48.

11. Ibid., 51–52.

12. Ibid., 7.

13. Ibid., 128.

14. Bufithis, *Norman Mailer,* 74.

15. Ibid., 102.

16. Norman Mailer, *Ancient Evenings* (Boston: Little, Brown, 1983), 632.

## Chapter Twenty-three. Yukio Mishima

1. For this description of Yukio Mishima's death, the author has drawn on the accounts of Nathan, Ross, Stokes, and Yourcenar. John Nathan, *Mishima: A Biography* (Cambridge, Mass.: De Capo Press, 2000); Christopher Ross, *Mishima's Sword: Travels in Search of a Samurai Legend* (Cambridge, Mass.: Da Capo Press/Perseus Books Group, 2006); Henry Scott Stokes, *The Life and Death of Yukio Mishima* (New York: Cooper Square Press, 1999); Marguerite Yourcenar, *Mishima: A Vision of the Void* (Chicago: University of Chicago Press, 2001).

2. Stokes, *Life and Death,* 250.

3. Columbia Encyclopedia, www.encyclopedia.com/doc/1E1-MishimaY.html.

4. Yourcenar, *Vision of the Void,* 149.

5. Yukio Mishima, *Confessions of a Mask* (New York: New Directions, 1958), 5.

6. Ibid., 5–6.

7. Ibid., 38–41.

8. Ibid., 218.

9. Ross, *Mishima's Sword,* 86.

10. Nathan, *Mishima,* 104.

11. Ibid., 132–33.

12. Ibid., footnote, 118.

13. Ibid., 131–32.

14. Yukio Mishima, *The Temple of Dawn* (New York: Vintage International, 1990), 23–24.

15. Hans TenDam, *Exploring Reincarnation* (London: Arkana, 1990), 38.

16. Ramon G. Mendoza, "Metempsychosis and Monism in Bruno's *nova filosofia,*" in *Giordano Bruno: Philosopher of the Renaissance,* Hilary Gatti, ed. (Burlington, Vt.: Ashgate, 2003), 288.

17. Mishima, *Temple of Dawn,* 120.

18. Yourcenar, *Vision of the Void,* 26–27.

19. Yukio Mishima, *Runaway Horses* (New York: Vintage International, 1990), 42–43.

20. Stokes, *Life and Death,* 161.

21. Yukio Mishima, *Spring Snow* (New York: Vintage International, 1990), 25–27.

22. Ibid., 389.

23. Mishima, *Runaway Horses,* 40.

24. Mishima, *Spring Snow,* 43.

25. Yourcenar, *Vision of the Void,* 72.

26. Ibid., 72–74.

27. Mishima, *Runaway Horses,* 409.

28. Ibid., 253.

29. Mishima, *Spring Snow,* 236.

30. Mishima, *Temple of Dawn*, 320.

31. Stokes, *Life and Death*, 140.

32. Yukio Mishima, *The Decay of the Angel* (New York: Vintage International, 1990), 236.

33. Ross, *Mishima's Sword*, 247.

34. Yourcenar, *Vision of the Void*, 65.

35. Ibid., 77.

36. Ibid., 67–68.

37. George Grant, *Time as History*, Massey Lectures, Ninth Series (Toronto, Ont.: Canadian Broadcasting Corporation Learning Systems, 1969), 35.

38. Doris Lessing, *The Sirian Experiments (The Report by Ambien II, of the Five), Canopus in Argos: Archives* 3 (New York: Knopf, 1980), 14.

39. Mishima, *Spring Snow*, 289.

40. Grant, *Time as History*, 29.

41. Ibid., 33.

42. Ibid., 34.

43. Stokes, *Life and Death*, 259.

44. Ibid., 260.

45. Henry Scott Stokes, personal e-mail communication, April 8, 2008.

## Chapter Twenty-four. James Merrill

1. James Merrill, *The Changing Light at Sandover* (New York: Knopf, 1982), 131.

2. Ibid., 225.

3. Chester A. Starr, *A History of the Ancient World* (New York/Oxford: Oxford University Press, 1991), 93.

4. Merrill, *Sandover*, 8.

5. Ibid., 143.

6. Ibid., 151–52.

7. Ibid., 145–46.

8. Ibid., 189.

9. Ibid., 131.

10. Ibid.

11. Ibid., 142–43.

12. Ibid., 126.

13. Ibid., 127.

14. Ibid.

15. Judith Moffett, *James Merrill: An Introduction to the Poetry* (New York: Columbia University Press, 1984), 198.

16. Merrill, *Sandover,* 476.

17. Ibid., 512.

18. Quoted in John Chambers, *Victor Hugo's Conversations with the Spirit World: A Literary Genius's Hidden Life* (Rochester, Vt.: Destiny Books, 2008), 264.

19. Ibid.

20. *Recitative,* J. D. McClatchy, ed. (San Francisco: North Point Press, 1986), 68.

21. Moffett, *James Merrill,* 191–92.

22. Merrill, *Sandover,* 330.

23. Ibid., 392.

24. Ibid., 293.

25. Ibid., 360.

26. Ibid., 362.

27. Merrill, *Divine Comedies,* 41.

28. Moffett, 179.

29. Merrill, *Sandover,* 124.

30. Ibid., 130.

31. Ibid., 155.

32. Ibid., 157.

33. Ibid., 363.

34. Jung, *Memories,* 339.

35. Ibid.

36. Merrill, *Sandover,* 155.

# Bibliography

Adams, M. H., ed. *The Norton Anthology of English Literature,* sixth edition, volume 2. New York: Norton, 1993.

Anka, Darryl. *Bashar: Blueprint for Change: A Message from Our Future.* Luana Ewing, ed. Redmond, Wash.: New Solutions, 1900.

Anton, Ted. *Eros, Magic, and the Murder of Professor Culianu.* Evanston, Ill.: Northwestern University Press, 1996.

Applebaum, Stanley, ed. *Introduction to French Poetry: A Dual-Language Book.* New York: Dover, 1969.

Arnold, Matthew. "Shelley." In *The Portable Matthew Arnold.* Edited by Lionel Trilling. New York: Viking, 1949.

Artz-Wegman, Dita. *Nostradamus' Dream Interpretation Guide: 500th Anniversary, 1503–2003: A Tribute to His Achievements, His Life and Legacy.* Oakville, Canada: Vasitha, 2003.

Balzac, Honoré de. *Louis Lambert.* In *The Short Novels of Balzac.* New York: Dial Press, 1948.

———. *The Quest of the Absolute.* London: J. M. Dent, 1932.

———. *Seraphita.* Introduction by Paul M. Allen. Blauvelt, N.Y.: Steinerbooks, 1976.

———. *The Wild Ass's Skin.* London: Penguin Books, 1977.

Baschera, Renzo. *Guide des recettes magiques de Nostradamus et autres sages contemporains.* Rome: Casa Editrice MEB, 1980.

Bayley, John, ed. *The Portable Tolstoy.* Harmondsworth, Middlesex, U.K.: Penguin, 1978.

Berlitz, Charles. *Doomsday 1999 A.D.* Garden City, N.Y.: Doubleday, 1981.

Berry, Thomas E. *Spiritualism in Tsarist Society and Literature.* Baltimore: Edgar Allan Poe Society, 1985.

Best, Geoffrey. *Churchill: A Study in Greatness*. Oxford: Oxford University Press, 2002.

Blavatsky, H. P. *Isis Unveiled: Madame Blavatsky's First Work*. Michael Gomes, ed. Wheaton, Ill.: Quest Books, 1997.

———. *The Secret Doctrine*. Unabridged, vols. 1 and 2. Los Angeles: Theosophical Company, 1982.

———. *An Abridgement of the Secret Doctrine*. E. Preston and C. Humphries, eds. London: Theosophical Publishing, 1966.

Bloom, Harold, ed. *Ben Jonson's* Volpone, or the Fox. New York: Chelsea House, 1988.

———. *The Western Canon: The Books and School of the Ages*. New York: Harcourt Brace, 1994.

Boas, George, trans. *The Hieroglyphics of Horapollo*. Bollingen Series 23. Princeton, N.J.: Princeton University Press, 1993.

Boeser, Knut, ed. *The Elixirs of Nostradamus: Nostradamus' Original Recipes for Elixirs, Scented Water, Beauty Potions and Sweetmeats*. London: Bloomsbury, 1995.

Boyle, Nicholas. *Goethe: The Poet and the Age*. In *The Poetry of Desire,* vol. 1. Oxford: Oxford University Press, 1992.

Brinkley, Dannion. *Saved by the Light*. New York: HarperCollins, 1994/2008.

Buckley, C. A. "Quantum Physics and the Ouija-Board: James Merrill's Holistic World View." *Mosaic: A Journal for the Interdisciplinary Study of Literature* 26 (2) (Spring 1993): 39–61.

Bufithis, Philip H. *Norman Mailer*. New York: Frederick Ungar, 1978.

Burckhardt, Jacob. *The Civilization of the Renaissance in Italy*. New York: Modern Library, 1954.

Butcher, William. *Jules Verne: The Definitive Biography*. New York: Thunder's Mouth Press, 2006.

Caldwell, David H., ed. *The Occult World of Madame Blavatsky*. Tucson, Ariz.: Impossible Dream, 1991.

Cary, Joyce. *The Horse's Mouth*. New York: Harper and Row, 1965.

Cellini, Benvenuto. *The Autobiography of Benvenuto Cellini*. Garden City, N.Y.: Doubleday, 1927.

Chambers, John. "Alien Lit 101: The Multiworlders and the Uniworlders." *The Anomalist* 10 (2002): 146–61.

———. *Prophecies for the New Millennium*. Lantana, Fla.: MicroMags, 1999.

———. *Victor Hugo's Conversations with the Spirit World: A Literary Genius's Hidden Life*. Rochester, Vt.: Destiny Books, 2008.

Christianson, Gale E. *In the Presence of the Creator: Isaac Newton and His Times*. New York: Free Press/Macmillan, 1984.

———. *Isaac Newton and the Scientific Revolution*. New York: Oxford University Press, 1996.

Churchill, Winston. *My Early Life: 1874–1904*. New York: Touchstone/Simon & Schuster, 1996.

Couliano, Ioan P. *Eros and Magic in the Renaissance*. Chicago: University of Chicago Press, 1987.

Cranston, Sylvia. *H.P.B.: The Extraordinary Life and Influence of Helena Blavatsky*. New York: Tarcher/Putnam, 1993.

Cranston, Sylvia, and Carey Williams. *Reincarnation: A New Horizon in Science, Religion, and Society*. New York: Julian Press, 1984.

Devlin, Mary. "The Nightmare Futures of Mary Shelley." *Atlantis Rising* 22 (2000): 30–31, 62–64.

Dobbs, B. J. T. *The Janus Faces of Genius: The Role of Alchemy in Newton's Thought*. Cambridge: Cambridge University Press, 2002.

Ebon, Martin. "C. G. Jung Among the Spirits." *Fate* 44 (1) (January 1991): 73–78.

———. "From Shakespeare to Shelley." Chapter 2. "Mann: Séance on *The Magic Mountain*." Chapter 19. "Yeats: A Poet's Lifetime Vision." Chapter 15. *They Knew the Unknown*. New York: World, 1971.

———. "Jung's First Medium." *Psychic Magazine* (May–June 1976): 42–47.

———. "Jung: Toward a Fourth Dimension." In *They Knew the Unknown*. Chapter 14. New York: World, 1971, 143–160.

———. "Nostradamus: Prophet for All Seasons." *Occult* 4 (4) (January 1974): 24–27, 100–102.

Eliade, Mircea. *The Two and the One*. New York: Harper Torchbooks, 1969.

Ellman, Richard. "At the Yeatses'." In *A Long the Riverrun: Selected Essays*. New York: Alfred A. Knopf, 1989.

Fackenheim, Emil L. *What Is Judaism? An Intepretation for the Present Age*. New York: Collier, 1987.

Fenwick, Peter, and Elizabeth Fenwick. *The Truth in the Light: An Investigation of Over 300 Near-Death Experiences*. New York: Berkley Books, 1997.

Flammarion, Camille. *Omega: The Last Days of the World*. Lincoln: University of Nebraska Press/Bison Books, 1999.

Flaubert, Gustave. *Bouvard et Pécuchet*. Norfolk, Conn.: New Directions, 1954.

Force, James E. "Newton, the 'Ancients,' and the 'Moderns.'" In *Newton and Religion: Context, Nature, and Influence*. James E. Force and Richard H. Popkin, eds. Dordrecht, The Netherlands: Kluwer Academic Publishers, 1999.

Foster, R. F. *W. B. Yeats: A Life. The Apprentice Mage, 1865–1914*, vol. 1. Oxford: Oxford University Press, 1997.

——. *W. B. Yeats: A Life. The Arch-Poet, 1915–1939,* vol. 2. Oxford: Oxford University Press, 2003.

Frye, Northrop. *Fearful Symmetry: A Study of William Blake.* Boston: Beacon Press, 1962.

Gassner, John. *Masters of the Drama.* New York: Dover, 1954.

Gassner, John, ed. *A Treasury of the Theatre: From Aeschylus to Turgenev.* New York: Dryden/Simon & Schuster, 1951.

——. *A Treasury of the Theatre: From Henrik Ibsen to Arthur Miller.* New York: Simon & Schuster, 1950.

Gaudart de Soulages, Michel, and Hubert Lamant. Dictionnaire des Francs-Maçons Français. Paris: Éditions Albatros, 1980.

Gerson, Noel B. *Daughter of Earth and Water: A Biography of Mary Wollstonecraft Shelley.* New York: William Morris, 1973.

Ginsburg, Seymour B., ed. *In Search of the Unitive Vision: Letters of Sri Madhava Ashish to an American Businessman, 1978–1997.* Boca Raton, Fla.: New Paradigm Books, 2001.

Gleick, James. *Isaac Newton.* New York: Pantheon Books, 2003.

Grant, George. *Time as History.* Massey Lectures, Ninth Series. Toronto: Canadian Broadcasting Corporation Learning Systems, 1969.

Grasset, Joseph. *The Marvels Beyond Science.* New York: Funk and Wagnalls, 1910.

Grosso, Michael. *The Millennium Myth: Love and Death at the End of Time.* Wheaton, Ill.: Quest Books, 1994.

Guillemin, Henri. *Lamartine.* Paris: Éditions du Seuil, 1987.

Hill, Calvin S., and Vernon J. Nordby. *A Primer of Jungian Psychology.* New York: A Mentor Book/New American Library, 1973.

Hogue, John. *Nostradamus: The Complete Prophecies.* Rockport, Mass.: Element Books, 1997.

Hugo, Adèle. *Le journal d'Adèle Hugo.* Frances Vernor Guille, ed. Paris: Lettres Modernes Minard, 1968–2000.

Hugo, Victor. *Oeuvres complètes.* Jean Massin, ed. *Édition chronologique.* Paris: Le Club Français du Livre, 1967–71.

Iyengar, K. R. Srinivasa, ed. *Indian Literature since Independence: A Symposium.* New Delhi: Sahitya Akademi, 1973.

Jaynes, Julian. *The Origin of Consciousness in the Breakdown of the Bicameral Mind.* Boston: Houghton Mifflin, 1990.

Johnson, K. Paul. *The Masters Revealed: Madame Blavatsky and the Myth of the Great White Lodge.* Albany: SUNY, 1994.

Johnson, Paul. *The Birth of the Modern: World Society 1815–1830.* New York: Harper Perennial, 1991.

———. *A History of the Jews*. New York: Harper and Row, 1988.

Jonson, Ben. "The Devil Is an Ass." In *The Works of Ben Jonson: In Nine Volumes*. W. Gifford, ed., vol. 5. London: W. Bulmer, 1816.

———. *Five Plays*. London: Oxford University Press, 1956.

———. "The Staple of News." In *The Works of Ben Jonson: In Nine Volumes*. W. Gifford, ed., vol. 5. London: W. Bulmer, 1816.

Jung, Carl. G. *An Answer to Job*. In *Collected Works*, vol. 11. Princeton, N.J.: Princeton University Press, 1973.

———. *Memories, Dreams, Reflections*. New York: Vintage Books/Random House, 1965.

Kalush, William, and Larry Sloman. *The Secret Life of Houdini: The Making of America's First Superhero*. New York: Atria Books, 2007.

Kaufmann, Walter. *Discovering the Mind*. Vol. 1, *Goethe, Kant, and Hegel*. New York: McGraw-Hill, 1980.

Keegan, John. *Winston Churchill: A Life*. New York: Penguin, 2002.

Keynes, Geoffrey, ed. *Poetry and Prose of William Blake*. London: Nonesuch Library, 1956.

Kuberski, Philip. "The Metaphysics of Postmodern Death: Mailer's *Ancient Evenings* and Merrill's *The Changing Light at Sandover*." *EHL* 56 (1) (Spring 1989): 229–54.

Küng, Hans. *Christianity: Essence, History, and Future*. New York: Continuum, 2003.

Lamartine, Alphonse de. *Oeuvres poétiques complètes*. F.-M. Guyard, ed. Paris: Bibliothèque de la Pléiade/Gallimard, 1963.

———. *A Pilgrimage to the Holy Land; Comprising Recollections, Sketches and Reflections, Made during a Tour in the East*, vol. 1. New York: Appleton, 1848.

Lamy, Michel. *The Secret Message of Jules Verne: Decoding His Masonic, Rosicrucian, and Occult Writings*. Rochester, Vt.: Destiny Books, 2007.

Lessing, Doris. *Alfred and Emily*. New York: Harper, 2008.

———. *The Four-Gated City* (*The Children of Violence*, Book 5). St. Albans, Hertfordshire, U.K.: Panther, 1972.

———. *The Making of the Representative for Planet 8. Canopus in Argos: Archives 4*. New York: Knopf, 1982.

———. *The Marriages Between Zones Three, Four, and Five. Canopus in Argos: Archives 2*. New York: Knopf, 1980.

———. *(Documents Relating to) The Sentimental Agents (In the Volyen Empire). Canopus in Argos: Archives 5*. New York: Knopf, 1980.

———. *(Re: Colonised Planet 5) Shikasta. Canopus in Argos: Archives 1*. New York: Knopf, 1979.

————. *The Sirian Experiments (The Report by Ambien II, of the Five). Canopus in Argos: Archives* 3. New York: Knopf, 1980.

Lichfield, John. "Jules Verne: Mythmaker of the Machine Age." *Independent* (London), March 14, 2005.

Lombard, Charles M. *Lamartine.* New York: Twayne, 1973.

Maddox, Brenda. *Yeats's Ghosts: The Secret Life of W. B. Yeats.* New York: HarperCollins, 1999.

Mailer, Norman. *Advertisements for Myself.* New York: G. P. Putnam's Sons, 1959.

————. *An American Dream.* New York: Dell, 1970.

————. *Ancient Evenings.* Boston: Little, Brown, 1983.

————. *The Deer Park.* New York: G. P. Putnam's Sons/Perigee Books, 1981.

————. *The Gospel According to the Son.* New York: Random House, 1997.

————. *Why Are We in Vietnam?* New York: G. P. Putnam's Sons/Berkley Medallion Edition, 1968.

Mailer, Norman, with Michael Lennon. *On God: An Uncommon Conversation.* New York: Random House, 2007.

Mann, Thomas. "An Experience in the Occult." In *Three Essays.* New York: Knopf, 1929.

————. "Goethe and Tolstoy." In *Three Essays.* New York: Knopf, 1929.

————. *The Magic Mountain.* New York: Vintage Books/Random House, 1969.

Manso, Peter. *Mailer: His Life and Times.* New York: Simon & Schuster, 1985.

Markley, Robert. "Newton, Corruption, and the Tradition of Universal History." In *Newton and Religion: Context, Nature, and Influence.* James E. Force and Richard H. Popkin, eds. Dordrecht, The Netherlands: Kluwer Academic Publishers, 1999, 121–43.

Marshall, Peter. *The Magic Circle of Rudolph II.* New York: Walker, 2006.

Mattlé, Robert. *Lamartine voyageur.* Paris: E. de Boccard, 1936.

Maudhuy, Roger. *Jules Verne: la face cachée.* Paris: France-Empire, 2005.

Maurois, André. *Prometheus: The Life of Balzac.* Harmondsworth, Middlesex, U.K.: Penguin, 1971.

McClatchy, J. D., ed. *Recitative.* San Francisco: North Point Press, 1986.

McMoneagle, Joseph W. "Jules Verne: Science Fiction Writer, Psychic, or Remote Viewer?" *The Anomalist* 5 (Summer 1997): 59–71.

Mendoza, Ramon G. "Metempsychosis and Monism in Bruno's *nova filosofia.*" In *Giordano Bruno: Philosopher of the Renaissance.* Hilary Gatti, ed. Burlington, Vt.: Ashgate, 2003.

Merrill, James. "The Art of Poetry, 31: James Merrill." *The Paris Review* 84 (Summer 1982).

————. *The Changing Light at Sandover.* New York: Knopf, 1982.

———. *Divine Comedies.* "The Will," New York: Atheneum, 1976.

Miner, Earl, Hiroko Odagiri, and Robert E. Morrell. *The Princeton Companion to Japanese Literature.* Princeton, N.J.: Princeton University Press, 1985.

Mishima, Yukio. *Confessions of a Mask.* New York: New Directions, 1958.

———. *The Decay of the Angel.* New York: Vintage International, 1990.

———. "Patriotism." In *Responding to Literature.* Judith A. Stanford, ed. Mountain View, Calif.: Mayfield, 1992.

———. *Patriotism.* DVD. South Burlington, Vt.: Criterion Collection, 1966.

———. *Runaway Horses.* New York: Vintage International, 1990.

———. *Spring Snow.* New York: Vintage International, 1990.

———. *The Temple of Dawn.* New York: Vintage International, 1990.

———. *The Temple of the Golden Pavilion.* New York: Vintage International, 1994.

Moffett, Judith. *James Merrill: An Introduction to the Poetry.* New York: Columbia University Press, 1984.

Monroe, Robert A. *Ultimate Journey.* Garden City, N.Y.: Doubleday, 1994.

Nabokov, Vladimir. *Lectures on Russian Literature.* Orlando, Fla.: Harvest/Harcourt, 1981.

Nathan, John. *Mishima: A Biography.* Cambridge, Mass.: De Capo Press, 2000.

Needham, Joseph. *Science and Civilisation in China.* Vol. 2, *History of Scientific Thought.* Cambridge: Cambridge University Press, 1956.

———. *Science and Civilisation in China.* Vol. 5, *Chemistry and Chemical Technology,* part 3, *Spagyrical Discovery and Invention: Historical Survey, from Cinnabar Elixirs to Synthetic Insulin.* Cambridge: Cambridge University Press, 1976.

———. *Science and Civilisation in China.* Vol. 5, *Chemistry and Chemical Technology,* part 4, Spagyrical *Discovery and Invention: Apparatus, Theories and Gifts.* Cambridge: Cambridge University Press, 1959.

Newton, Sir Isaac. *The Chronology of Ancient Kingdoms Amended.* London: Histories and Mysteries of Man, 1988.

———. *The Original of Religions.* (The Newton Project). www.newtonproject .ac.uk.

———. *Theologiae Gentiles Origines Philosophicae* (The Newton Project). www .newtonproject.sussex.ac.uk.

Nostradamus, M. Michel. *Le vrai et parfaict embellissement de la face.* Achevé d'imprimer le 15 août 1979 sur les presses des imprimeries réunies de Senlis pour le compte de Gutenberg reprint dépôt légal N° 917.

Neame, Ronald, dir., *The Horse's Mouth,* VHS Movie, 1958.

Pereira, Patricia. *Songs of the Arcturians: Arcturian Star Chronicles: Volume One.* Hillsboro, Ore.: Beyond Words, 1996.

Phillips, Charles, Michael Kerrigan, and David Gould. *The Eternal Cycle: Indian Myth (Myth and Mankind)*. London/Amsterdam: Time-Life Books, 1998.

Picknett, Lynn, and Clive Prince. *The Sion Revelation: The Truth About the Guardians of Christ's Sacred Bloodline*. New York: Touchstone/Simon & Schuster, 2006.

Poirier, Richard. *Mailer*. London: Fontana/Collins, 1972.

Rand, Rev. Silas Tertius. *Legends of the Micmacs,* vol. 2. New York: Longmans, Green, 1894.

Rauscher, William V. *The Houdini Code Mystery: A Spirit Secret Solved*. Pasadena, Calif.: Mike Caveney's Magic Words, 2000.

Robb, Graham. *Balzac: A Life*. New York: W. W. Norton, 1994.

Robinson, Charles E., ed., *Mary Shelley: Collected Tales and Stories with Original Engravings*. Baltimore: The Johns Hopkins University Press, 1990.

Ross, Christopher. *Mishima's Sword: Travels in Search of a Samurai Legend*. Cambridge, Mass.: Da Capo Press/Perseus Books Group, 2006.

Roy, Dilip Kumar. *Yogi Sri Krishnaprem*. Bombay: Bharatiya Vidya Bhavan, 1992.

Schorer, Mark. *William Blake: The Politics of Vision*. New York: Vintage Books, 1959.

Schrader, Paul, and Leonard Schrader. *Mishima: A Life in Four Chapters*. DVD. Directed by Paul Schrader. South Burlington, Vt.: Criterion Collection, 2008. First released in 1985.

Shelley, Mary. *Frankenstein, or The Modern Prometheus*. New York: Peter Bedrick Books, 1989.

———. *The Last Man*. Lincoln and London: Bison Books/University of Nebraska Press, 1993.

Smoley, Richard. "Isis a Little More Unveiled." *Gnosis Magazine* (Winter 1999): 64.

Starr, Chester A. *A History of the Ancient World*. New York/Oxford: Oxford University Press, 1991.

Steiner, George. *Tolstoy or Dostoevsky: An Essay in the Old Criticism*. New York: E. P. Dutton, 1959.

Stevenson, Ian. *Unlearned Language: New Studies in Xenoglossy*. Charlottesville: University Press of Virginia, 1984.

———. *Where Reincarnation and Biology Intersect*. Westport, Ct.: Praeger, 1997.

Stokes, Henry Scott. *The Life and Death of Yukio Mishima*. New York: Cooper Square Press, 1999.

Storr, Anthony. "Carl Gustav Jung." In *Feet of Clay: Saints, Sinners and Madmen: A Study of Gurus*. New York: Free Press Paperbacks/Simon & Schuster, 1997, 83–105.

Symons, Arthur. "Balzac." In *The Symbolist Movement in Literature*. New York: E. P. Dutton, 1958.

TenDam, Hans. *Exploring Reincarnation*. London: Arkana, 1990.

Tolstoy, Leo. *Anna Karenina*. New York: Penguin, 2002.

———. "The Fruits of Enlightenment." In *Darkness and Light: Three Short Works*. New York: Holt, Rinehart and Winston, 1965.

Troyat, Henri. *Tolstoy*. Garden City, N.Y.: Doubleday, 1967.

UNESCO. *Index Translationum*. http://databases.unesco.org/xtrans/stat /xTransStat.html.

Verne, Jules. *Clovis Dardentor*. London: Sampson Low, Marston, 1897.

———. "The Eternal Adam." N.p., 1905.

———. *From the Earth to the Moon*. Paris: Hachette/Livre de Poche, 1966.

———. *Michael Strogoff*. Paris: Hachette/Livre de Poche, 1966.

———. *Paris in the Twentieth Century: The Lost Novel*. New York: Random House, 1996.

———. *Twenty Thousand Leagues Under the Sea*. New York: Charles Scribner's Sons, 1925.

Weissman, Judith. "Vision, Madness, and Morality: Poetry and the Theory of the Bicameral Mind." *The Georgia Review* 33 (1) (1979): 118–48.

———. *Of Two Minds: Poets Who Hear Voices*. Hanover, N.H.: University Press of New England, 1993.

Wells, H. G. *Experiment in Autobiography*. New York: Macmillan, 1934.

———. *Collected Stories*. London: Penguin, 1971.

———. *The Last War: A World Set Free*. Introduction by Greg Bear. Lincoln: University of Nebraska Press, 2001.

———. *The War in the Air*. Harmondsworth, Middlesex, U.K.: Penguin, 1941.

Westfall, Richard S. *Never at Rest: A Biography of Isaac Newton*. Cambridge: Cambridge University Press, 1998.

Willoughby, L. A. "Goethe." *Man, Myth & Magic: An Illustrated Encyclopedia of the Supernatural* 40, 1124–1127. London: BPC Publishing, 1971.

Wilson, Colin. *The Psychic Detectives*. San Francisco: Mercury House, 1985.

Wilson, Edmund. "W. B. Yeats." In *Axel's Castle: A Study in the Imaginative Literature of 1870–1930*. New York: Charles Scribner's Sons, 1969.

Wilson, Ian. *Nostradamus: The Man Behind the Prophecies*. New York: St. Martin's Griffin, 2007.

Yates, Frances A. *Giordano Bruno and the Hermetic Tradition*. Chicago: The University of Chicago Press, 1964.

———. *The Rosicrucian Enlightenment*. London: Routledge and Kegan Paul, 1972.

Yeats, W. B. *Collected Works*. Vol. 4, *Early Essays*. Richard J. Finnerman and George Bornstein, eds. New York: Simon & Schuster, 2007–2008.

———. *Mythologies*. New York: Collier, 1959.

———. *A Vision*. New York: Collier Books, 1966.

———. *Selected Poems*. Stuart Miller, ed. New York: Barnes and Noble, 1994.

Yenser, Stephen. *The Consuming Myth: The Work of James Merrill.* Cambridge, Mass.: Harvard University Press, 1987.

Yourcenar, Marguerite. "Humanism and Occultism in Thomas Mann." In *The Dark Brain of Piranesi.* New York: Farrar Straus, 1984.

———. *Mishima: A Vision of the Void.* Chicago: University of Chicago Press, 2001.

Zeller, Eduard. *Outlines of the History of Greek Philosophy.* New York: Meridian, 1955.

Zweig, Stefan. *Balzac.* New York: Viking, 1946.

Zumstein-Preiswerk, Stefanie. *C. G. Jung's Medium.* Munich: Kindler-Verlag, 1975.